FORGOTTEN WARRIORS

of the Aleutian Campaign

ALSO BY JIM REARDEN

Alaska's Wolf Man
The 1915–55 Wilderness Adventures of Frank Glaser

Sam O. White Alaskan
Tales of a Legendary Wildlife Agent and Bush Pilot

Castner's Cutthroats
Saga of the Alaska Scouts

The Wolves of Alaska
A fact-based saga

Alaska's First Bush Pilots, 1923–30
And the Winter Search in Siberia for Eielson and Borland

Koga's Zero
The Fighter That Changed World War II

Slim Moore: Alaska Master Guide
A Sourdough's Hunting Adventures and Wisdom

Jim Rearden's Alaska
Fifty Years of Frontier Adventure

Travel Air NC9084
The History of a 75-Year-Old Working Airplane

Hunting Alaska's Far Places
Fifty Years with Rifle and Shotgun

Shadows on the Koyukuk
An Alaskan Native's Life Along the River

In the Shadow of Eagles
A Flyer's Story

All fourteen of these books can be found in most Alaska book stores.
The above twelve may be ordered directly from the publisher (406) 549-8488.
See copyright page for address, website, e-mail, and fax number.

Arctic Bush Pilot
From Navy Combat to Flying Alaska's Northern Wilderness

Tales of Alaska's Big Bears

FORGOTTEN WARRIORS

of the Aleutian Campaign

by Jim Rearden

Pictorial Histories Pubishing Company, Inc.
Missoula, Montana

Library of Congress
Control Number 2005905610

ISBN 978-1-57510-120-0

FIRST PRINTING August 2005
SECOND PRINTING March 2012

COVER PHOTO BY CHARLES ARNESON
William Charles House, Lieut. Commdr. USN (ret.), on Kiska in July 1985. Behind him are remnants of the bombed *Nozima Maru* beached at the head of Kiska Harbor.

TYPOGRAPHY, BOOK DESIGN AND COVER GRAPHICS
Arrow Graphics, Missoula, Montana

PRINTED BY
Friesens, Altona, Manitoba, Canada

PRINTED IN CANADA

PUBLISHED BY
Pictorial Histories Publishing Company, Inc.
713 South Third Street West, Missoula, Montana 59801
PHONE (406) 549-8488, FAX (406) 728-9280
EMAIL phpc@montana.com
www.pictorialhistoriespublishing.com

CONTENTS

ABOUT THE AUTHOR

A SIXTY-TWO-YEAR resident of Alaska, Jim Rearden has written twenty-seven books. In addition, he has written more than 500 magazine articles about Alaska for about forty magazines in seven countries around the world. He has received many awards for his writing, the most prestigious being named "Historian of the Year 1999" from the Alaska Historical Society for his book *Alaska's Wolf Man*. Two of his books, an early version of *Koga's Zero*, and *Shadows on the Koyukuk*, have been published in the Japanese language in Japan.

He is a Navy veteran of World War II, and served aboard the destroyer escort *USS Lovering* in the Central Pacific war zone.

Rearden studied fish and game management at Oregon State College and the University of Maine, receiving degrees from both. For four years he was head of the Department of Wildlife Management at the University of Alaska Fairbanks, and for eleven years he was a state fishery biologist responsible for the management of the commercial fisheries of Cook Inlet.

He served twelve years as a member of the Alaska Board of Fish and Game and the Board of Game. In 1976 President Gerald Ford appointed him to the National Advisory Committee on Oceans and Atmosphere, where he served for a year and a half.

He was Outdoors Editor for *Alaska* Magazine for twenty years; simultaneously he was a Field Editor for *Outdoor Life*.

In May 2005 the University of Alaska Fairbanks awarded Rearden an honorary doctorate in science for his teaching, conservation work, and writings.

He lives at Homer with his wife Audrey, in a log house he built himself.

ACKNOWLEDGMENTS

THANKS SEEMS A WEAK WORD to acknowledge the generous help I have received from so many in assembling this book.

When I asked John H. Cloe, Chief of History for the Eleventh Air Force at Elmendorf Air Force Base, Alaska, to review a draft for historical accuracy, I didn't think he'd find many errors. But he did. He not only spent hours ferreting out my many attempts to alter history, he sent me 304 pages of single-spaced typewritten notes on the Aleutian Campaign. "Here, check it out yourself," was the message.

I have long wondered how John managed to write his eloquent and encyclopedic *The Aleutian Warriors; A History of the 11th Air Force and Fleet Air Wing 4*. It was simple; he read every conceivable reference, wrote condensations in chronological order, and worked from that. Just a few years of intensive work, that's all. And he shared it with me to insure that this volume of Aleutian Campaign stories is historically accurate.

Submariner George Herold permitted me to use the article he wrote about the S-27, wrote me multiple times answering questions, and provided photos to illustrate the story of that ill-fated submarine.

Dr. Paul Eneboe, my family physician for nearly four decades, reviewed a draft and made many helpful suggestions. Paul is a fast reader, and he can go right to the heart of a writing problem, and he did. He demanded quality, accuracy, and detail. He wouldn't let me skip over things he thought needed explaining.

Rick Rosenthal, who invited Charlie House and me to accompany him and his crew at Kiska back in 1985, was a gracious host on the beautiful *Manutea*. He also contributed significantly to the photos used herein, and shared with me secrets he discovered on the sea floor at Kiska.

Bill Thies and Bob Larson, former Aleutian Campaign Navy pilots, have been contributors to my work—and friends—ever since I wrote *Koga's Zero* in 1987. Their perspective on the Aleutian Campaign and their memories of it should be celebrated as national treasures.

Janet LeGore, daughter of my friend Stig Palm, spent much time rummaging through Stig's files to find photos I could use, and she generously allowed me to reprint Stig's letters, as well as his fine article about Squeaky Anderson.

Earl Acuff, former Alaska Scout, reviewed the manuscript for accuracy on my report on Castner's Cutthroats. He even wrote a cover blurb. This isn't the first time I've called on Earl for help—as early as 1956 when I moved to the Kenai, Earl Acuff helped make my life easier.

I was a stranger to Heather Lende, a talented writer at Haines, Alaska, when I asked her if she would help me learn what happened to Alaska Scout Leo Land. She did so, with dispatch.

David Land, of Haines, Alaska, son of Alaska Scout Leo Land, was helpful in providing information on his father.

Barbara Evison, daughter of Charlie House, reviewed my write-up of her father, and provided helpful information.

Jeff Davis, bless him, spent weeks typing Russell Annabel's dispatches in chronological order—and generously gave me a disk of his work, with a generous "go ahead" when I checked to see if he minded if I used some of Annabel's writings in this volume.

And last, but certainly not least, my daughter, English teacher Nancy Kleine, and my wife, Audrey, the most important person in my life, both spent days proofreading and correcting grammar and muddy syntax, as well as commenting on the contents of the manuscript as it was produced. Their help and encouragement made the difference on a day-to-day basis.

To all of these I offer my very grateful thank you.

—Jim Rearden

INTRODUCTION

THIS VOLUME, IN EFFECT, is a memorial. Many, if not most, of those whose names appear herein are gone. Others will soon be, for in this year of 2005, World War II veterans are dying at the rate of about 1,000 a day. (The Department of Veterans Affairs estimates it at 32,000 a month.)

Though historic, this is not a history of the Aleutian Campaign, a minor conflict by World War II standards. Rather, it is an attempt to let readers accompany those who fought there, to take to the skies as pilots of PBY Catalinas, to dodge bullets while lying on their bellies on wet tundra, to breathe the stale air of a long-submerged submarine, to glory in the performance of a powerful fighter plane. It is a salute to those young men who fought in that campaign, many of whom were in their late teens, others mostly in their early twenties.

I started this book in 1957 when I interviewed Homer, Alaska, resident George Bishop, and learned about Castner's Cutthroats, also known as the Alaska Scouts.

I first met Bishop in 1956 when I moved from Fairbanks to Homer. He owned and ran the Inlet Trading Post, a general store. He was somewhat roly-poly, cherubic-appearing, with the beginning of a double chin and an enlarged waistline. He was jolly, relaxed, friendly, appearing to be an ordinary businessman-storekeeper. I didn't dream that as a younger man he had carved a reputation as a crack woodsman, a gutsy soldier who, only thirteen years earlier, had been a heroic, mountain-climbing, expert-rifleman member of Castner's famed Scouts.

I didn't learn of that background for about a year. When I did, I interviewed him with a tape recorder. That interview is chapter twelve in this volume. It also led to my writing the historical novel, *Castner's Cutthroats's, Saga of the Alaska Scouts.*

Writing that book resulted in my becoming acquainted with about a dozen other former members of the Alaska Scouts. Contributions by some of these men to events in the Aleutian campaign are also found herein.

In July 1985, while on a writing assignment for the *National Geographic* magazine, I was in the Aleutian Islands, where I became acquainted with the extraordinary then-retired Admiral James Russell. I never called him "Jim" as he suggested I do. He was too imposing and impressive—it was always a respectful "Admiral." My time as an enlisted man in the Navy during World War II emphasized our different backgrounds.

The Admiral told me about the Zero fighter airplane, lost by the Japanese during their second Dutch Harbor raid, prompting me to write my book *Koga's Zero, The Fighter That Changed World War II.*

That, in turn, led me to pilots Bill Thies and Bob Larson, who were flying the PBY Catalina from which the downed Zero was discovered, and their contributions to this volume.

Thies and Larson put me in touch with others who had served in the Aleutians, and my files on the Aleutian Campaign snowballed.

Another turn of fate brought me the historically significant treasure of press releases on the Aleutian Campaign by United Press correspondent Russell Annabel. In 1957, by chance, I met Cliff Cernick, who had once roomed with Annabel. Cernick was then editor of the *Anchorage Daily News*. As we chatted, mostly about writing, he invited me to stay overnight with him at his home.

At the time Annabel was known mostly for his sometimes outrageously fictionized Alaska stories presented as fact in national outdoor magazines. His writing was lively, picturesque, and so descriptive that even though most Alaskans were aware the stories were fiction, they enjoyed them anyway. Outdoorsmen in the South-48 got an over-romantic and distorted view of Alaska from Rusty's articles.

Before leaving Alaska, Annabel stored a box of papers in Cernick's basement, saying, "If I don't send for them in six months, do with them whatever you want."

That evening "whatever Cliff wanted" was to give me that cardboard egg carton full of papers (and an in-need-of-cleaning Pendleton wool shirt, which I still wear occasionally).

The papers were onion-skin carbon copies of about 600 press releases, mostly on the Aleutian Campaign, filed by Annabel with the United Press between 1942 and late 1945.

Over the years I used information from these papers in various magazine articles relating to the Aleutians. I attempted to put them into book form, but it didn't make a compelling read.

In the late 1990s Cliff asked, "Do you still have Annabel's papers?" He wanted them back, for he was planning to write a book about his friend Rusty Annabel.

I sent them. Tragically, Cliff had a debilitating stroke, and was unable to complete the planned book. If he had, it would have been a good one; he wrote some fine books over the years. He died soon after. I miss him. He was a good friend, and, among other favors, he edited a number of my books.

Jeff Davis, a former Air Force officer friend of Cliff's, assembled Annabel's releases chronologically and retyped all 230,000 words. He generously provided me with a disk of his work.

I have included in this volume a sprinkling of Annabel's Aleutian Campaign press releases, most of which carry my theme of "Forgotten Warriors." I like being able to include the names of those he wrote about, with their home towns. Perhaps some of these former warriors, or their families, will read the book.

I refer to Annabel's press releases as "historically significant." That needs explanation. The news media is famous for mangling history. Annabel's releases are significant because it was from them that many newspapers disseminated details of the Aleutian Campaign. Some call the releases from war correspondents "history on the run."

Postwar study of military records, compared with his releases, make clear that Annabel often shot from the hip, as it were. He often missed, as, of course, did other war correspondents. The historical significance of a wartime press release is that *often it is the only information the public receives on an event.*

It isn't necessarily history. Clearly, it not always true.

The fog of war was very real in the Aleutians, in two senses: the war was fought in one of the foggiest regions of the world. And the other meaning—the confusion surrounding events described differently by participants—was also prominent.

A news release, hurriedly typed in a dugout, or aboard an airplane or ship, and written to meet the requirements of censors who were particularly hard-nosed in the Aleutian Campaign, shouldn't be viewed as an accurate history of an event.

Also, unseen to the reading public is the "fog" of editing. Annabel's releases were written in telegram-ese shorthand. These "telegrams," I presume, were sent by the military, using Morse code. His editors filled in the blanks. When Jeff Davis typed the 600 Annabel releases from the onion-skin flimsies, he "filled in," the telegrams, as editors had to in running the stories in their newspapers. This "filling in" could easily change meaning.

In short, newspapers are generally a poor source for a demanding historian. Postwar studies of the military records kept by both sides of a war give a more accurate picture of what really happened.

Annabel, like other war correspondents, relied

on interviews from the low ranked enlistees to top-ranked officers, as well as Public Information Officers. Low-rankers in the military seldom know the big picture. Clearly, too, he sometimes filled in the blanks with his own version of an event. He was expected to provide his editors with publishable copy, which he did. He wasn't writing history; he was doing a job.

Annabel used his imagination and picturesque wording to spice his press releases. On events that were clear cut, it is revealing to compare the dull-as-dishwater official release with the scintillating Annabel story of the same event. On these he did a fine job.

Some of Annabel's press releases were most likely pure fiction, events dreamed up by Annabel—material to fill columns for his editors. None of these appear in this volume.

I have been selective in my choice of Annabel releases, and, as far as possible, have used straightforward, verifiable, accounts; on some, I have included author's comments.

Russell Annabel died in Los Tepames, Mexico, in January 1979.

One more subject: the word Jap. Today it isn't politically correct, and has racist overtones. This volume, however, represents the world of 1941–45 when that word was commonly used. Jeff Davis changed "Jap" to "Japanese" when he typed Annabel's releases, ". . . out of respect for today's political realities."

Annabel's releases, written during World War II, are history. If I altered his wording I would be altering history. I've generally left the word as Annabel used it. I want the reader to find himself drawn back to World War II years. Military men of World War II (including myself) didn't talk politely about the enemy.

Our Jap enemy was trying to kill us, and we were doing our best to kill him. In the war zone, every pilot, soldier, and sailor knew he could die at any time from a Jap bomb, bullet, mortar, grenade, or torpedo. Our verbiage about our enemy wasn't polite. When we said "Jap," it was most often accompanied by expletives.

I have omitted the expletives.

The same thinking applies to stories herein, other than Annabel's releases. It wouldn't be realistic if I tiptoed through them trying to be politically correct. The period 1941–45 wouldn't be honestly represented.

I have used a mix of "Jap" and "Japanese," in this book, depending on context, and source. For this I make no apology.

—JIM REARDEN
Sprucewood
Homer, Alaska
May 2005

PROLOGUE

The Aleutian Islands was a helluva place to fight a war.

From the tip of the 400-mile, scimitar-shaped Alaska Peninsula, the Aleutians, like a string of oddly-shaped beads, arc 1,000 miles west toward Kamchatka, dividing the icy Bering Sea from the turbulent North Pacific Ocean. Attu, the westernmost, is at the same longitude as the North Island of New Zealand.

This string of about forty main islands are volcanic mountains that rise 4,000 or more feet above the sea surface. Many of these peaks are commonly snow-covered year-around; most have knife-sharp edges. Some vent steam, and occasionally, lava. Violent eruptions occur occasionally.

These mountainous islands' shores are generally bold, with almost uncountable off-lying islets, rocks, and reefs.

It is, "One of the stormiest regions in the world," says the *United States Coast Pilot*, the Bible of mariners. "Heavy weather with rain or snow is common. Violent winds over the Aleutians, especially in fall and winter, frequently make navigation extremely hazardous."

All passes between islands from the Bering Sea to the Pacific have currents with velocities up to twelve knots.

The Aleutians appear as tiny dots on a map; fifty by twenty-three mile Unimak, the largest, is about the size of Rhode Island. Unalaska is sixty-seven miles long, and from thirty-five to fifteen miles wide. Umnak is sixty-five miles long and averages about fifteen miles wide.

"Williwaw" is a crazy name for a violent wind which frequently occurs on the leeward side of Aleutian mountains. Air dams on the windward side of a mountain, then suddenly breaks loose, to spill over as an overwhelming, swift, destructive air avalanche.

It can flip a large boat, turn any airplane upside down, or knock a man down.

Villagers in the Aleutians often string anchored cables across their houses to keep them or their roofs from blowing away.

What's it like when wind blows at 100 mph or more? Warriors who served in the Aleutians during World War II learned; outside latrines toppled and sometimes flew off; a 100-foot steel antenna mast which snapped at its base disappeared—blown somewhere. Full barrels of oil lying in the open blew around like empty cardboard boxes. Airplanes tied to huge tractors lifted into the air and dragged the tractors about.

Soldiers leaving an island mess hall opened the door—only to watch the door, and the front porch, fly into the night.

Men cannot stand erect against such wind; they must crouch and hold one another, or crawl. A mess hall only 150 yards distant can take twenty minutes to reach.

A flying sheet of metal roofing can cut a man's head off.

Half-round military huts vibrated, creaked, and groaned in high wind. When heavy snow arrived with such wind, huts could become snow-locked. Wind-blasted drifts may become so hard they must be chopped to break them up. Those inside have to be freed by men with shovels and axes.

During World War II a pilot new to the Aleutians landed on the Shemya runway. "What's that for?" he asked a local, pointing to post from which a logging chain hung.

"Oh, that's our wind sock," was the reply.

Fog dominates Aleutian weather; cold surface water, under warm moist air, produces sea fog throughout the islands, and even gale force winds may not blow it away.

Clear weather over large areas is seldom encountered. At Dutch Harbor, skies average nearly eighty percent cloud cover year-round.

The Aleutians form the longest archipelago in the world. From Unimak, the easternmost, to Attu, the westernmost, it is 1,000 miles—the distance from New York to Minneapolis.

The United States had three major military bases on the drive toward the Jap-held islands of Kiska and Attu. Dutch Harbor, roughly one-seventh the way from the mainland, was the first. Adak, the second, was 450 miles farther—about the distance from San Francisco to Salt Lake City. The next, Amchitka, was 170 miles beyond Adak.

Our planes regularly bombed Attu from Amchitka—a round trip of 550 miles.

So much for the gee-whizzes.

There is another, less-often recognized side to the Aleutians. They are beautiful. Though all the Aleutians are treeless, the abundant moisture and long summer daylight hours produce luxuriant green growth on the lower elevations. Colorful flowers stain hillsides red, blue, pink, and yellow.

The sea around the Aleutians is rich with salmon, halibut, and cod. There are sea otter, sea lions, harbor seals, whales, porpoises, and millions upon millions of sea birds. The Bering Sea is one of the richest commercial fisheries in the world.

Valleys and lower slopes are commonly tundra, a muskeg-like growth of moss, grass and flowering plants. Among the several hundred plant species are crowberries, tiny, black, slightly bitter, with small hard seeds; luscious, abundant blueberries; thimbleberries, red, shiny, tart and sweet, with big leaves; too, there are lingonberries (wild cranberries) that hug the ground. When ripe, they may color a hillside red.

Nevertheless, though the islands are alluring, especially in summer with snowcapped peaks and lush plant growth, because of their ruggedness, the sprawling vast distances, rip-roaring climate, and icy, churning seas, the Aleutians was a helluva place to fight a war.

SUCKER MOVE

ON JUNE 3, 1942, six months almost to the day after the Jap sneak attack on Pearl Harbor, their carrier planes bombed and machine-gunned our military base at Dutch Harbor, initiating the fifteen-month Aleutian Campaign. These planes raided Dutch again the next day.

The Japs occupied the islands of Kiska and Attu on June 7.

A post-war statement by Japanese writer Chihaya Masataka said Japan seized these islands in order to ". . . frustrate and repel possible allied attacks on Japan from the Aleutians."

Other Japanese writers say that seizing Alaska islands ". . . was to advance the Japanese defensive perimeter to Midway and the Aleutians."

The attack on the Aleutians, one day before their bombing of Midway, was also planned to be a diversion, a sucker move, part of the complex Japanese plan for the Battle of Midway. It was an attempt to draw some of our fighting ships north from Pearl Harbor to protect Alaska, thus weakening our fleet for the Battle at Midway the Japs were planning.

Their attack on Midway, the Japs thought, would lure the remnants of our Pearl Harbor fleet there in defense—another sucker move. They were confident they would then destroy what was left of our fighting ships.

They attacked Midway June 4, the day after the first Dutch Harbor raid.

Our enemy was unaware their radio codes had

been broken, and that the U.S. knew their plans. At Midway, the extraordinary courage and sacrifices of our torpedo-bomber pilots, and the skill of our dive-bomber pilots, plus a great deal of luck, allowed our Navy to sink four of Japan's first-line aircraft carriers.

After their cataclysmic defeat at Midway, seizing two Aleutian islands partly became a face-saving action; to "save face" is important to the Japanese.

An event worrisome to the Japs was the Doolittle bombing raid on Japan the previous April. Although they knew Doolittle's sixteen B-25 Mitchell bombers flew from the aircraft carrier *Hornet,* they feared that long-range bombers based in the Aleutians could reach the Japanese islands.

The Battle of Midway was the turning point of the war in the Pacific. After that, Japan was largely on the defensive.

In the meantime, Japan clung to those two rugged Aleutian islands. Was this Aleutian foothold a first move toward mainland North America for the Japanese? No one knew. To insure against this, and to drive the enemy from Alaska, the U.S. mounted the offensive we call the Aleutian Campaign.

THE ALEUTIAN ISLANDS

UNIMAK ISLAND

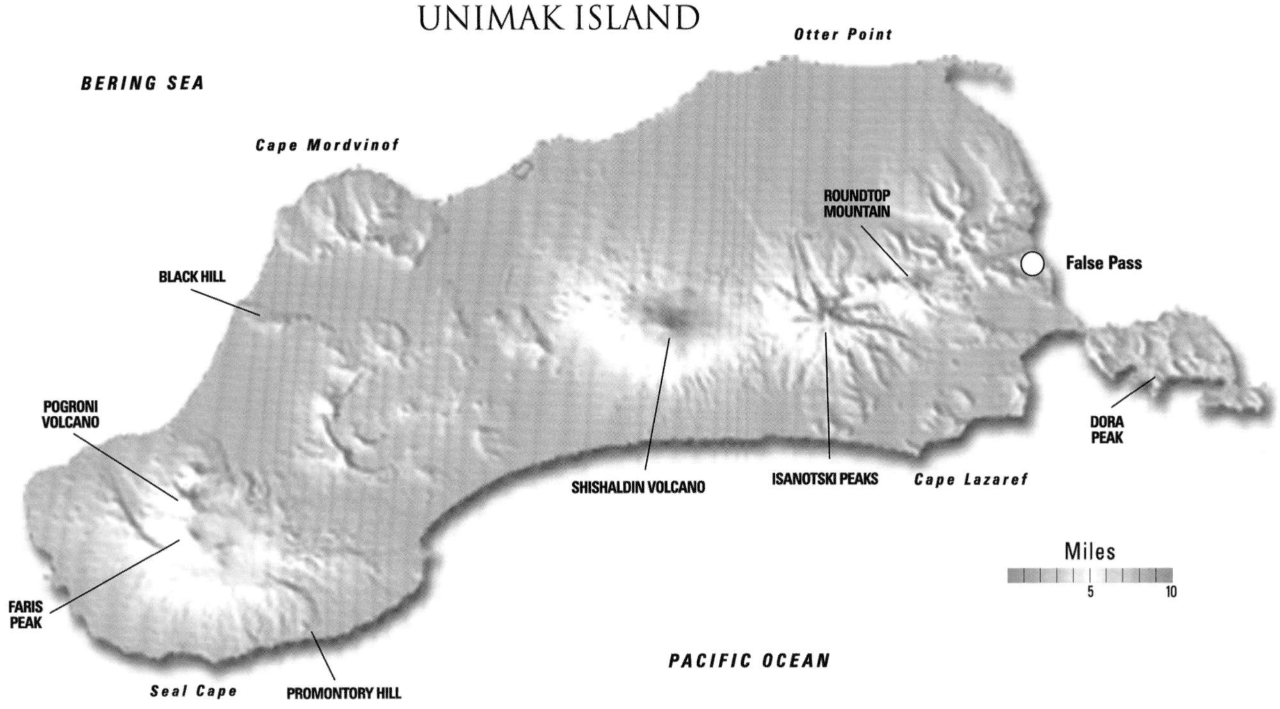

AKUTAN & AKUN ISLANDS

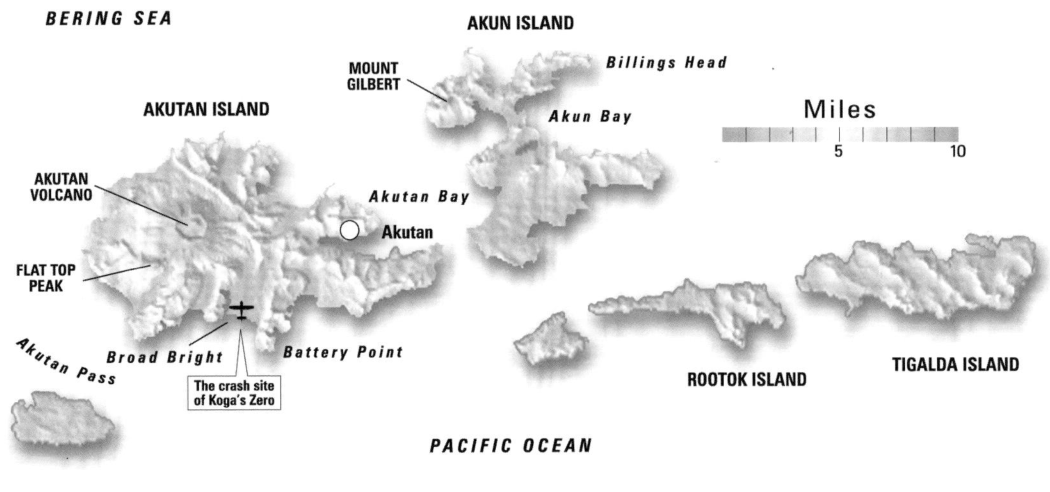

UNALASKA ISLAND

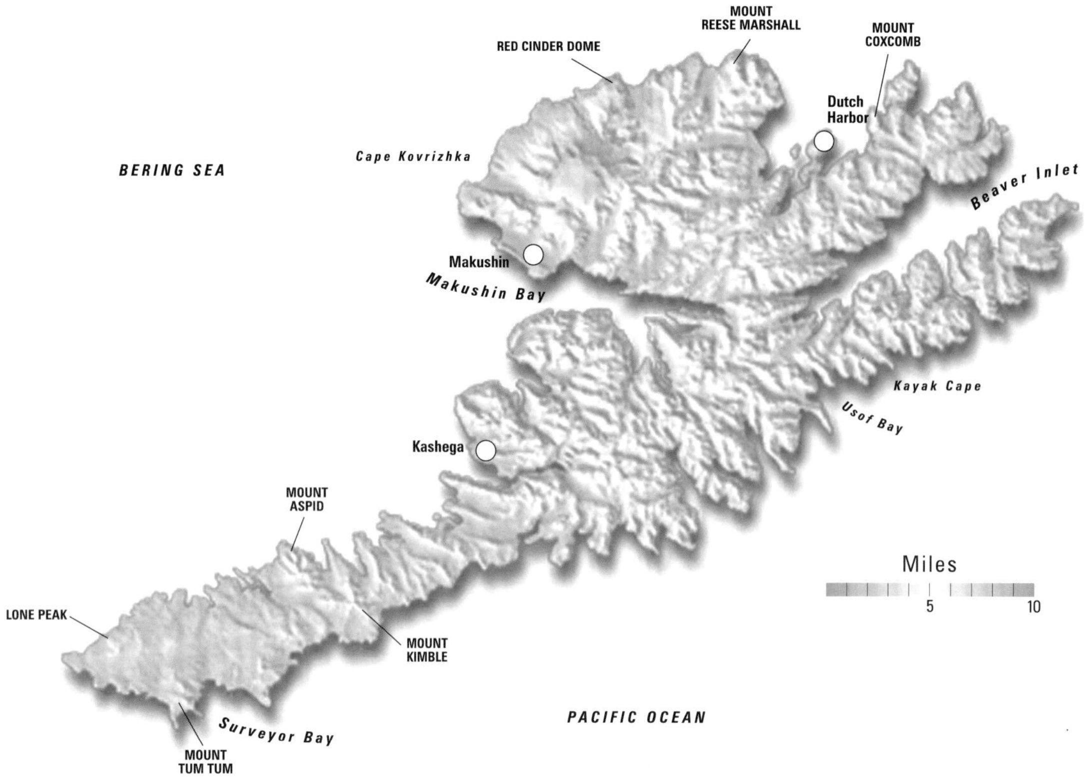

UMNAK ISLAND

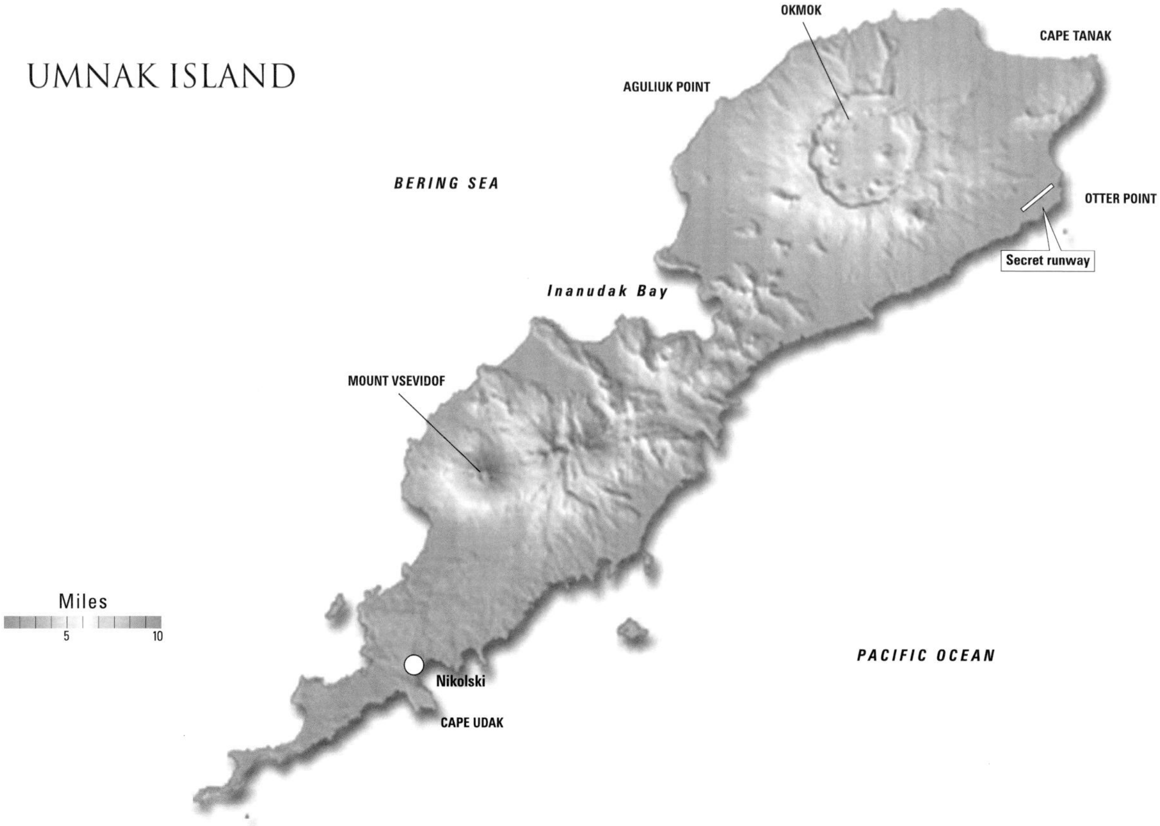

ATKA ISLAND

ADAK ISLAND

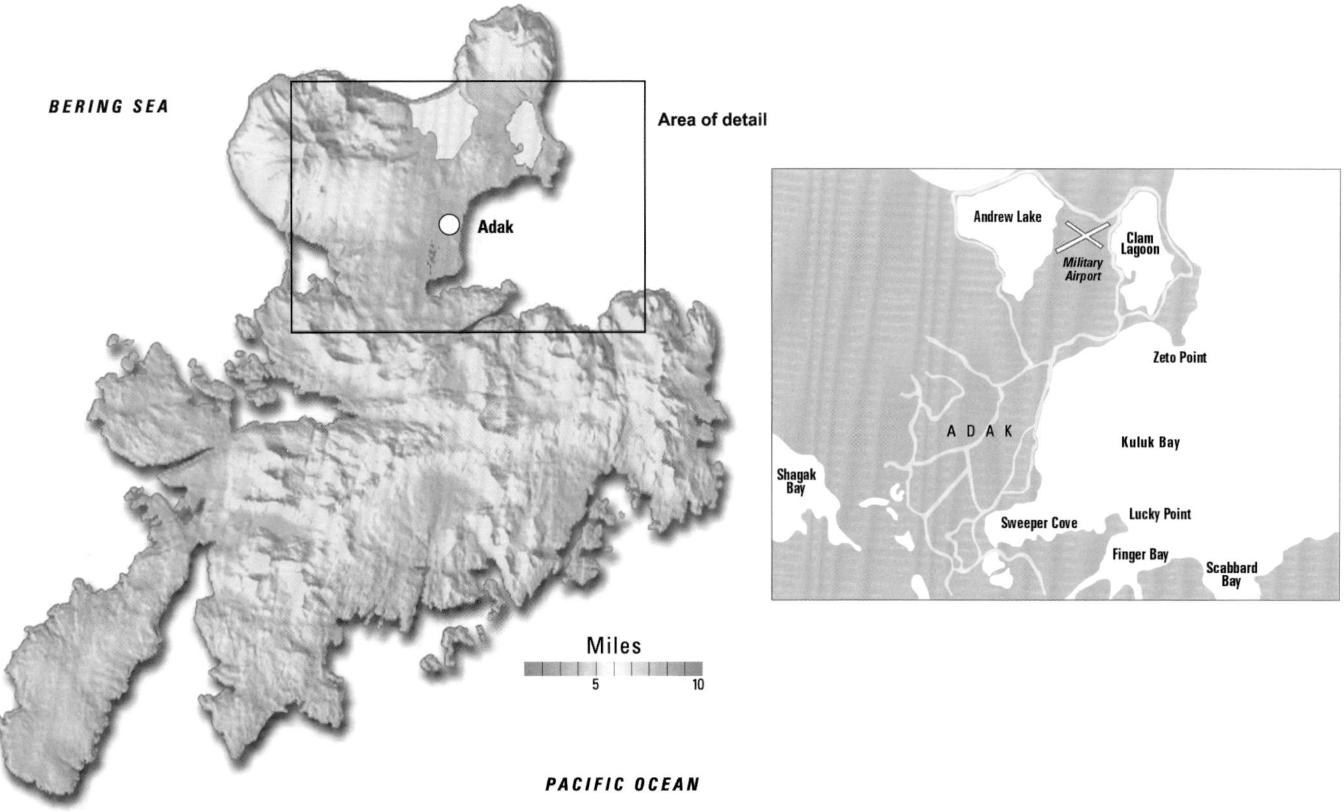

KISKA ISLAND

AMCHITA ISLAND

ATTU ISLAND

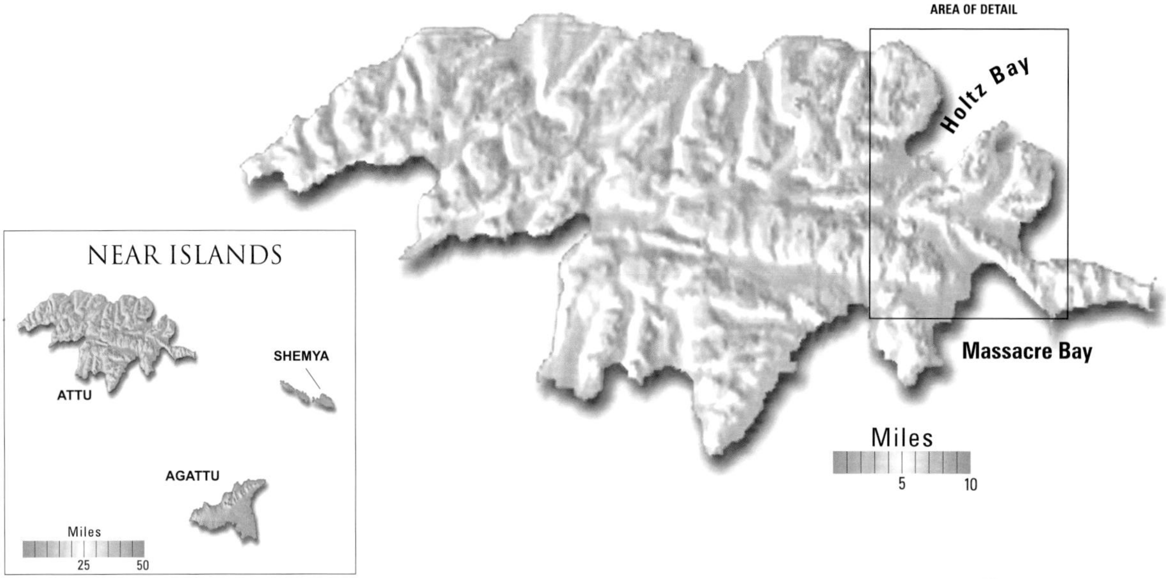

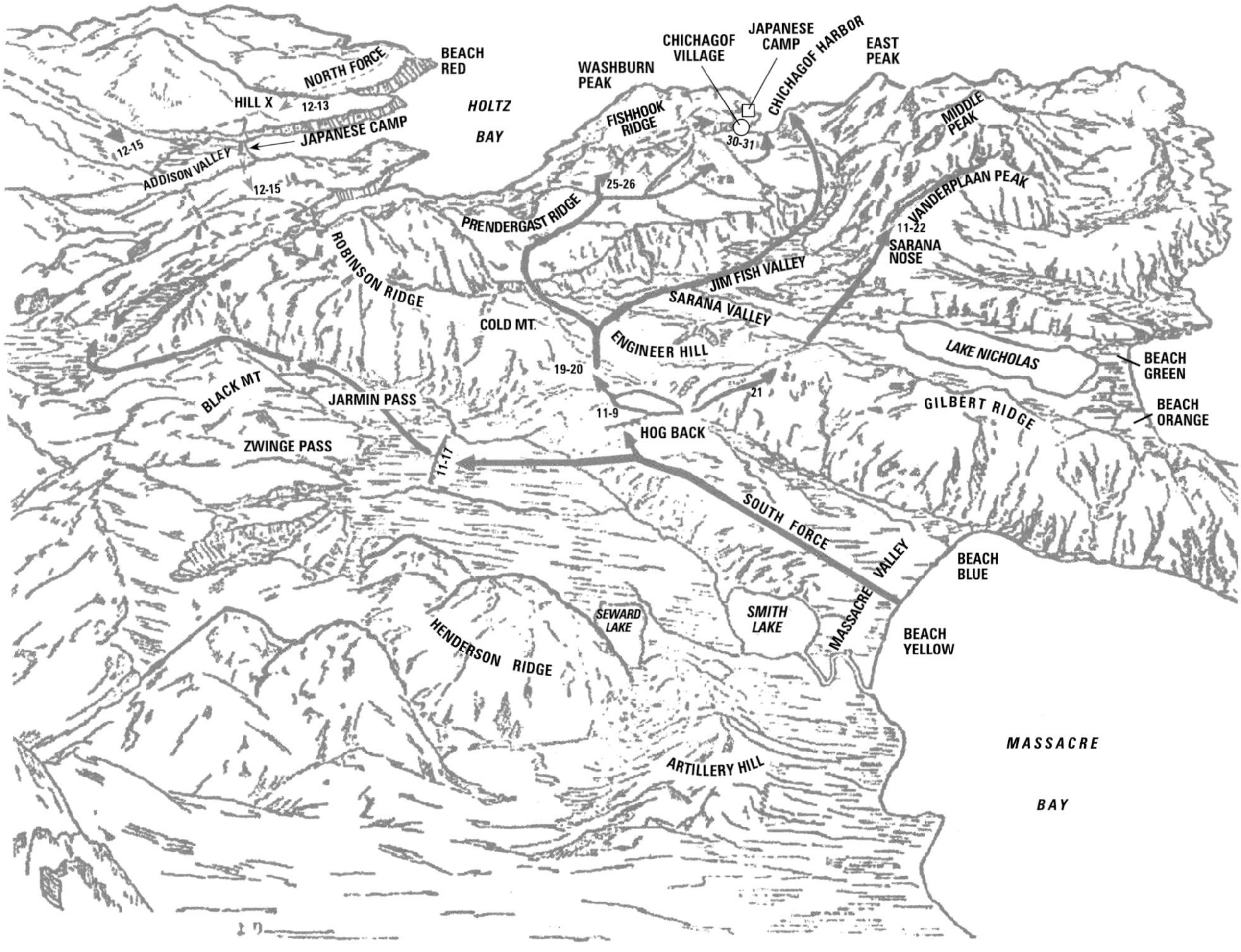

Bottom: A map of Attu Island captured from a Japanese soldier.

1

WAR AT SEA

UP RELEASE BY RUSSELL ANNABEL, ABOARD AN ARMY FREIGHTER AT SEA, SEPTEMBER 10, 1942

THE GUNNER LEANING against the breech of the antiaircraft piece, hands thrust into the pockets of his peajacket, was very blase' regarding submarines. He admitted there probably were some enemy subs in these waters and that they might make a pass at us. But so what? This was war, wasn't it?

"If a guy's number is up, he'll get it. If it isn't—" he shrugged.

The gunner was not more than twenty-one, but he was already a veteran in this business of navigating sub-haunted seas. A few weeks ago he had been on a ship that was shelled for six hours by a Jap sub and he had come through the engagement without a scratch. He said he had been in so many alerts that he felt undressed when he wasn't wearing a life preserver and a tin hat. His name was Don Wilson and his home was in Granite Falls, Washington.

"I was standing in the bow one day when we saw a torpedo coming," he said. "It was on the surface and was tearing through the water so fast we didn't have time to turn out of its path. If it had hit us the old orange crate we were in would have gone up in a shower of splinters. But it missed by ten feet. I heard the swish as it went under the bow. Our number wasn't up, that's all."

You get the same reaction from all these kids in the transport service. They are on the front line constantly and they take it in their stride. They tell you it's their job, their part in winning the war. But it's hard for a landlubber to match their attitude. It's hard even to get used to the ships, many of them former passenger liners built for the luxury trade. The deserted lounges, the unused pianos in the social salons, the absence of women and children aboard, the complete blackout between dusk and daybreak, all contribute to the grim and strange atmosphere of war.

The fact that you are here in the gale-swept Pacific on a nameless ship, that you have departed from a nameless port and are bound for another nameless port [thanks to military censors], makes you feel like a sub-Arctic Flying Dutchman. You are about to mention this when you observe that the conveying warship up ahead is flashing a message with its signal lamp. The gunner beside you stiffens and you realize it is no routine message. The dots and dashes are coming so fast the beam of light is almost unbroken.

"They've spotted one," the gunner says.

The freighter abruptly comes around on full rudder and begins to circle. Somewhere a warning bell clangs. You sprint to your room for your life preserver and tin hat. The warship meanwhile has slewed around and is slamming back along her wake. A depth charge shivers the freighter. Then another. You can't hear them but you can feel them, like earthquake shocks. The loudspeaker on the bridge sputters and crackles.

"Submarine on the starboard bow," the captain says in conversational tones.

Okay, you think, here it comes. And you try to remember what you are supposed to do when a ship is torpedoed. Somewhere on a bulletin board you've read an admonition against jumping overboard. The bulletin stated the concussion of depth charges was very dangerous to a person in the water. You also recall that somebody warned you against going over the rail feet first. The idea was that when you hit the water, the cork life preserver would catch you a nasty clip on the chin. The thing to do was to dive in. Ok, you would remember to dive in.

You haven't seen the submarine yet, but somebody must have seen or heard it because the warship is coming past again like a bat out of hell, her cheese-knife bow splitting the green waves cleanly, and black smoke rolling from her stacks.

Another depth charge lifts the freighter and shakes her so violently the rigging rattles.

A seaman hurries along the deck carrying the ship's cat, a white kitten named Kiska, and tosses it into a lifeboat. This apparently annoys the cat because it arches its back and snarls. The seaman grins at it. Obviously he is a very blase' individual, too. In fact, nobody seems particularly excited or perturbed, and it occurs to you this definitely is not the way Hollywood and the fiction magazines handle a submarine attack.

A half hour passes and still you haven't seen either the wake of a torpedo or the sinister black column of a periscope. Then suddenly the warship takes the lead again and her signal lamp flashes. The alarm is over. The freighter resumes her course and the kid gunner comes back from the foredeck and looks at you and smiles.

"They've got hot coffee in the galley," he says, "If you want some."

"A gallon of it," you tell him.

In the galley, the cooks and mess boys are talking about an experience they had a couple of months ago on another freighter. The ship was pretty thoroughly shelled and the boys are unable to agree as to whether the shells contained shrapnel, or were of the fragmentation type. One of the mess boys, Bill Darter, of Bothell, Washington, said they were fragmentation shells. He said he ought to know, because a chunk of one hit him and split his side open. You gulp your coffee and wonder what it would take to frighten these kids, and you decide that probably nothing would.

"Did they get the submarine they were dropping depth bombs on out there?" you ask.

"Maybe—maybe not," the gunner says. "The thing is, it didn't get us."

"Our number wasn't up," you say, trying to make it sound convincing.

"Sure. That's it," the gunner says.

2 THE GIANT OF KISKA

In July, 1985, the 112-foot, steel sailing schooner *Manutea* (White Dove) eased into the harbor of Kiska Island in Alaska's western Aleutians. Aboard were five professional scuba diver/photographers hoping to photograph ships, warplanes, and perhaps other military residue known to have disappeared beneath the waters of the harbor during the savage Aleutian Campaign of World War II.

The editors of *National Geographic Magazine* assigned me to write an article describing their findings.

Accompanying me on the journey to the *Manutea* at Kiska was retired Navy Lieut. Commander William Charles House. House was the U.S. Navy petty officer in command of a ten-man weather crew on Kiska when, on June 7, 1942, Japs stormed ashore there and quickly turned it into a military stronghold. Now, forty-three years later, he was to help me with historic details.

Based on his phoned description, I immediately recognized the slim, 150-pound, 72-year-old House when I met him at the Anchorage airport. He had mostly recovered from a heart bypass he had undergone four months earlier. When he smiled his whole face lit up. His eyes sparkled with wit and good humor. He was friendly, modest, easy to like—an extrovert. He enjoyed life.

Orin Seybert, our pilot for the 1,150-mile flight to Kiska, was waiting for us the next day when we arrived at the Alaska Peninsula village of King Salmon, a small weather-beaten village on the Bering Sea coast that sprang up around a World War II aircraft runway. Seybert is founder and president of Peninsula Airways, Inc., and our airplane for the flight was a twin-engine Grumman Widgeon amphibian. Appropriate to our mission, the Grumman was built during World War II.

Orin lifted the Widgeon off the King Salmon runway, and, under the fog layer, climbed to an altitude of just ninety feet, and at 145 mph pointed its nose southeast to follow the Bering Sea shoreline of the Alaska Peninsula. At Izembek Lagoon, near Cold Bay, we roared over several huge brown bears. Were they fishing? Couldn't tell.

Navigating by Loran, we then flew for 100 miles through fog about ten feet above the sea to land at Dutch Harbor to refuel. From Dutch Harbor at Unalaska Island to Adak Island we flew above solid fog. With 900 miles behind us, we spent the night at Adak, a large U.S. Navy base, only 250 miles from Kiska.

Next day, July 20, we flew past the snowy tops of several volcanoes that poked through solid white clouds. On instruments, twenty miles from Kiska, Orin descended and found the sea, but fog lay on the water too dense for safe flying. He climbed back on top. Somehow, he found his way into Kiska Harbor, where the sky was clear, although the island was surrounded by fog. He landed near the anchored *Manutea*. A skiff came for Charlie and me.

Even today, twenty years later, Orin says, to his knowledge, only one other non-military plane has landed at remote Kiska since World War II. Kiska is remote, even by Alaska standards.

The mast of the *Nisson Maru*, a 400-foot-long

The U.S. Navy weather detachment at Kiska Island in May 1942. All were taken prisoner by Japanese troops in June of that year. First Class Aerographer William Charles House (third from left, standing) fled into the hills with the rest of the crew when the Japs landed. House remained free for forty-nine days; the others were captured within eleven days. Left to right, standing: Turner, Copperfield, House, Mull, Echols, Yaconelli and Courtney. Mull and Yaconelli were from a supply ship, and not part of the weather detachment. Left to right, kneeling: McCandless, Christiansen, Winfrey (with dog Explosion), Palmer and Gaffney. NATIONAL ARCHIVES

freighter sunk in ninety feet, poked out of the water in Kiska harbor. Hulls of two other bombed and shot-up Jap ships lay on the beach. Jap coastal and anti-aircraft guns pointed skyward and to sea from surrounding ridge tops, now handy perches for gulls and bald eagles. Huge live shells and empty brass casings lay near some of the guns. Entrances to dozens of caves dug by the Japs rimmed the north side of the harbor. Zero fighter plane engines and floats, old trucks, wire and rusted guns lay about. Hundreds of grass-grown bomb craters sprinkled the island.

For the next week, Charlie and I wandered parts of Kiska. He showed me where the three shacks for his Navy weather crew had been, as well as the Japanese camp. The island is a wildlife refuge, and

The Peninsula Airways Grumman Widgeon, at Kiska Harbor, in which the author and Charlie House were flown by Orin Seybert from King Salmon to Kiska. CHUCK NICKLIN

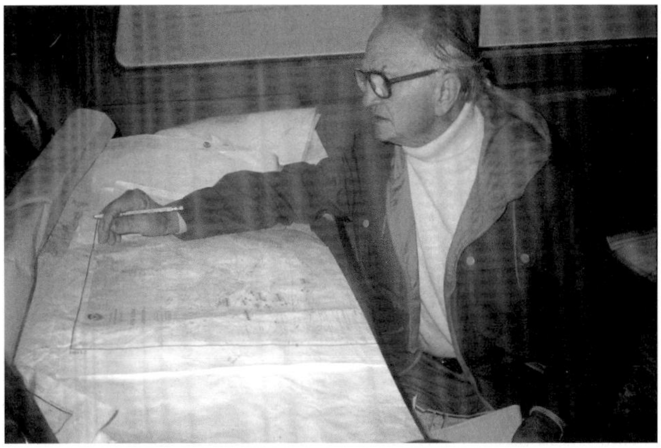

Charlie House, aboard the schooner *Manutea*, in Kiska Harbor, studying a marine chart of the harbor which was marked with underwater targets for divers. AUTHOR

Charlie House relaxes on the July greenery of Kiska. He visited the island with the author forty-three years after he was forced to surrender there to the invading Japanese. AUTHOR

all buildings had been removed by the U.S. Fish and Wildlife Service, save for a storage warehouse.

The diving and exploring done, we raised sails for the 250-mile cruise to Adak, where we were greeted by retired Admiral James S. Russell, a Lieutenant Commander when he served early in the Aleutian Campaign. Russell and House were old friends.

I interviewed Russell about Kiska, and other aspects of the Aleutian Campaign while at Adak, and again in 1987 at his home at Tacoma, Washington. We also corresponded until his death at age 93 in 1996.

After our trip to Kiska, Charlie and I stayed in touch. At Christmas, 1985, he wrote: ". . . you said we would have a fun trip. It was. The eastern Aleutians were beautiful with the emerald green grass, black cliffs and white breakers.

"Kiska looked pretty with all of the green grass. The scars will mostly disappear in time—only the guns and concrete will remain to remind future generations of the futility of war.

"I enjoyed my stint at the wheel on the *Manutea*, and the ride through the storm in the Bering Sea."

SINCERELY, CHARLES

THE U.S. NAVAL WEATHER STATION, KISKA ISLAND. JUNE 7, 1942. JUST AFTER TWO A.M.

Charlie House, U.S. Navy Aerographer (Navy lingo for weatherman), petty officer first class, ranking member of the ten-man weather station, was awakened by shouts "Japs! Japs! Japs!"

The shouts came from Walter M.(Wimpy) Winfrey, Aerographer's mate third class, who occupied the top of their two-man bunk.

"Go back to sleep, Wimpy. You're having a bad dream," Charlie growled. Sleep had been hard to come by for several days.

Wimpy, in his skivvies, switched on a light. Blood ran from a bullet hole in his right thigh. "Look, Charlie," he said. "Is this a dream?"

As Charlie stared at the wound, a bunkhouse window was shattered by another machine gun bullet.

More bullets penetrated the plywood walls about four feet above the floor. Charlie and others in the bunkroom frantically dressed while lying on the floor below the zinging bullets.

All but House and Aerographer's Mate second class J.L. Turner, immediately fled into the dawn.

House and Turner turned the oil burning heating stove to high and stuffed it with radio communication ciphers. As they worked, another bullet shattered the glass case covering the selsyn wind-recorder in the adjacent radio shack.

Turner waited momentarily for House, who made sure all critical papers had burned. House snatched two gray wool blankets from his bunk, grabbed the radio coding board, and fled. "I didn't have time to get my outdoor clothing," he told me.

He was stunned to see many Jap landing craft beetling across the harbor. From each, machine guns rattled fire toward the three small buildings of the weather station.

"We'd better separate and get into the clouds," Turner suggested.

Charlie fled uphill one way, Turner another.

Jap machine gunners hosed bullets at the ten distant, scattered, fleeing weather crew. House, peering over his shoulder, saw glowing tracers approaching. He dropped to his belly. The tracers stopped.

In moments, he was running again, peering back fearfully. The tracers re-started.

"In the dim light, they looked like flaming baseballs," Charlie told me. "I saw them coming and stepped aside so they'd miss. Because of the distance, phosphorous on the tracers burned off and they became lighter and carried farther than the non-tracers, which I saw hitting the ground short."

Three hundred yards up the ridge, Charlie ran into low clouds. He continued to scramble until he was exhausted. Gasping, he threw himself down to rest.

The shock of being asleep one minute, and having to dodge bullets the next, had his mind whirling. All had been peaceful on Kiska. The weather crew was the only human presence on the island, and their routine had been easy and simple.

"I heard 'thump! thump!' the loud sound of footsteps. They seemed to be nearing. I pressed my ear to the ground—and realized I had heard my racing heart," he said, laughing at himself.

"After catching my breath, I climbed higher, and near a pile of gray rocks covered myself with my two blankets. I assumed the Japs would knock out our facilities and leave. My duty was to evade them. I remained under the gray blankets near gray rocks until dark," he remembered.

Lightly dressed, his warmest clothing item was a canvas hunting jacket with a zip-off hood. His rubber-bottom shoepacks kept his feet dry on the wet tundra; his main warmth came from the blankets.

The fog burned off. "From my ridge-top perch, I watched Jap troops swarm ashore. It was a beehive. Cargo ships arrived and started to unload. Cruisers and destroyers anchored. Jap carrier planes flew over. Later, an aircraft carrier came into the harbor and anchored.

"Summer days in Alaska are long—this one was especially so. I was alone, in danger, and my world had just been pulled out from under me.

"I heard occasional rifle shots and worried that members of my crew had been killed." He now realized the Japs had come to Kiska to stay.

This was a moment of destiny for Charlie House;

One of the Japanese guns on Little Kiska Island, with Charlie House (left) and diver-photographer-explorer Rick Rosenthall. CHUCK NICKLIN

his escape into the Kiska fog began an adventure that made him a legend to those familiar with the history of the Aleutian Campaign of World War II.

SEAMAN TO WEATHERMAN

HOUSE WAS A low-ranked seaman in the fall of 1934 when he was transferred from the cruiser *USS Portland* to the U.S. Naval Air Station Lighter Than Air School at Lakehurst, New Jersey. After training, he hoped to become a crewmember of the huge navy dirigible *USS Macon*.

However, on February 12, 1935, before House completed his schooling, the *Macon* crashed, ending the navy's large-dirigible program. Charlie was lucky he wasn't aboard.

Perhaps Charlie was born (August 17, 1913) under a special star that thrust him into pivotal historic events. At Lakehurst, he was one of the ground-handling crew clinging to ropes beneath the giant German hydrogen-filled dirigible *Hindenburg* when it exploded into flame on May 6, 1937.

"When she started to burn and fall, I dropped my line and ran like hell. I was lucky to get out from under. It was a horrible scene."

Thirty-six died.

In January 1937, he was sent to the navy's Primary Aerographer's School. He graduated in May, 1937.

As an Aerographer, he served with weather units on the aircraft carrier *Saratoga*, the battleship *California*, and at the Naval Air Station, San Diego, California. He was at San Diego December 7, 1941, when the Japs made their sneak attack on Pearl Harbor.

Suddenly, wartime security required ships at sea to maintain radio silence. The lack of at-sea weather reports created huge blank spots on weather maps of the Pacific. Without these, there was no way to predict eastward-moving weather for the west coast of the U.S. and Alaska.

ASSIGNMENT ALASKA

TO COMPENSATE for the lack of forecasting in Alaska, a chain of Navy weather stations was planned for the Aleutian Islands. Aerographer Mates House, Hudson, Lynch, and Omang were to run these stations.

These weathermen were assigned to Patrol Wing Four at Naval Air Station Seattle to await equipment and transportation to Alaska. The wing flew the lumbering twin-engine PBY seaplane; the later model, PBY-5, of this long-range patrol plane was amphibious.

The weathermen left Seattle April 14, 1942, aboard the troop transport *USS Grant* bound for Dutch Harbor, adjacent to the Aleutian Island of Unalaska. At Dutch, assignments were made by drawing slips from a hat. House drew Kiska; chance had again put him in harm's way.

House and his crew left Dutch Harbor in early May, bound for Kiska on the seaplane tender *USS Williamson*, a former World War I four-stack destroyer from which two forward boilers had been removed to make room for aviation gasoline tanks; thus it had only two stacks.

The *Williamson* was short-handed, and the weathermen were pressed into service as gun crews. As they steamed the 650 miles west to Kiska, an Officer of the Deck told them, "Shoot at anything you see. There are no friendly ships here."

"That brought me into the war," Charlie told me. "After that, when on gun watch I kept my finger on the trigger and constantly combed the horizon for enemy ships and planes."

KISKA

RUGGED AND mountainous, Kiska is about twenty-two miles long and varies in width from one-and-a-half to six miles. Kiska Volcano, on the northern end, rises to 4,000 feet.

Each summer three to six million least and crested auklets (six, and nine-and-a-half-inch-long, respectively) nest in the rugged lava at Sirius Point at the northern tip of Kiska. Flocks awing near nesting cliffs are so dense, from a distance they look like smoke. Sea otters, seals, sea lions, whales, and porpoises frolic in the seas around the island. Blue arctic foxes live on the island.

Immediately south of the volcano is a two-mile-wide valley that nearly spans the island, in which there are several salt water lakes.

Flat-topped boulder-strewn ridges of 1,000 to 1,400 feet lie between the salt water lakes and Kiska Harbor, which opens about midway along the east shore of the island. Valleys and lower slopes of the island are covered with tundra and grass; higher elevations are generally bare and are strewn with boulders. Shores of the island are mostly rocky and steep.

Kiska Harbor, roughly circular and about one and three-tenth miles in diameter, is one of the finest big ship harbors in the Aleutians. Because it is exposed to easterly winds, it can become extremely rough for boats under about fifty feet. The Japs learned it wasn't a good place for seaplanes, which do best with calm water.

The *Williamson* steamed into Kiska Harbor May 18. Charlie expected the three small, new, Seabee-built plywood buildings of the weather station would be his home for several years.

Chief Petty Officer William C. Jones, a radio technician, accompanied the weather crew from Dutch to help install radios. With him was Explosion, a mixed-breed dog—a gift mascot for the weather crew. Months earlier, while Explosion was being whelped at Dutch, an explosives storage shed had detonated, hence the dog's name. Explosion was to see history made, although he probably didn't appreciate it; first he was a mascot of the American weather crew, then he became a mascot to the Japs; and he was there to welcome American and Canadian troops when they arrived to retake Kiska.

While the *Williamson* was being unloaded, Commander K. Kivette, the skipper, sent a signalman and a quartermaster to a high ridge overlooking the sea outside the harbor.

"If you see any unidentified ship or airplane, signal immediately. I'll steam to sea so I can do battle in unrestricted waters," he told them. "We'll have to abandon you and you'll have to join the weather crew. Hopefully, we'll be able to pick you up later," he said, somberly.

A six-month supply of provisions was lightered to the beach, but a strong easterly and its accompanying surf made beaching impossible. While supplies were off-loaded, for forty-five minutes, House and several of his crew stood chest-deep in the thirty-eight-degree water, holding the motor launch so it wouldn't broach.

While the *Williamson* was unloading, two PBY Navy patrol planes touched down. Bound for Attu, a storm had forced them back to Kiska. One was piloted by Lt. Commander James S. Russell, Commanding Officer of VP-42 (Squadron 42, Patrol Wing 4). His passengers were Lieut. General Simon Bolivar Buckner, Commanding Officer of the Alaska Defense Command, and Navy Commander Paul L. Foster, an emissary sent by President Roosevelt to evaluate General Buckner's view that Alaska could be a military gateway to Japan. The other PBY was flown by Lieutenant Samuel E. Coleman.

Russell told me, "If there was any excitement, Buckner wanted to be there. I was quite concerned when he decided to join us [on the Aleutian trip]. He invited himself, and at Kodiak climbed into my plane with a hunting rifle and a down sleeping bag."

Russell's concern for the lives of Buckner and Foster was based on the expectation of a Jap force arriving in the Aleutians. The Navy's Combat Intelligence Unit at Pearl Harbor had, for weeks, been able to read Jap military codes. The Navy was only too aware of the Jap's plans to attack the Aleutians.

Referring to Foster, Russell, who often understated, told me, "A person with a letter in his pocket from the President was of considerable interest."

Russell recounted for me, "What happened was what one expects in the Aleutians—we got weather-bound at Kiska. The Aleutians is a place for the exercise of patience."

General Buckner and Charlie House spent most of a wet, windy day walking about the island studying the terrain.

"General Buckner impressed on me that the most important thing outside of our regular weather reporting was to immediately report enemy sightings," Charlie told me. "He also promised to send me some tree seeds. I was going to plant them in sheltered canyons."

During the storm that kept the PBYs at Kiska, Russell continued to worry over the safety of his distinguished passengers.

"I came up with various schemes to get them away. I went as far as loading them into the plane, leaving the mooring, and taxiing at high speed to make sure the plane's engines would wind up. Some of the crew on the *Williamson* became terribly worried, thinking I was planning to fly into the storm," Russell told me.

Eventually, Russell convinced the reluctant Buckner and Foster to return to Kodiak on the *Williamson*, instead of waiting for suitable flying weather.

The weather broke four days after Buckner and Foster left, and Russell and Coleman then scouted with their PBYs for Jap forces on long-range patrols from Kiska.

The Navy had cached aviation gasoline in barrels on the Kiska beach. "With a skiff, we towed barrels of gasoline out to the anchored planes," Charlie told me. "The barrels floated upright while we pumped fuel into the planes, a seven or eight hour task. But it did give the air crews some rest time."

While Charlie and his crew refueled the PBYs, Russell caught some sleep in House's bunk.

The seaplane tender *USS Casco*, returning from Attu, stopped briefly at Kiska. Aboard was Chief Petty officer William C. Jones, who had installed the radio at Kiska. He went ashore to check it out again.

Russell told House, "If the Japs come, head for the hills. If possible, we'll pick you up after they leave."

Charlie had reason to remember that promise.

Russell told me, "We took off, made a brief circle, and headed for Dutch Harbor. We were no sooner airborne than the *Casco* got under way."

It too was headed for Dutch Harbor, then the major base of the U.S. in the Aleutians.

ON THEIR OWN

House and his crew—ten men and a dog—were now on their own on remote Kiska. The crew sent a weather report to Dutch Harbor every three hours.

On May 24, one of the crew, outside, called, "I hear an airplane." They all rushed out. Charlie, with binoculars, identified it as a Jap plane by the rising sun wing-and-fuselage markings (meatballs, our pilots called them) as the low-wing twin-float plane circled lazily over Kiska harbor. From their *Enemy Plane Identification Book* Charlie and crew decided it was a Yokosuka reconnaissance seaplane ("Glen").

After-war records revealed it had come from the huge submarine I-9. It also made survey flights over the islands of Attu and Adak. The plane was housed in a watertight hangar on the submarine. Wings and floats were detachable. It was catapulted into flight from the deck, and lifted back aboard with a crane.

House reported the sighting to Dutch.

"Report altitude, course, and speed of plane," Dutch requested. This done, Dutch radioed back, "Are you sure you saw a plane?"

Charlie thought this a ridiculous query and ignored it.

That midnight all hands listened to a shortwave news broadcast from San Francisco which predicted the Japs would attack Alaska and the West Coast of the U.S. within ten days. Was their aircraft sighting the basis of that prediction?

Charlie and his crew never knew.

They then listened to the Jap version of the news in English, broadcast from Tokyo.

Spurred by sight of the enemy plane, Charlie's crew dug zig-zag trenches, hopefully to provide protection against bombing or strafing. They pitched two tents in distant ravines and stocked them with food, rifles, and ammunition.

Early on the morning of June 3, one of the radiomen awoke everyone, yelling "The Japs are attacking Dutch!" At that moment the Dutch Harbor radio was reporting a Jap bombing raid; Dutch reported the second bombing raid the following day. They were the only enemy carrier plane bombings made on North American soil during World War II.

House and crew guessed at the position of the Jap raiders. Using a ten-knot speed, they estimated the time it would take for them to reach Kiska. For three nights, rifles ready, they slept in their clothes.

By June 6, Charlie figured the Japs were well beyond Kiska if they were returning to Japan, so he allowed the crew to relax and undress for bed.

The fog-shrouded *Borneo Maru* lies in Gertrude Cove, a few miles south of Kiska Harbor, where it was beached after being bombed. AUTHOR

Next morning he was awakened by shouts from the wounded Winfrey. Shortly, he found himself alone atop a ridge overlooking Kiska Harbor.

ON THE RUN: SURVIVAL

BY THE TIME dark fell June 7, Charlie House's mind was made up. He wouldn't give up without a struggle. Perhaps help would arrive and drive the enemy from the island. He remembered Russell's orders for the crew to flee to the hills ("If possible, we'll pick you up later").

During the three-hour-long dusky June night he tried to locate one of their tent caches. He moved swiftly and became overheated. He gulped water from small streams and ate snow from drifts. He became nauseated and vomited what little food his stomach held.

He couldn't locate the tent. When the eastern sky started to lighten, he headed toward the northeast coast, aiming for Reynard Cove, remembering it from a marine chart. At daylight he started across what he thought was a shallow stream and found himself chest-deep.

"I threw my blankets ashore, crawled out on the bank, and spread my sopping clothes to dry. Then I rolled up in the blankets in high grass to stay out of sight."

Fortunately for Charlie, that day happened to be one of the rare sunshiny days that come to Kiska.

A Jap patrol boat dropped bow and stern anchors within a few hundred yards offshore. "That pinned me down. I didn't dare move. I remained in the creek bed all day."

At dark, rested, and with dry clothes, he hiked uphill, heading inland. He found a bank that looked as if it would make a sheltering cave if he dug it out. But digging in the wet clay with his fingers was slow, and he gave up.

Next day, he remained on a small meadow by a stream. He could see the harbor, but it also meant he could be seen from boats in the harbor. He tried to sleep curled in his gray blankets next to gray rocks.

He saw fifteen or twenty ships sail in and out of Kiska Harbor, and watched the patrol boat that had pinned him down methodically take lead-line soundings of the outer harbor.

He hadn't eaten for two days. While at Dutch he had talked with a trapper who had been on Kiska. "Nothing poisonous grows in the Aleutians," the man told him. [Not precisely true. Three plants known to grow in the Aleutians that may be poisonous include the narcissus-flowered anemone, nootka lupine, and vetch or locoweed. JR]

He tried eating lupine bulbs, but didn't like the taste. Next he ate what he called "tundra." The plant Charlie called "tundra" was cow parsnip or wild celery (*Heracleum lanatum*). After eating his fill of it, he became nauseated, with an urge for a bowel movement. His stool was mostly undigested "tundra," mixed with clotted blood.

He was within view of several ships in the harbor, but since he hadn't been disturbed by searching soldiers, he uneasily remained there four days.

Then the bombing started.

"At first PBYs bombed the Japs. On cloudy days (most of the time) they flew above the clouds, usually starting from Kiska Volcano, which usually showed above the clouds, set a course, and timed themselves until they were over the harbor or the Jap camp. They would then dive out of the clouds, drop bombs, and instantly climb back into concealment.

"Ships shot at them, and so did shore-based anti-aircraft guns. Flak fell all around me. Some of it was big enough to kill. I had to get out of there.

"That night it poured cats and dogs," he said.

All night he sloshed and trudged to a cove near Conquer Point on the northwest coast.

"I found a little ledge and a cave. I crawled up in the cave and rolled up in my blankets and got to sleep. But a cold front came through, and it snowed heavy, wet, flakes. My feet were cold. All I could do was stick it out. By morning the cave was dripping. I was a mess.

"I had to wear my clothes wet—no choice. In a creek I found nice long angle worms which I cleaned and ate. They were bitter, but I figured they were protein.

He realized his chances of surviving were poor, that the constant fog, rain, clouds, wind, and cool temperatures would keep him chilled and wet. The Aleutian Islands have no trees for shelter, or fuel. There was no obvious way to create warmth.

Or was there?

It was at this point that Charlie House's ingenuity enabled him to survive the challenging Aleutian climate. He was tired of being wet and cold. That discomfort prompted him to an imaginative and unique solution.

He was raised on a farm at Fruitland, Washington. Perhaps his memory of haystacks pointed him toward that solution.

The spring greening was just taking place. There was also an abundance of dry, winter-dead vegetation in his steep-banked valley. He piled this in a two-foot-high heap and folded his blankets over it. He then covered the blankets with another eighteen inches of dry vegetation. This gave him the equivalent of a thatched roof atop a soft mattress that insulated him from wet ground.

"The dry grass kept the rain off me—it absorbed it and got wet only a little way down, and it allowed it to drain away.

"After I figured out how to keep dry and warm with a small "haystack" I wasn't particularly bothered by the weather. Over several days I made a really big pad to sleep on. I put the folded blankets over it, and more dry grass on top. That bed lasted me the rest of the time I was there. It was comfortable. It was warm. It kept the rain off, and it kept the Japs from seeing me. I could crawl into my blankets and sleep secure," he told me.

There he remained for the next six weeks. "It rained all but one of those days."

Cow parsnip was abundant. "The roots and the inside tender parts of the new growth stem were soft and sweet and not so coarse. I nibbled at it almost full time. It was tasty, something like fresh corn," he said.

Each morning he gathered the tender parts of cow parsnip and rush (*Juncus*), filled the zip-off canvas hood from his jacket with water from a creek, and picked up, rinsed, and ate ten or fifteen earthworms. He then returned to his "haystack."

"I'd eat and sleep, and think and watch planes fly over."

How could he get out of this situation? There didn't seem to be any desirable alternatives. An early counter-invasion by American forces seemed improbable. His crew had scattered, with no way of communicating.

Despite Russell's promise of a pick-up, he realized it was unlikely. He thought longingly of his wife Marie and their baby daughter Barbara, and wondered if he would ever see them again. He took satisfaction that he had taken out the maximum $10,000 of National Service life insurance for Marie. He thought about and sometimes dreamed of food.

He had a pencil, but nothing to write on. He kept track of time by making a mark on the pencil each day.

One day an Irish setter dog ran near. It stopped and stared at him. Its Jap master, carrying a shotgun, was some distance away, probably hunting ptarmigan. After a moment, the dog rejoined his master. The hunter didn't see the crouching Charlie.

"He wasn't a very good hunter," Charlie remarked.

On another day a rocketing, machine-gun stuttering, Zero fighter skimmed down the floor of the valley. For a moment Charlie thought he was the target, but the plane, still spraying bullets, continued seaward. It didn't return.

On July fifth he was awakened by sharp explosions from the east side of the island. "It rocked the whole island," Charlie said.

Howard W. Gilmore, skipper of the new submarine *USS Growler* had slipped up on the destroyers *Arare, Kasumi* and *Shiranuhi* anchored near Reynard Cove on Kiska's eastern shore. *Growler* fired three torpedoes simultaneously, hitting all three enemy ships. One of the destroyers fired two torpedoes back. Gilmore took the *Growler* deep and the crew heard the deadly whine of torpedoes passing their boat.[1]

Arare sank; the bow of *Kasumi* was smashed; the hull of *Shiranuhi* appeared broken in half as Commander Gilmore left.

Postwar Jap records revealed that *Arare* was a total loss; the other two destroyers were refloated, towed back to Japan, and rebuilt.

Raids by PBYs ceased, and those by B-17 Flying Fortresses became frequent. Charlie became accustomed to hearing their exploding bombs. One B-17 painted a white contrail as it circled the island; it then formed a contrail cross within the circle—to indicate a target, he decided.

Food became a preoccupation, and was constantly on his mind. Next to that, loneliness sometimes overcame him. Like most enlisted Navy men, he was accustomed to living in close quarters with many others.

He talked to himself, arguing. "Should I surrender? Yeah, but what if they decide to shoot me?

"What am I accomplishing here? Am I doing my duty? What are the Japs doing at the harbor? What happened to my crew?"

---

1. Captain Gilmore became a submarine legend on Feb. 7, 1943. While operating out of Australia with the *Growler* on the surface charging batteries, the 900-ton provision ship *Hayasaki* loomed near and attempted to ram. Confusion reigned, and *Growler*, doing 17 knots, slammed into the *Hayasaki*. The impact knocked everyone below decks off his feet, and *Growler* heeled fifty degrees.

The crew of *Hayasaki* sprayed machine gun fire at the bridge of the *Growler*. Ensign William Williams and lookout W. F. Kelley were killed instantly. Captain Gilmore, wounded, clung to the bridge frame. He shouted, "Clear the bridge."

The officer of the deck, the quartermaster, and two wounded lookouts plunged down the hatch into the conning tower. For thirty seconds Arnold Schade, the executive officer, stood at the foot of the ladder, waiting for Gilmore. Then came the shout from Gilmore that became submarine legend: "Take her down!"

Schade had to make a terrible decision—save the boat or save the captain? He followed the captain's last order and gave orders to dive, leaving the wounded Gilmore and the bodies of Williams and Kelley topside to disappear into the sea.

Howard Gilmore was posthumously awarded the Medal of Honor.

At times he thought he heard voices, then realized it was his imagination. Sometimes he awoke during the short Alaskan night, empty belly aching, in a cold sweat, thinking he heard approaching Jap soldiers. "Would they see my haystack and shoot into it to see what it was?

"On the 48th day I was on my way to the creek for water when I fainted. I realized if I remained there I would die. I wrote my name on my jacket so my remains could be identified.

"I thought the Japs might kill me if I gave myself up, but it was my only choice. Even with the possibility of execution, and the shame, humiliation, and uncertainties, it was my only option."

A Japanese gun overlooking Kiska Harbor. This is the gun emplacement where Charlie House surrendered, forty-nine days after enemy troops landed on Kiska. AUTHOR

SURRENDER

"On the next day, July 26, I slowly climbed the nearby ridge. I was weak, and fell, slid, and rolled to the bottom of a steep slope. I had to climb a longer, less steep route.

"At mid-morning, on the ridgetop, I saw a sandbagged Jap anti-aircraft gun and its crew. The drifting fog was patchy; when it cleared I dropped to hide in tall grass; when the fog returned, I walked toward the gun.

"It was scary. I was afraid the gun crew would shoot me if I startled them. I had no white flag, so I tore off a piece of my shorts. The fog cleared and I was standing within thirty feet of the gun, holding my little white rag," he remembered. "Actually, the rag was gray—I had worn those shorts for seven weeks," he grinned.

"Two of the Jap marines at the gun ran and held me up by the elbows and assisted me to the emplacement. I was staggering.

"They sat me on one of the sandbags that ringed the gun and brought biscuits. I was eating biscuits and drinking tea when one of our B-17 bombers came over.

"Two of the gun crew took me a short distance and remained with me while their anti-aircraft gun fired at the plane. The B-17 dropped its bombs and left.

"The little Jap officer in charge seemed to be in a nasty mood. He barked orders to two soldiers, and they jammed their bayonets into place. Those cold clicks of steel startled and alarmed me. He then motioned me to follow him. I was apprehensive and thought he might take me down the path and have the soldiers bayonet me. The four of us started toward Kiska harbor.

"Camp headquarters came into view and I felt I had been spared."

Charlie was amazed at what he saw; Kiska had become a fortress. There were twenty-five or thirty buildings, where before there had only been three small weather crew shacks. There was a road network, submarine and seaplane bases, machine shops, a water and power system with fire hydrants, three radio stations, and a telephone system. About a dozen float Zero fighters (Rufes) were on the beach or anchored offshore, as well as four huge four-engine Kawanishi ("Mavis") seaplanes. Freighters and warships were anchored in the harbor. Anti-aircraft, machine, and coastal artillery guns lined the ridges. Caves had been dug into the sandstone for living space, hospitals, storage, and shelter.

The entrance to one of the more than fifty caves dug into sandstone by the Japanese on Kiska during their occupation. They used caves for a hospital, for living quarters, storage, and bomb shelters. AUTHOR

"They sat me on a grass-filled sack at Jap headquarters. Soon, a ring of fur-hatted Jap soldiers three or four deep surrounded me. They stared. They didn't smile. They didn't talk. They just stood and looked, and they looked mean. I felt like a monkey in a zoo."

He was served tea and dinner, then later, tea and biscuits. The circle of gawking soldiers remained for several hours.

"Late in the afternoon I was put into our old power house and given some grass-filled sacks and blankets for a bed."

Charlie House had survived forty nine-days in the hostile Kiska climate, wearing light clothing, without adequate food, and with makeshift shelter. It was a nearly incredible feat. He had lost more than eighty pounds.

A line of curious Japs formed at the two windows of the power house. Each stared at Charlie for a minute or so and left, to be replaced by the next in line. Darkness put an end to the staring, and Charlie luxuriated in the protection of a building. A steady rain beat on the shingled roof that night. "It sure felt cozy to have shelter again." A guard checked on him every half-hour by shining a flashlight in his eyes.

A Jap doctor examined him next morning. He told Charlie that J.C. "Mac" McCandless, ship's cook 3rd class, and aerographer 2nd class W. I. Gaffney, were captured on the morning of the landing.

"In dense fog, they ran smack into a group of soldiers marching from North Head to the campsite," Charlie said.

"After the war, McCandless told me he had been carrying a .22 handgun, which was taken away from him. He and Gaffney were marched back to the camp, where one of the Japs asked Mac if he had eaten lately."

"Not since yesterday," he answered.

"Go into the kitchen and make yourself breakfast," he was told.

"Mac opened the walk-in refrigerator, sliced off a big steak, and fried it. One of his captors eyed the steak and promptly padlocked the refrigerator," Charlie recounted.

Chief Pharmacist Mate R. L. Copperfield and aerographer 3rd class W. M. Winfrey—with Explosion, who had attached himself to Winfrey—surrendered after a couple of days. They had survived on food found in several trappers' cabins. They were taken aboard a cruiser where a doctor removed the bullet from Winfrey's leg. They were fed rice and soup, and questioned.

"Is the harbor mined? Where are the other men? Do you know of any other food caches?"

Within eleven days of the Jap landing, nine of the ten-man weather crew were prisoners. All had been sent to Japan as prisoners of war. The Japs had presumed Charlie was dead. Explosion remained on Kiska, a mascot for the invaders. Now Charlie and Explosion were the only Americans on Kiska.

Charlie was treated with courtesy and respect. He slept in the power house, was allowed to go to the toilet whenever necessary, and used the pond between headquarters and the bay for washing himself, his dishes, and clothes.

He was given all he could eat, and his weight and strength quickly returned. The line of gawkers at his window dwindled, returning only when a ship arrived, when a new line formed.

THE GIANT OF KISKA

Jap reporters and photographers occasionally arrived at Kiska. Mikizo Fukazawa, War Correspondent for the Jap newspaper *Domei*, wrote about Charlie. His account was later found on Kiska, when it was retaken by the U.S. It was partially translated by military intelligence. A copy of the two-page, single-spaced translated material, headed "Restricted: Advance CP, Hq Alaska Defense Command, 14 Aug. 1943," was sent to me by Admiral Russell.

It reads: "With the guidance of Captain Kanzaki we were taken to our barracks and told, 'Yesterday, after fifty days, an American soldier on Kiska surrendered. Would you like to see him tomorrow? He's weak and weary.'

"Upon my entering the room with Captain Kanzaki, the man beneath the blanket flung the blanket aside, sat up, and, together with a personality smile, executed a doubtful salute to the visitors.

"He who had goggling eyes and sunken cheeks, whose arms and legs were so thin that the expression "thin as string" fitted him perfectly, with a long, brown beard was "the man who was hiding for fifty days."

"The medical officer said, 'Because he hadn't eaten anything resembling food, but survived on grasses which grew on the beach, and when we gave him rice mush, he got a stomach ache.'

"He showed us by pressing his stomach which stuck to his back like a board as if he understood Captain Kanzaki's explanation.

"He said, 'Because I didn't have any food, and though I existed by eating grasses (called "buski" which the natives eat ["pushki, or pooshki is the Russianized Alaska Native term for cow parsnip—JR]) which grow along the shore, I couldn't bear it any longer so I surrendered. Please look at these skinny legs.'

"The thigh which he grabbed was no larger than a child's arm.

"He stated that his name was William Charhaus, age 29, and in his home in California a pretty wife and a girl are awaiting his return.

"When we mentioned that we were correspondents of a Tokyo newspaper and that we are planning to return to Tokyo soon, he stared at us with a serious look and asked, 'Which newspaper?'

"And when we said *Domei*, he said, 'I know about *Domei*. If you return, I want you to send a wire to my family that I am well and in the care of the Japanese forces and they are not to worry.'

"He repeated word-for-word his wife's and child's names and addresses in California.

"I felt sorry for him, but from my heart came another thought. Suppose he were a Japanese? I cannot think that with a healthy body they [the Japanese] would be taken captive, except in the case of being wounded. If he were a Japanese, he would never show his personality nor even in a dream ask to have his family notified of his well being.

The Japanese shrine on Kiska, September 7, 1943. It represented considerable labor by the island occupiers. Makeshift Jap housing and tents are the background. NATIONAL ARCHIVES

Charlie House at what remains of the Japanese shrine on Kiska. RICK ROSENTHAL

"While listening to his words, I clearly understood the difference between the Japanese and the Americans."

Another correspondent who wrote about Charlie referred to him as "The Giant of Kiska." At 5 feet 11-1/2 inches, he towered over most Japs.

FRIENDS

SEVERAL JAP military men visited Charlie frequently. One, nicknamed "BF" by Charlie for "Best Friend," had a homely wit, and reminded Charlie of Benjamin Franklin. He had been a reporter for a Tokyo newspaper before being drafted. At Kiska, he was a servant in the officer's quarters adjacent to the power house.

The former reporter was unhappy that the war had disrupted his life and landed him at Kiska. He liked booze, which he pinched from the officer's mess and stored in the attic of the power house. He entered through a window with a bag full of liquor bottles, and climbed into the attic to hide them. He always put his finger on his lips and said to Charlie, "No speak."

He usually brought Charlie food tidbits. On one occasion, eggs in his pocket broke as he crawled through the window. He withdrew his hand from his pocket, dripping with egg and shell, and extended it toward Charlie, saying, "For you."

"It took a bit of doing to show appreciation without laughing," Charlie said.

On another occasion he decided the two of them should get drunk. Charlie participated sparingly, but his Jap friend became maudlin and spent several hours telling Charlie about his life. Shortly after, he disappeared from Charlie's sphere; he never knew what happened to the man.

A Zero pilot drew Charlie's portrait, and helped him to start learning the Japanese language. One evening this pilot excitedly pointed east, and sketched American-type destroyers. "Three of your country's warships are right out there," he said.

The next day Charlie gleefully watched American naval shells walk across the tundra in the camp; one shell exploded within thirty feet of command headquarters.

"I was watching out the window as a soldier jumped into the shell holes for protection. He kept diving from one hole to the next, and it looked humorous to me and I laughed. He saw me, and the next day he pushed me off the walkway on my return from the washing pond. The executive officer saw this, and chewed him out.

"Almost every morning I watched the commander, Captain Kanzaki, at his exercise. He prayed aloud and swung his samurai sword. It made me uneasy, watching this old guy slicing that big sword around," he recalled.

Charlie asked a bomber pilot wistfully, "Maybe you could drop me at Dutch Harbor with a parachute?"

The Jap smiled and replied, "I can't do that."

The captain of a submarine bragged to Charlie that his boat had shelled the Oregon Coast. This must have been Meiji Tagoni, and his boat the I-25, for postwar records showed that on June 21, 1942, that submarine shelled Fort Stevens, an historical dot on the map at the mouth of the Columbia River. The I-25 also launched a plane on September 9 and 29 to drop bombs in Oregon forests, hoping to start fires.

An officer who spoke broken English with a German accent interrogated Charlie. After many questions he asked, "Who do you tink vill vin da var?"

Charlie replied, "I hope someone does soon."

That officer's report was left in his quarters when the Japs departed hurriedly from Kiska the following year. Found by U.S. intelligence, it was translated and sent to Washington D.C., where it was shown to Charlie's brother Robert who was on duty with the Navy Photographic Lab.

After Charlie recovered his health, and was near normal weight, an officer told him, "All healthy people in Japan must work. That includes you."

For the next three weeks, each morning he went to the head of the harbor to fill sandbags, which were piled around buildings for bomb protection. Most of the fifteen or twenty workers on the detail were civilians. "We had a good time talking and working together," Charlie remembered.

AIR RAIDS

On September 14, Charlie and his civilian friends were on the beach, filling sandbags. "I heard a noise and looked up and saw fourteen P-39 Bell Airacobra fighters about 700 feet above the harbor, just zipping along. It was the first raid from the new American base on Adak Island.

"They machine-gunned the Mavis seaplanes and came through the camp with guns blazing and dropping bombs. They dive-bombed guns on the east end of the island. Then they made another pass.

"Next, twelve B-24 Liberator bombers dropped bombs, and fourteen P-38 Lockheed Lightnings strafed and bombed the camp," he said.

Charlie had been told to go to his power house bedroom when bombs fell. As the raid started, he looked in that direction, but, "I was reluctant to run through that mess of gunfire and dropping bombs," he told me with a smile.

The Jap workers fled to a nearby cave. "I crawled in behind them. I had a hard time squirming into that little tunnel—my legs were too long to stand. We stayed for a couple of hours, and there were many bombing runs. The ground shook again and again," Charlie remembered.

"When things became quiet, we crawled out. It was a very good raid. Ten or twelve buildings were burning. A bomb had slammed through the power house roof. It landed on my blankets and knocked the entire north wall out," he told me.

The executive officer stood staring at the destroyed power house—Charlie's former bedroom. "You're a very lucky man, House," he said.

That night, Charlie slept in a bullet-riddled bathhouse. "I curled up in a big wooden tub, but couldn't get comfortable," he remembered.

Lt. Col. Charles M. McCorkle, flight leader of the P-39 Airacobras, reported that his planes shot down two float Zero fighters, devastated positions on Little Kiska Island, damaged three submarines, destroyed a Mavis flying boat, strafed four anti-aircraft positions, and killed or wounded about 400 Japs.[2]

During World War II, the Bell Airacobra fighter plane, with a 37mm cannon firing through the propeller hub, and two fifty and four thirty caliber machine guns, was especially effective at ground strafing.

Two of the P-38 Lightning fighters collided during the raid. The pilots were Lt. Dewey E. Crowe and Major Thomas W. Jackson, the latter the squadron's first commanding officer. Both crashed into the ocean. Neither survived. No other American losses were reported.

The Jap dead were buried the next day. "They broke legs and arms and stuffed the bodies into boxes about two feet square and twenty-eight or thirty inches high. They put the boxes on stretchers, and pallbearers carried them through camp bound for a cemetery," Charlie said.

As they passed, workers and soldiers—and Charlie—stood at attention and saluted the dead. The parade of death continued all day. "The Japs seem to have more respect for the dead than the living," Charlie commented.

Remembering McCorkle's report, I asked Charlie if he thought 400 Japs had been killed.

"That's about right," he answered.

One day, a bomb plunged into the dining hall from which Charlie's food came. Remnants of the cooking stove came through a wall.

That day, lunch was sent to the Jap workers, but none arrived for Charlie. He asked the German-accented officer, "Where's my lunch?"

"You vait," he was told.

After a bit he asked again, and got a, "Keep vaiting."

Finally, the officer sent Charlie to a mess hall on his own. On his return, he heard a bomb whistling down. He carefully placed his filled rice dish on the ground and covered it with his body. The bomb landed about fifteen feet away, penetrating four or five feet into the soggy ground. The blast was up, and the sides of the crater absorbed shrapnel.

"It tossed mud all over me, but I saved my chow. One of the Japs who saw it laughed at me. I picked up my chow, found a place to sit, and ate every bite," he said.

Charlie House and Admiral James Russell at Adak, July, 1985. Russell was among the last Americans that House saw on Kiska before having to surrender to the Japanese. After the war, Russell recommended House for a bronze star for burning communication ciphers while under enemy fire. AUTHOR

Charlie continued working on the sandbag detail until September 19, when the executive officer informed him he was leaving for Japan the next day. He told Charlie to shave (Charlie, with a full beard, hadn't shaved since June 7).

"I don't have a razor," Charlie told him.

The man gave him a razor, and the next morning Charlie was clean-shaven, with his worn clothing clean and ready for travel.

As he left for the collier that was to take him to Japan, his civilian laborer friends cheered, clapped, and said goodbye.

2. A copy of this report is in the archives of the 11th Air Force Bomber Command at Maxwell Air Force Base, Montgomery, Alabama.

"I was glad to leave. I doubt if I could have survived many more of those raids from Adak," he said.

LAST THOUGHTS

One afternoon Charlie and I sat on a hillside overlooking a calm Kiska Harbor. Colorful wildflowers surrounded us. The island was green, peaceful, quiet and beautiful. Charlie was thoughtful.

"Kiska looks nice today. From a distance, it's hard to see the damage that took place half a century ago. Time does heal the land.

"Sometimes I think I was kind of nuts to hide out for forty-nine days, with nothing to do and nothing to eat. I hoped someone would come get me, but they didn't. Finally I gave in. I probably think more about that place than any other," he said.

"When I came home after the war I was determined to never be cold, hungry, or in a hurry again. I've managed that," he grinned.

"I'm glad I came to see Kiska again, but I wouldn't want to spend another forty-nine days here alone."

REFERENCES

Blair, Clay, Jr., *Silent Victory; The U.S. Submarine War Against Japan.* Vols I and II. J.B. Lippincott Company, 1974.

Cloe, John, *The Aleutian Warriors; A History of the 11th Air Force and Fleet Wing 4. Part I.* Joint publication by Anchorage Chapter of the Air Force Association and Pictorial Histories Publishing Company, Inc.

Cohen, Stan. *The Forgotten War.* Vol. II. Pictorial Histories Publishing Company. 1989.

Francillon, Rene J., *Japanese Aircraft of the Pacific War.* Naval Institute Press, 1988.

Fukazawa, Mikizo, Translation, House, William C.: *Advance CP. HQ Alaska Defense Command, Office of the Assistant Chief of Staff for Military Intelligence, G-2, I & I Detachment, c/o PM, Seattle, Washington.* 14 August, 1943.

Heller, Christine A., Edible and Poisonous Plants of Alaska. Cooperative Agriculture Extension Service, University of Alaska. 1953.

House, William Charles, *Report to Neil F. O'Connor, USN, Naval War College, College of Naval Warfare, Newport, Rhode Island 02840.* Postwar. Not dated. (19 typewritten, double-spaced first-person account of House's experiences on Kiska.)

McCombs, Don, and Worth, Fred L., *World War II Super Facts.* Warner Books, 1983.

Parrish, Thomas (Editor), S.L.A. Marshall, Chief Consultant Editor, *The Simon and Schuster Encyclopedia of World War II.* 1978.

Rearden, Jim, "Kiska: One Island's Moment in History," *Alaska Magazine, 1986,* September, p. 18, and October, p. 26.

Rearden, Jim, Tape recordings of House and personal interview notes while at Kiska Island. 1985.

Turner, J. L. "The Attack on Kiska Island." A postwar report written for Admiral James Russell by a member of the Navy weather crew who was on Kiska June 7, 1942. 4 pp., typewritten (copy in author's files).

Winfrey, W. M. "Aleutian Attack of 7 June 1942." A postwar report written for Admiral James Russell by a member of the Navy weather crew who was on Kiska June 7, 1942. 8 pp., typewritten (copy in author's files).

3 A PRISONER IN JAPAN

Bound for Japan, a grimy Japanese collier sailed from Kiska Harbor September 20, 1942, with forty-one American prisoners aboard—forty Aleut Natives from the village of Attu, and Charlie House.

Charlie was made to clean toilets, and given other menial tasks, including washing the ship captain's clothing. Was this what he could expect as a prisoner of war in Japan? The well-known brutalities of the Japs in their China campaign were foremost on his mind.

"I ripped the captain's collar and cuffs where they were already worn," he told me with a grin.

He was free to roam over most of the ship (where else could he go?), and at night he went into the hold where the Aleuts were kept. He enjoyed talking with Mike Hodikoff, the village leader from Attu. He remembered Mike's son, little Stephan Hodikoff, who was 11, and Innokenty Golodof, who was 25.

"In May 1979, when I gave a high school commencement address at the Adak naval base, Innokenty told me he had thought I was one of the Japs," Charlie remembered.

"Brutal" doesn't adequately describe the Japanese treatment of allied prisoners of war during World War II. Beheadings with swords, bayonet practice on live prisoners, beatings with clubs, bizarre medical experiments, physical torture, starvation rations, cannibalism (eating prisoner's livers), and slave labor of prisoners, were all documented after the war.

Nearly one out of three (27 percent) Allied prisoners of war (POW) died in Japan. The death rate for WWII POW in German camps was only one out of twenty-five (4 percent) and Germans weren't noted for their humanitarianism.

The Attuans were taken off the collier at Otaru on Hokkaido Island. The terrible treatment they received there until their release on September 21, 1945, can be summarized by figures; forty were taken to Japan; only twenty-four survived (forty percent died, not counting newborn, of which three out of four died).

They were forced to dig clay for a pottery factory, under guard, while living in what Aleut prisoner Mike E. Lokanin described as ". . . a house that looked like chicken or pigs' house to me."

The Aleuts died of tuberculosis, beriberi, food poisoning, pneumonia, and other causes because of lack of food, decent housing, improper clothing.

The Jap treatment of these innocent American civilians had a horrendous impact on their health and well-being for the remainder of their lives.

The collier next arrived at a secret naval base about twenty miles southwest of Tokyo. A Jap petty officer blindfolded Charlie. "Can you see?" he asked.

"No," he answered.

"You see, I shoot," he warned.

He was taken to Ofuna, a camp thirty miles southwest of Tokyo. The blindfold was removed and the first person he saw was Mac McCandless, the cook from Kiska.

"Hi, Mac. How are you?" he called.

Chichagof Village on Attu was home to forty-one Aleut Natives when the Japanese took them captive. The village Russian Orthodox church, built in 1932, held valuable religious icons. The entire village was destroyed during the war. It was not rebuilt. NATIONAL ARCHIVES

Mac looked stricken, held his fingers to his lips, and went *shsshh*.

That puzzled Charlie.

He was locked in a tiny cell. "There was barely room for me to stretch out diagonally on the two-inch-thick mattress provided."

Breakfast next morning was a small cup of rice delivered to the cell door. Next came an interview with the Commandant, who sat behind a desk on which a samurai sword lay.

"You are not a prisoner of war. You are an enemy of Japan. We reserve the right to kill you at any time. You are not to talk to any other prisoner," he told Charlie.

Charlie now knew why McCandless had shushed him.

The Commandant asked Charlie a few perfunctory questions. "Where are you from? Are you in the reserves? Are you a weather man?"

Though Charlie spent six months in Ofuna, that was the only time he was questioned.

The razor given to him at Kiska was confiscated; the Japs feared Charlie would commit suicide.

The Commandant somehow learned that Japanese

reporters had interviewed Charlie at Kiska. "Did they take your picture?" he asked one day.

"Yes, many," Charlie assured him.

Charlie thought that may have saved his life. The photos left a trail. If he disappeared while at Ofuna, as did many prisoners, it might have been difficult to explain.

Marine fighter pilot Major Greg (Pappy) Boyington, famed for his Black Sheep Squadron which fought brilliantly in the South Pacific, was held at Ofuna the winter and spring of 1944, months after Charlie had left. In his book Boyington called it an "intimidation" camp. His account of the Ofuna treatment agrees with that of House.

Names of Ofuna prisoners were not reported to the International Red Cross. They were fed three-quarters the amount of food that POWs were supposed to receive. They did not receive clothing POWs were supposed to receive. The idea, according to Boyington, was to make them so miserable they would disclose military information.

Prisoners were selected for Ofuna because they supposedly had a special value to the Japs. They included submarine survivors, pilots, and various technicians. Charlie never understood why he and McCandless were taken there.

Commander Richard O'Kane, Captain of the submarine *USS Tang* (Rear Admiral O'Kane after the war—and recipient of the Medal of Honor), was one of the submariners imprisoned at Ofuna. His description of Ofuna agrees with that of Boyington and Charlie.

When O'Kane arrived he said other prisoners looked like ". . . walking skeletons." He said that, "Sometimes under orders but at other times on their own, gangs of guards roamed the corridors to beat prisoners who had been singled out for "special" treatment, and others whom they apparently simply disliked."

Referring to the skimpy daily ration of food, O'Kane wrote, "During war crimes trials, this ration was adjudged to have averaged 300 calories per day, and this was actually a quarter less than the Japanese authorities had planned."

When freed at the end of the war (from the Omori POW camp near Yokohama), "We all weighed in the 90s . . ." O'Kane said.

Despite the "no talking" edict, prisoners at Ofuna managed to communicate with notes on toilet paper, and whispers.

"A guard saw me whisper to another prisoner. He slammed me in the mouth with the butt of his rifle, knocking out all my front teeth," Charlie said.

A U.S. Navy commander at Ofuna (from the cruiser *Houston*) got word to the other prisoners that the correct answer to questions was name, rank, and serial number.

"If prisoners did that, they got the hell beat out of them," Charlie said.

After a time, prisoners learned to lie. "We told them more, or less, and made up stories. Many of us were beaten, regardless."

The prisoners' rule became never tell the truth.

An Australian navy lieutenant, in the cell adjacent to Charlie's, was told to diagram the defenses of the Sidney harbor. His work didn't satisfy the Japs.

They lined up the prisoners and stood the Australian in front, a guard on each side.

The Commandant announced, "He lies to us. We punish."

With fresh-cut green cherry limbs about an inch and a half in diameter, the two guards beat on his back. He finally fell. The guards then kicked and stomped him, and dragged him to his cell.

"He groaned and moaned all night," Charlie remembered.

The camp doctor spent the next day with the beaten man, and during the following week trays of food went into his cell.

At the end of the week, prisoners were ordered to close the shutters of their cell windows so they couldn't see. Guards again beat the Australian.

"He cried all that night. They had crushed his kidneys—he was urinating blood," Charlie said.

The man was tough; he survived.

Such treatment was common. Prisoners were routinely beaten and tortured. Charlie lost the weight he had gained at Kiska, and became skin and bones again. Sometimes there was what was called a trial, most times not. Either way there were executions, often in batches, at a rifle range in Nagoya or near Osaka. Those prisoners simply disappeared. There was no record of their being in Japan.

Charlie remembered three members of a PBY Catalina seaplane crew that had been captured in the South Pacific—the pilot, a radarman, and a mechanic. The copilot of the plane had been killed.

"The Japs made the pilot draw the radar setup for a PBY. Then they made the radarman draw it. Then the mechanic.

"They beat hell out of each; their drawings hadn't agreed.

"Then they called the pilot in again and told him, 'You're a naval officer. That's a sloppy drawing. We'll excuse the enlisted men, but not an officer.'"

"They beat him again," Charlie said.

Punishment for minor infractions, or sometimes no obvious infraction, was to be hit in the face and knocked down. One type of formal punishment, described by Boyington, required a prisoner to bend over; a guard would then repeatedly slam him in the rear with a baseball-bat-size club hard enough to knock him down.

When a prisoner needed to go to the latrine, he had to find a guard, bow from the waist, and ask permission in polite Japanese. Afterward he had to return to the guard, bow again, and thank him respectfully.

Charlie remembered, "We were so hungry we drank a lot of water to kill hunger pangs. As a result, at night we had to make frequent trips to the toilet.

"One night I knocked on my cell door three or four times and in polite Japanese asked, 'Please may I go to the toilet?'"

"They often pretended they didn't understand us; they didn't like our accent.

"I was ignored. The guard pretended he didn't understand me. Finally, I'm jumping up and down, really needing to go. The guard finally opened the door, and I ran down the hall. As I came back I saw a track of pee on the floor all the way to my cell.

"That made the guard angry. He stopped me and ordered me to stand at attention. As I stood there, he slapped me across the face and cheeks, their habitual response when they were annoyed.

"After he had slapped me on both sides of the face half a dozen times, I ducked and jumped into my cell and held the door shut. He tried to pull it open. I hung on. We tussled for some time.

"He finally let go and locked the door.

"I won that one," Charlie said.

Each morning, all prisoners stood in formation facing Tokyo and the Emperor's palace. They were forced to bow as one to the Emperor. The guards also bowed. While guards had heads down, POW's, with heads-down, unknown to the guards, spat in the appropriate direction.

Every two weeks women barbers arrived at the prison to shave prisoners' faces and heads; except for eyebrows every hair was removed.

One morning, because of the cold and his bald head, during the bowing routine Charlie didn't remove his hat. Guards beat him savagely for it.

"I had insulted the Emperor," he explained.

WORK CAMP

In February 1943, after six months at Ofuna, Charlie was taken to the Mitsubishi Dispatch Camp Number One in downtown Yokohama. As he walked into the camp, one of the prisoners called, "Hello Charlie. How are you?"

"I'm fine. Who are you?"

"Pete."

"Pete who?" Charlie asked.

"Pete Vaneer," he answered.

He was a radioman who had served with Charlie at Lakehurst, New Jersey, 1934-37.

Charlie hadn't recognized him. "He was nothing but skin and skeleton," Charlie said.

Pete died a week later.

The camp had a contract to provide prisoner labor for the Mitsubishi Shipyard. Charlie was assigned to the painting gang, which, daily, marched three miles to the shipyard and scraped and painted ships.

"We were systematically starved while being forced to work. Prisoners died at the rate of three a day. That's ninety a month, and there were only 500 of us. You'd get up in the morning and the guy sleeping next to you might be dead.

"If he was, we just covered him up, drew his rice ration, and reported him dead after breakfast.

"I quit thinking about it; I had to think about something else," Charlie remembered.

The Japs housed forty Aleut prisoners in this ramshackle building. Mike E. Lokanin, one of the Aleuts, commented that the building, "Looked like a chicken or pigs' house." it was cold in winter, and a small charcoal stove didn't help much.
ALEUTIAN/PRIBILOF ISLANDS ASSOCIATION, INC.

"The rate of dying dropped off in the spring, with warmer weather."

"Some of those who died were not survival-minded. They didn't have a will to live. If some guy was talking to you and getting sentimental, he might look perfectly healthy, but he might not be alive next morning. He was talking home."

I asked Charlie if he had considered trying to escape.

"Escape? We could have walked out of prison camp any night we wanted to, but where would be go?" he responded.

"There was no chance. Most POWs were a head or more taller than most Japs and would stand out wherever they went. You would have had to make your way to the seacoast, and it's a long way by raft to the U.S. or China," Charlie explained.

He worked at the Mitsubishi Shipyard seven days a week from February 1943, until that fall, "I got sick and the shipyard doctor diagnosed me with diphtheria."

When Charlie told the camp Commandant this, the man jumped back from him, exclaiming, "Stay away from me."

The Commandant put Charlie on a mattress on the floor in a corner of the building where the prisoners slept. Food was brought to him daily. Two British doctors, also prisoners, did what they could for him. There was no medicine.

The only Red Cross representative Charlie saw

during the war arrived in the form of a Jap medical doctor, who came to inspect the building.

"What's the matter with him?" the doctor asked the Commandant, pointing to the bed-ridden Charlie.

"Diphtheria? He should be in a hospital," the doctor exclaimed.

About twenty minutes later a medical sergeant showed up, handed Charlie a mask, told him to get dressed, and took him via train, bus, and streetcar to the Tokyo Military hospital on the west side of Tokyo. One ward there held ten or fifteen American prisoners.

TOKYO MILITARY HOSPITAL

A DOCTOR EXAMINED him and asked, "Where did our powerful Japanese forces capture you?"

This was in the fall of 1943, soon after about 2,500 Japs had been killed on Attu.

"At Kiska, Alaska.

"I saw his face tighten, and he said 'That will be all,' " Charlie remembered.

He checked Charlie every day, gave him injections, and as soon as there was a negative throat smear, sent him back to work camp.

PARALYZED

"I WAS SKINNY and weak, and the work camp doctor told me I wasn't fit to work. He put me in the kitchen, washing dishes."

It was warm, and, after the dinner dishes, Charlie often went outside to sun bathe.

"One evening I couldn't get up to go back inside. I could only crawl."

The camp doctor told him, "You have paralysis."

"My hands quit working. It affected my eyesight—closeup vision was blurred. In a couple of days I couldn't eat. I couldn't use a spoon or feed myself. I couldn't swallow," he said.

He was fed glucose intravenously and given massive doses of vitamins.

"They had a death watch on me at night. Another prisoner sat with me, waiting . . ."

The paralysis began leaving. "I didn't want them to know it. I kept exercising, moving my muscles, trying to get back on my feet. On August 17, my birthday, I crawled a ways, stood up, and fell flat. I was like a skeleton hanging by a string; cut the string and that was me, sprawled on the floor."

He crawled back to bed.

SHINAGAWA

HE WAS TAKEN to Shinagawa, a POW hospital located between Tokyo and Yokohama. There, the Japs had pooled thirty-five U.S. Army doctors who had been captured in the Philippines.

Shinagawa was an evil place, with stories of medical experiments, of prisoners arriving and never leaving. Postwar findings revealed that the head Jap doctor did experimental operations and gave prisoners experimental injections of caproic acid, soybean extract, sulfur and castor oil, serum from malaria sufferers, and urine. He bled men to death for plasma.

That doctor, tried before the International Military Tribunal of the Far East, was given a death sentence for using POWs for medical experiments. At the verdict, he went catatonic. When the sentence was commuted he came back to life; in two weeks he asked for his medical books.

"I was lucky to survive the hospital, much less the diphtheria. I faked paralysis and other health problems there for a year. Shortly after I arrived I weighed eighty-eight pounds. They had a plentiful supply of vitamins, and the food was a little better than at the work camp. In about six weeks, I felt pretty good. One foot dragged when I walked, but I started to get around a bit.

"I started washing clothes for patients. Later I was assigned as a ward orderly.

"The Jap Commandant figured I was getting to be a bit of a fixture. Occasionally he'd look me over and comment on how well I looked. I'd then arrange to have dysentery or some other pretext of illness, and he'd allow me to stay.

"By this time I had a good idea how the Japs operated. An American army medical orderly and I looked the camp over and figured out where Red Cross parcels were warehoused. They were supposed to be distributed to prisoners.

They weren't, of course.

"We smoked a small piece of metal, and followed one of the guards. When he had inspected and passed the building, we inserted the metal into the lock and moved it about. We then took it back to the hospital and filed on it. We repeated this several times. One day the lock opened.

"The building was full of food, clothing, packages, medicine—items desperately needed by prisoners.

"We got sweaters, new shoes, sulpha drugs, bread and other things that we shared with prisoners who could keep their mouths shut. We filled pillow cases and hid the stuff under our beds. We ate all night there for a while, and did very well.

"We found some suicide pills, one of which I carried in a pocket until the war's end. If I became mutilated, or without hope of recovery, I always had that damned pill.

"We stopped raiding the Red Cross warehouse when the lock on the door was changed; someone had gotten suspicious, and we didn't dare chance going back.

"I spent a year at that hospital and had largely recovered from paralysis, and had gained some weight, although I was still a walking skeleton."

SLAVE MARKET

"They sent me back to the Mitsubishi Dispatch Camp in Yokohama. By then I had learned how that camp operated. Prisoners could accept their job-assignment, as I had painting ships for the Mitsubishi Shipyard, or they could go to the slave market and get a change.

"Jap contractors and business operators could bid on POWs at the slave market. I watched faces of the bidders. They looked critically as each prisoner was brought up. The extremely skinny ones were always last to be bought. Those who had some meat on them, and therefore some energy, were bought first.

"Thoughts of the bidders showed on their faces. 'I like the looks of that guy—he could probably lift a lot.' Or, 'I'll bid low on that guy—he's kind of skinny and looks weak,' and so on.

"I wasn't getting enough outside chow on the job I had as a painter for Mitsubishi, so I went to the slave market. The guy who bid on me was Anisam, a little guy who had a small building near the drydock. With his other slaves, I'd get there in the morning. First, he would read us the paper with the Japanese slant on the news, and make a pot of tea for us.

"About ten o'clock, we left his building with an old cart, one slave between the shafts, two others, one on each side, pulled the cart with a rope over their shoulders. Several other slaves followed.

"We dragged that cart around the drydock to pick up empty acetylene and oxygen bottles. We'd call off the bottle numbers in Japanese and our boss recorded them in a little book. With each load we'd haul fifteen or twenty bottles to the gate, where a truck picked them up.

"We'd go back to his shack and wait for lunch. Armed guards would take us to a central area for lunch, which was mostly rice in a little box about half the size of a cigar box.

"When we had eaten, Anisam came for us and took us back to his shack, and that afternoon we'd make another round to pick up empties.

"Collecting empty acetylene and oxygen bottles was boring and we didn't get any outside chow. For us half-starved prisoners, food—chow—was all-important.

"I told his other slaves to tell Anisam I was sick and couldn't work. I knew the gang I wanted into. Without going to the slave market, one day I simply joined the Warehouse Movers, whose job was to move items in and out of warehouses. Sometimes this included food. These prisoners were all British.

"We don't want you. We have our own gang," they told me.

"I'm here and I'm staying," I responded, and remained with them. "I hung around them for a week before they accepted me.

"With that gang, food became available from time to time. One day we got our fill of frozen strawberries. On another, we moved a bunch of sacks of sugar. We hid one sack on our cart and stalled long enough to meet guys coming out of the camp to get rice, and added our sack of sugar to his load.

"A week or so later a guy from camp brought me a little cake—my share of the sugar.

"We handled piles of leather. Some of the Japs wanted leather to make belts and other items. We swapped leather for rice or cigarettes. I didn't smoke, but I used the cigarettes to trade for food."

B-29 BOMBING RAIDS

"Raids of B-29 bombers started; I counted 143 raids while I worked in Yokohama. When the bombers arrived, it really frightened the Japs.

"On November 23rd, 1944, there was a big stir in the yard. Sirens blew and bull horns blew, speakers blared, '*Ka ki, Ka ko. Bene jaku*' (air raid, B-29s).

"Here comes a lone B-29 at about 35,000 feet, apparently spotting and taking pictures.

"A few days later another came. This frightened them. Then one day 240 B-29s flew over. They went to a steel mill to the north of us. We took cover and I was in a good position to see the planes. I counted them aloud for the POWs crouched out of sight below me.

"After I had counted for a time, one of the guys warned, 'Not so loud, House. You're enjoying yourself too much. The Japs'll take it out on you.'

"Because of the frequent bombing raids, the Japs decided to create more space between warehouses to prevent fires from spreading, so they tore down every other one. The stuff that had been stored in the warehouses was hauled into the country and covered with canvas.

"As Warehouse Movers, we loaded the trucks hauling this stuff. A lot of it was food, from which we managed to pilfer enough to make a significant difference in our diets.

"I'll never forget one raid on Yokohama. It started about six o'clock at night. The B-29s flew at about 6,000 feet and arrived single file, one-by-one, until three the next morning.

"A searchlight picked up each bomber as it arrived. Anti-aircraft guns blasted, and Zero fighters dived and fired into the bombers' wing tanks trying to set the gasoline afire.

"Eleven B-29s were shot down over us that night.

"One of these plummeted down, afire, just over my head. I thought for a moment it would land on a bunch of us prisoners crouched in a ditch, but it veered and landed about three blocks away. The explosion of the plane and its bombs rocked the area. Fire and a huge plume of smoke marked the spot.

"An anti-aircraft shell exploded in the bomb bay of another B-29, causing its bombs to explode. The sky lit up like daylight, and the thunderous sound was almost unbearable. Airplane parts, including wings, fluttered to the ground. The crew was probably dead, for we saw some of them tumbling through the air. No parachutes opened. Pieces of the plane were scattered everywhere.

"By midnight the ack-acks had run out of ammunition. The Zeros were out of gas. B-29s arrived without opposition.

"On April 6, 1944, B-29s dropped incendiary bombs on Tokyo. I could have read a newspaper in Yokohama by the light of fires in thirty-mile-distant Tokyo.

"A sometimes guard, who had lived in Baltimore for forty-nine years as an importer of Jap sporting goods, was gungho for Japan in the war. He didn't like American POW's.

"He spent three days at Tokyo fighting fires from that raid, which burned fifty-four square miles of the city. On his return, he told us, 'These dumb bastards don't know when they're licked.'

"He knew the war was lost. He got the message.

"About then, a major change took place in the Mitsubishi Shipyard. Keels had been laid for several new ships. One day we saw workers using acetylene torches to cut these keels into four or five pieces.

"On the day of President Roosevelt's death, a Jap interpreter called in all the prisoners who were working in and around the yard.

"'Roosevelto has died. You are leaving the shipyard,' he announced.

"That sounded good to me. We walked back to camp, not knowing what to expect next. Next morning, guards walked us about fifteen miles into the country to a beautiful golf course. With spades, we were to turn it into a turnip patch.

"Next day, when we were about half way to the turnip patch, a couple hundred B-29s flew over and we ran into the woods. There was no need; they raided an aircraft factory at Kawasiki.

"I don't know what kind of bombs they dropped, but even though the explosions were fifteen miles away, those bombs were the noisiest suckers I have ever heard; they crackled impressively."

KAMAISHI

"AFTER A WEEK of spading the golf course, we were taken by train to be slave laborers at a steel mill at Kamaishi, on Honshu Island's northeast coast.

"We hadn't been there long when an American task force of carriers, battleships, cruisers and destroyers arrived offshore. About nine in the morning, airplanes from the carriers arrived over the steel mill.

"First, they dive-bombed and eliminated the anti-aircraft guns. There was a lull, during which all the steel mill workers fled, leaving us POW's behind with old Honcho, the main guard.

"The rolling mills were old Krupp type—three-feet-thick steel with seven feet of concrete underneath. During the bombing, Honcho took us under the concrete.

"We had barely arrived there when the first of many dozens of 2,000-pound sixteen-inch shells from our battleships *South Dakota, Indiana*, and *Massachusetts* rocked the place. The first ones landed near the beach; then they crept inland, each shell a bit farther from the beach. Those great battlewagons put a sixteen-inch shell in every ten square yards of that mill. Old Honcho was so frightened he cried, and continued to cry, during the entire bombardment.

"As we crouched, holding our ears, just above us were several tanks of molten steel. If a shell had hit one of those we'd have all died instantly."

As the shells roared in, Charlie remembered the captain of the submarine I-25 at Kiska who had bragged about shelling the Oregon coast. "This is a bit different," he thought with satisfaction, as he cowered from the earth-shaking explosions.

"That shelling was my most terrifying experience," he told me.

"When the shelling ended, that steel mill's yard looked like Hiroshima must have looked. Smoke rose everywhere. There was complete devastation.

"Our guard led us out of the yard. Some of the workers had returned. They were angry with us and threw rocks and other stuff at us.

"We passed unexploded sixteen-inch shells. That frightened us. We half expected them to explode momentarily.

"We arrived where our camp had been. It had been obliterated.

"There was no water, no electricity. All civilians had fled.

"We returned to a gravel pit at the steel mill. The Commandant put machine guns in various points around us.

"This is your camp for the night. If you cross the lines, we shoot," he warned.

The shelling killed ten or fifteen POW—and, according to Charlie, "A lot of Japs."

"We were the only coolies left, and we were forced to dispose of the bodies. One trench was filled with little girls wearing school uniform middies. They had gone into the trench for shelter, and an exploding shell had buried them. We dug them all out and threw their bodies on trucks. They were driven into the country, where they were tossed into huge fires. They were not identified.

"We then went through the shipyard and picked up all the loose bodies and tossed them on trucks to be hauled off and burned.

"Two or three days later, after all the obvious bodies had been removed, a Jap we called "Pluto" (for his sensitive nose) arrived. Sniffing, he crawled into old covered air raid trenches, and into railroad tunnels where people had run for shelter only to be buried by a hit from one of those big shells.

"He located bodies and told us where to dig, and he'd usually be right," Charlie remembered.

"It was grim," he told me. "But it was the way we were forced to live. Though we didn't get used to it, we learned how to cope," Charlie told me, shaking his head.

"We constantly reminded ourselves of Pearl Harbor, and who had started the war.

"At the time, the only clothing I had was a pair of pants and shoes. No shirt, no socks," Charlie remembered. "I managed to salvage a sweater and some socks from a couple of the bodies. I felt I was rich with a warm sweater to wear.

"One of the POW took a cap from a body. A guard saw him wearing it, read the message on it, and beat hell out of the guy. The cap was a twenty-year award to a worker who had never missed a day of work. The POW had "dishonored" the dead worker by wearing the cap.

"After the bodies were disposed of, Honcho took us into the steel mill's yard and pointed to a dud sixteen-inch shell. 'Dig hole' he said. We were all nervous, afraid to even touch that shell lest it explode.

"When the hole was dug he ordered, 'Push it in.'

"I was scared to death, but, with several other prisoners, I got behind the shell and rolled it into the hole."

"'Cover it,' the commandant ordered.

"For several days we went around burying dud shells. I have always hoped that one day Honcho or some other former guard digging up one of those shells with a forklift blows himself to kingdom come.

"Next we were forced to dig up and repair pipelines the shells had ruptured.

"At night they put us in a gymnasium that had but three sides; the fourth side had been blown out by a sixteen-inch shell. Walsh, a marine, and I, were sweeping the floor in that gymnasium when another carrier plane raid started.

"I heard a bomber diving. It sounded directly overhead, and I was sure the gymnasium was the target. I dropped to the floor, and if I could have, I'd have dug right through that floor with my fingernails.

"The target was a nearby bridge. The bomb hit it squarely.

"Walsh ran toward the open side of the gym. Rocks, tossed high by the explosion, thundered on the gym's roof. A watermelon-sized one busted through and hit Walsh on the head, killing him instantly.

"I ran outside. All around me Navy planes, machine guns clattering, were repeatedly diving. I panicked and ran like hell. I didn't know what I was doing. I suddenly realized how silly it was to run.

"I said 'To hell with it,' and sat. 'Go ahead, shoot me. I'm ready to die,' I thought.

"I sat for a few minutes while the strafing continued, and I suddenly realized I wasn't ready to die. I got up and got the hell out of sight," Charlie said.

"War's end was near, and we prisoners sensed it. We even knew within twenty minutes about the bombs that fell on Hiroshima and Nagasaki.

"The Japs talked about atoms and bombs that could destroy entire cities. They were damned scared.

"Kamaishi had been shelled and bombed twice. A rumor started that there were 2,200 ships offshore and there was to be an American landing. We all believed it, probably because we wanted to.

"At two a. m. that night all 300 of us prisoners fled from the gymnasium into the hills. It sounded logical, and we wanted desperately for it to be true.

"As I crouched among the trees and brush on that hillside, I worried how I was going to get through the American lines without getting shot.

"There was no landing, of course, and no 2,200 ships. Why would there be a major landing in that tiny valley at an outmoded and newly-destroyed steel mill?" Charlie asked.

"Next afternoon guards arrived in the hills, shouting *'Horyos, horyos'* (prisoners) to round us up.

"Not sure what their mood was, I remained in the bushes until other prisoners had been gathered up. When I didn't see anyone getting beaten, I joined them.

WAR'S END

"One morning the guards didn't arrive to take us to the mill. Another prisoner told me, 'Something good or bad has happened; either the Emperor is dead, or the war's over. Something's hot.'

"That day most of the guards mustered themselves out of their jobs and lined up for the train to Tokyo. However, Honcho, the old commandant, and a few others, remained. For many hours no one told us what had happened.

"About three o'clock, Honcho said, 'There's a truce. But Japan will never give in. It will haggle for a hundred years.'

"Shortly he said, 'There's a train here for you. It leaves in ten minutes.'

"All 300 of us were on that narrow-gauge train in ten minutes. The engine used water and wood, and had to stop frequently for water.

"We arrived at some little town and stopped for the night. As usual, we slept on the ground. A few snoozed on steps in a park. Some of the prisoners sat close together, smoking and talking. The few guards left ignored them, which was unusual. We couldn't figure out what was going on.

"Next morning, fighter planes from a carrier made a pass over us and dropped a message with three colored flags.

"Tell us what you need. A red flag for food. Yellow flag for clothes. Green for medicine." An added sentence read, 'Bear in mind that we've been at sea for fifty-six days and we're short on everything.'

"We knew then for sure the war was over. We were tired, half-starved, some were crippled. Some celebrated with yells, but most of the guys were simply relieved and thankful.

"Our next reaction was to wish we could respond to the dropped message by, 'Bear in mind that we've been here for three years and we're *really* short on everything.'

"We put all the flags out. Soon food, clothing, and medicine rained from overhead planes.

"We got new army uniforms, including boots. When we put them on and went into that little town, the Japs thought we were the occupation forces. They saluted us, or ran from us, depending.

"Barrels of food were dropped from B-29s. Some barrels parted from the chutes and came down like bombs. Two POW's were killed. What an irony; being abused and starved prisoners for years, then getting killed by a falling barrel of chow.

"A few Japs were killed too. That didn't bother us.

"Several of us grabbed some Jap coolies, a turnabout we enjoyed, and went up in the hills to retrieve some of the food, to bring it down to the others, some of whom were crippled, or too weak to climb.

"I found a bunch of C rations that were labeled "breakfast," "lunch," and "supper."

"I immediately sat and had a breakfast, a lunch, and a supper. And a breakfast, a lunch, and a supper. All in one grand, hoggish celebration.

"My stomach couldn't handle it. I lost it all. There was a little stream there where I washed my mouth out.

"Then I sat and ate a sensible dinner, which stayed with me.

"We turned our train around and went back to Kamaishi where we took over a barracks that had been occupied by anti-aircraft gun crews. We slaughtered a cow, and POWs who were cooks made some wonderful stews.

Other POWs went to a local bakery and made it clear that we expected an abundance of bread. Then, while we ate well for the first time in months or years, we waited.

"Two weeks later, one of our minesweepers swept the harbor, and a hospital ship and several destroyers arrived.

"The mayor of Kamaishi built a big stand. It looked like something you'd see on the 4th of July with ribbons and bunting. He wore a top hat and long tails. He expected a big ceremony.

"A Navy Commodore, with a gaggle of war correspondents, came ashore driving a Jeep. He swung by the mayor's stand.

'I won't talk to you. Get that crap out of here,' the Commodore growled, pointing to the stand.

"Where are the prisoners?" he asked.

"When he located us, he called, 'Bring the worst ones out.'

"There were plenty of skeletal, crippled, 'worst ones,' so the Commodore, and the correspondents got a graphic idea of the treatment we had received as "the worst ones" paraded.

"We boarded a hospital ship. They tossed all our new clothes over the side, sprayed us with what I now think was DDT, and outfitted us with new Navy dungarees.

"I rode a destroyer to Yokohama; then a troop transport to Guam. On that leg, we survived a terrible typhoon, which was so violent that some Navy ships sank. From Guam, I was flown to Honolulu, and after that, to San Francisco where I crawled off the plane and kissed the ground.

"The pilot of a C-54 told me I could fly with him to Los Angeles. I phoned my wife and told her to meet me at the San Pedro Naval Station.

"The C-54 landed at an airport about thirty miles short of Los Angeles. I walked out to the highway and stuck out my thunb. A guy stopped and asked me where I was going. I explained.

"'I'll take you there,'" he said, and he did. And

there was my wife, standing at the gate, with my daughter."

AFTERWORD

Charlie House survived thirty-nine months as a prisoner of the Japs, including his time alone at Kiska.

"I don't think I could have survived another winter as a prisoner of war in Japan," he told me. "The atomic bombs saved my life, and that of the 146,000 other Allied POWs in Japan—108,000 British and Imperial, 23,000 Dutch, and 15,000 American.

"If there had been an invasion, the Japs would have killed every one of us," he told me.

All ten members of the Kiska navy weather detachment managed to survive captivity in Japan.

After the war, Charlie remained in the Navy. He was soon commissioned—a jump up from first class petty officer.

In 1946, based on Admiral Russell's recommendation, he was awarded a bronze star for burning communication ciphers at Kiska while under enemy fire.

"I had signed for those ciphers, and I wasn't about to let the enemy have them," he told me.

Lieutenant Commander William Charles House retired from the Navy in 1959, after 27 years of service. He and his wife Marie bought a small piece of land in southern California. For the rest of his life he was a commercial grape grower, cultivating, pruning, and picking grapes himself.

After the war, Admiral James Russell worked on General Douglas McArthur's staff in Japan interviewing Japanese military to clarify historic events. He asked Captain Kanzaki, the one-time Kiska commander, if he remembered Charles House.

"Yes, he was a fine fellow and we all liked him," Kanzaki replied.

While we were at Kiska in July 1985, I asked Charlie, "After all you have been through, what do you think of the Japs now?"

"Some Japs treated me very well, but many were cruel, with no apparent sense of humanity," he said.

After a few moments he added, "I've never bought a Jap made car."

Charlie House died at age 83, October 31, 1996. His daughter, Barbara, told me that toward the end he occasionally hallucinated, believing he was again a prisoner of the Japs.

The Japanese reporter who interviewed Charlie on Kiska was closer to the truth than he could possibly have known when he called Charlie House "the Giant of Kiska."

REFERENCES

Boyington, Gregory, *Baa Baa Black Sheep,* Wilson Press, Inc. 1958.

Bradley, James, *Flyboys; A True Story of Courage.* Little, Brown and Company, 2003.

Cloe, John, *The Aleutian Warriors; A History of the 11th Air Force & Fleet Air Wing 4.* Anchorage Chapter—Air Force Association and Pictorial Histories Publishing Company, Inc., 1991.

Daws, Gavan, *Prisoners of the Japanese; POWs of World War II in the Pacific.* William Morrow, 1994.

Golodoff, Innokenty, as-told-to Karl W. Kenyon, "Last Days of Attu Village," *Alaska Sportsman*, December, 1966.

O'Kane, Richard H., *Clear the Bridge; The War Patrols of the USS Tang.* Presidio Press. 1977.

Oliver, Ethel Ross, *Journal of an Aleutian Year.* University of Washington Press, 1988.

Parrish, Thomas, Editor, and S.L.A. Marshall, Chief Consultant Editor, *The Simon and Schuster Encyclopedia of World War II.* 1978.

Rearden, Jim, Tape recordings of House and interview notes taken while at Kiska Island, 1985. Misc. papers provided the author by House.

4 UNDERSEA AT KISKA

FOR YEARS MY friend Rick Rosenthal, Adjunct Professor of Science and Natural History Filmmaking at Montana State University, heard stories from Alaska's commercial fishermen about the many sunken war ships and airplanes in Kiska Harbor. There was even a yarn about a sunken Zero fighter plane with the pilot still in it. The stories ballooned until it sounded as if Kiska Harbor was another Truk Lagoon, world famous for its fleet of sunken Japanese ships from World War II, and long a magnet for scuba divers.

Scuba diver Bill Evans, an ex-professional football player who once played for the Eagles, also heard the stories. He approached Rosenthal, proposing an underwater expedition to Kiska.

In January 1985, they chartered a commercial fishing vessel at Dutch Harbor and sailed to Kiska. Rosenthal, Evans, and Ron Kuiper, another scuba expert, did the diving and underwater filming on that preliminary probe.

"The water was near 36 degrees at the surface. Dry suits were a must," Rosenthal told me.

"We used a side-scan sonar to locate targets and check out bottom terrain. We found many underwater targets with it, and in a hurried four days explored and photographed several. Low winter-light levels and short days hindered the work. Also, the commercial vessel chartered for the job couldn't linger.

For the summer 1985 expedition, they chartered the 112-foot schooner *Manutea*. It arrived at Kiska in July with five divers (Rosenthal, Evans, Ron Kuiper, Charles Arneson, Chuck Nicklin), to film a documentary of Kiska's underwater treasures from World War II. It was this expedition that Charlie House and I joined (see chapter two).

RESULTS

THE FOLLOWING came largely from an oral report to the author from Rosenthal, who is internationally known as a cinematographer and marine biologist. He received a Primetime Emmy in 2002 for Outstanding Cinematography for the non-fiction programming of *The Blue Planet, Seas of Life* (BBC and the Discovery Channel). He has made or participated in fifty-five wildlife and nature films around the world.

"In January, we explored two sixty-foot patrol boats. They were in about seventy feet of water. Their wood hulls had pretty well collapsed on the sea floor. There was no cargo on either," Rosenthal told me.

The transport *Nissan Maru*'s mast sticks out of the water roughly in the center of Kiska Harbor.

In diving on her, Rosenthal found that, "The *Nissan's* cargo was hundreds of barrels of gasoline in the cargo hold. The ship was still leaking gasoline after forty-three years. The ship burned, and was probably scuttled. The deck is fifty feet beneath the surface; the hold is ninety plus feet down."

Ron Kuiper, after diving on the *Nissan*, swore he had found a compartment full of doorknobs. Another compartment was full of beer bottles, said Bill Evans.

The 112-foot steel schooner *Manutea* at the north end of Kiska Island. Divers worked from this ship to explore the bottom of Kiska Harbor for war-time relics. CHUCK NICKLIN

From the *Nissan*, divers brought up dishes, empty brass from a deck gun, and one tiny, lovely sake server.

Rosenthal related, "The Japanese submarine RO-65, in Kiska Harbor, is ninety feet below the surface. I found the conning tower separated from the hull and lying on the ocean floor, spun the wheel to the conning tower hatch, and it opened easily. The brass inside was still shiny and instruments and controls looked almost ready for use," he said.

"From the gear it is rigged with, it appeared that the sub might have been under tow. We found the anchor way out in front.

"I entered the conning tower and the control room with movie camera and lights. Rust and silt stirred up. A huge resident cod fish swam at me through the rust and gloom. At one time near the end of the dive, I was perched on the bow of the sub, looking back along the rusted hull. I remember wondering what had become of the crew. Did anyone survive the bombing and sinking?

"She had been hit in a number of places by bombs or shells, with holes along the sides. You can go through the hatch and into the periscope control room. We didn't get into the living quarters; the fit was too tight for scuba tanks."

I-boat Captain Zenji Orita, in his book, *I-Boat Captain; How Japan's Submarines Almost Defeated the U.S. Navy in the Pacific* [a nonsensical title if ever there was one—JR], written with Joseph D. Harrington (Major Books, 1976), claimed that the RO-65, ". . . sank accidentally in Kiska Harbor, November 4 [1942]. All hands were lost."

The holes seen in the hull by Rosenthal probably confirm that the sub was damaged by bombs. Orita's book listed the captain of RO-65 as Lieutenant Shoichi Egi.

A diver finds dinner plates on the deck of the *Nissan Maru*, fifty feet below the surface of Kiska Harbor. RICK ROSENTHAL

The transport *Kano Maru*, lying in the shallows on the south side of Kiska Harbor, was first hit with a torpedo from the fleet submarine *Grunion*. The *Grunion* was lost on a war patrol off Kiska on or about July 30, 1942.

After being damaged by the *Grunion*, the *Kano* caught fire during a U.S. naval bombardment on August 7, 1942. Later that day she was sunk by one or more bombs from PBY airplanes.

"It appears she was run up on the beach," said Rosenthal. "She's in shallow water, down to about thirty feet. She's broken up all over the reef."

The freighter *Nozima Maru*, at the head of Kiska Harbor, was apparently intact at the end of the war. Storms tore her in half. The front half was still there. Instead of jagged edges, some of her steel appeared to have been cut. Parts of her may have been salvaged, an observation passed on to me by John Cloe, Chief of History for the Eleventh Air Force at Elmendorf AFB, Alaska.

Rosenthal continued, "We dived on a Japanese landing ship of around forty feet, which may have been lost in a storm. It may have been used in the invasion of Kiska, or it could have been one of the barges used to evacuate personnel," Rosenthal said.

"We found an upside-down hull of a 200-foot-long boat in ninety feet of water. It was V-shaped, and didn't appear to be a barge. We have no idea what it was, nor could we find an entrance. The hull was intact," according to Rosenthal.

A diver at 60 feet, on the deck of the *Nisson Maru*, with what appears to be a large caliber shell. The ship carried hundreds of barrels of aviation gasoline. RICK ROSENTHAL

The *Borneo Maru*, in Gertrude Cove, a few miles southwest of Kiska Harbor, sits high out of the water, a square-bowed, old-fashioned freighter, with the tide washing in and out of her rusty, broken sides.

"On our first dive on the *Borneo*, we were accompanied by a large bull fur seal that swam in and out of the old submerged hull," Rosenthal told me.

"It is like a cathedral inside the *Borneo Maru*. It is calm, peaceful, and beautiful. The plant and animal life is every bit as colorful as tropical coral and algae," Bill Evans told me.

Rosenthal said, "The *Borneo* looked like it had been hauling coal and other types of supplies. It had coal in the bottom of its hold. She's sitting in about twenty feet of water, and appears to have been deliberately beached. Fire was intense on that ship; shoes were melted to the deck, and bottles had melted."

The destroyer *Arare*, sunk by the U.S. submarine *Growler* (the torpedo explosions heard July 5, 1942, by Charlie House) evaded discovery by Rosenthal and crew, despite days of searching. The

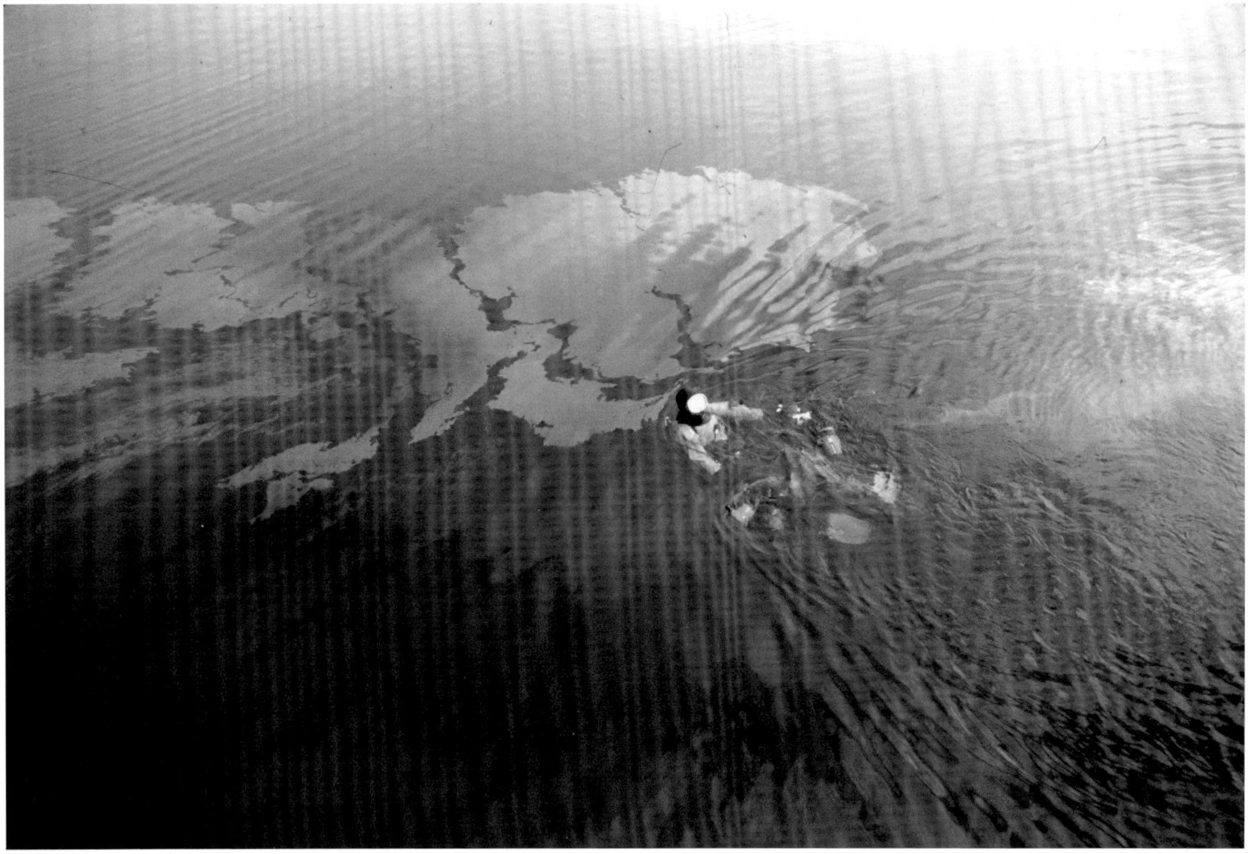

A diver on the surface above the *Nisson Maru* in Kiska Harbor, with a gasoline slick that had bubbled to the surface from the sunken ship. AUTHOR

three destroyers (*Arare, Kasumi* and *Shiranuhi*) reportedly left Kiska Harbor in dense fog and decided to wait for the fog to clear. They anchored near shore off the Salmon Lagoon area, where the *Growler* found them. Reports vary on where they sank.

The divers were unable to find any of the warplanes reportedly shot down in Kiska harbor.

Nor did the divers find any of the "piles of rifles and pistols" dumped by the fleeing Japs and reported by American and Canadian troops who landed on Kiska. Those visible in shallows were probably grabbed as souvenirs by soldiers later stationed on the island.

Kiska Harbor is not another Truk Lagoon.

[AUTHOR'S NOTE: *During the Aleutian Campaign, U.S. air attacks sank the RO-65, although after the war, as noted by Captain Orita, the Japanese claimed it sank accidentally, perhaps after being damaged by bombing. Air attacks sank the cargo ships* Nisson Maru, Nozima Maru, *and* Borneo Maru. *As noted, the cargo ship* Kano Maru *was first torpedoed by the American submarine* Grunion, *then set afire by naval bombardment, and finished off with bombs from PBYs. Source:* Campaigns of the Pacific War, *pp. 83 and 90 (notes by John Cloe), and Morison, Samuel Eliot,* Aleutians, Gilberts and Marshalls, *pp. 10–12.*]

5 WILD BILL THIES: PILOT

I WAS WRITING *Koga's Zero*, my book about the Japanese Zero fighter plane that Bill Thies and his crew found crashed on Akutan Island, and I wanted him to tell me about the discovery.

I drove from Alaska in November 1987, to interview him—a retired Navy Captain—at his pleasant Monterey, California, home.

I learned much about him during that tape-recorded interview. Over the past eighteen years I have maintained telephone, mail, and E-mail correspondence with him, learning more, some of which I have incorporated into this chapter.

In 2005, Bill Thies was 89—and still going strong.

FINDING KOGA'S ZERO

At dusk, July 9, 1942, Lieutenant Bill Thies, with his crew of seven, lifted a PBY patrol plane off the water at Dutch Harbor.[1] All night they flew over the Pacific, watching their radar scope (one of the earliest aircraft radar installations), searching for enemy ships.

Their commanding officer, Commander Paul Foley, had decided on night patrols to avoid the heavy loss of aircraft that PBY squadrons had incurred in daytime operations against Jap carrier planes in the Southwest Pacific. In Alaska the planes depended on radar to sniff out targets encountered in darkness. Planes flew darkened, and observed radio silence except for contact reports.

It had only been five weeks since Jap planes had bombed Dutch, and the Japanese military became entrenched on Kiska and Attu Islands.

Navigation for Thies' plane that night was by dead reckoning with an unknown wind; at dusk as they left Dutch, it blew strongly from the east; at dawn, after they had flown all night, it was blowing from the west. The night was dark, the sea rough. There was a solid overcast. No stars were visible.

At daylight Thies and crew had only a vague idea where they were. Where were they when they encountered the 180-degree wind change?

Copilot Bob Larson, navigator, took a sight through the copilot's side window and calculated

1. Built by Consolidated Aircraft Company in San Diego, California, the PBY-5 was a flying boat (seaplane) with wheels. Patrol range about 2,000 miles. It had wingtip floats and two 1,200 horsepower Pratt and Whitney engines. The hull was connected to the 104-foot wing by a cabane strut, which housed the flight engineer and all the engine instruments.

The nose housed the bombardier's station, and a thirty-caliber machine gun. Behind that was the cockpit for two pilots who sat high above the walkway between them. Further aft were the navigator's table and the radioman's station.

In the center of the hull beneath the flight engineer's station was a two-cycle gas engine which furnished electricity when the main engines were not running. There was also a two-burner electric hot plate for cooking. Aft the bunk compartments, and following that, the waist compartment. There were port and starboard plexiglass blisters at the waist that could be opened to allow firing of two fifty-caliber machine guns. Toward the tail section was the tunnel hatch in the bottom of the hull which could be opened and had a thirty caliber machine gun.

Bombs and aerial torpedoes were carried under the wings.

Normal crew of a Navy PBY in the Aleutians was eight: Patrol Plane Commander, copilot, navigator, relief pilot and bow gunner, radio/radar operator, second radioman, ordanceman and gunner, and plane captain.

The plane captain (an enlisted man) was responsible for maintaining the aircraft on the ground, and to have his crew trained to man all stations except pilot and navigator spots when it was airborne.

Lieutenant William N. Thies, in 1942. Thies was patrol plane commander of the PBY that discovered Koga's Zero on Akutan Island. "Wild Bill" Thies, holder of the Navy Cross for bombing a Japanese ship in Kiska Harbor with a slow, lumbering, PBY, told the author he though his most significant contribution to World War II was finding the downed enemy Zero. JOE RYCHETNIK

that the plane was 240 miles east of their intended course. That was a suspicious figure, so Larson recalculated and came up with the same number.

That day, July 10, while returning to Dutch, Thies flew over Akutan Island, twenty-five miles east of Dutch. Al Knack, the plane captain, in a waist blister, called, "Skipper, there's a plane down there."

Thies descended and circled an upside-down silver-gray airplane lying on the ground. It had rising sun emblems on wings and fuselage, and it appeared relatively undamaged. Larson marked its location on a chart, and Thies flew back to Dutch.

"I was excited over the find," Thies told me. "But Commander Paul Foley, my Commanding Officer, balked when I asked to be released from patrol duty to take a party to Akutan to examine the plane to see if it could be salvaged.

"This was understandable, because we were short of crews and planes due both to losses to the Japanese and to the weather.[2] But I persisted, and pushed so hard I was almost insubordinate. Foley finally relented and allowed me to take my air crew to examine the plane," he told me.

Neither knew they had just participated in a major turning point in the Pacific aerial war.

We traveled to Akutan with the YP-151, the *Mary Anne*, a converted fishing boat used for patrol. For all we knew there was a Jap crew on the loose on the island, so we all went armed. Since we had located the plane from the air, we had no difficulty in walking directly to it on the ground.

"From the air, the valley where the plane had landed appeared as smooth as a golf course; not easily seen was the foot or so of water beneath the dense grass. Tadayoshi Koga, the Zero's pilot (whose name was unknown in the U.S. until after the war), had landed his plane wheels down. The wheels hit the water and the plane flipped onto its back. Koga, dead, was still strapped in his seat with his head submerged," Thies remembered.

The Japanese Zero then dominated the skies in the Pacific war zone. It outmaneuvered our fighter planes in almost every encounter. A few badly wrecked Zeros had been examined after the sneak attack on Pearl Harbor, but little had been learned from them. It was a mystery plane to the U.S. and its Allies.

2. Of twelve crews that arrived at Dutch Harbor to fly patrols in PBYs in June 1942, nine were lost—mostly to weather, but some to enemy action.

In the literature of World War II, the plane Thies and his crew found—the first Zero captured and flown by test pilots in the U.S. during WWII—has been called the Aleutian Zero, the Akutan Zero, and Koga's Zero. It was shipped to the North Island Naval Air Station, San Diego, for repair and test flights.

A PBY under Japanese anti-aircraft fire at Kiska, June, 1942. The big, slow, seaplanes were easy targets. JAPANESE PHOTO

On September 20, 1942, Lt. Commander Eddie R. Sanders was the first American to fly Koga's repaired Zero. That first flight, from North Island, exposed weaknesses which our pilots could exploit. Before he died in 1992, then Rear Admiral Sanders told me [JR], "The Zero had superior maneuverability only at the lower speeds used in dog fighting, with short turning radius and excellent aileron control at very low speeds.

"However, immediately apparent was the fact that the ailerons froze up at speeds above 200 knots so that rolling maneuvers at those speeds were slow and required much force on the control stick.

"It rolled to the left much easier than to the right. Also, its engine cut out under negative acceleration due to its float-type carburetor.

"We now had an answer for our pilots who were being outmaneuvered and unable to escape a pursuing Zero. Go into a vertical power dive, using negative acceleration if possible to open the range quickly, and gain advantageous speed while the Zero's engine was stopped by the acceleration. At about 200 knots, roll hard right before the Zero pilot could get his sights lined up.

"This recommended tactic was radioed to the fleet after the first flight, and soon the welcome answer came back, 'It works!' " Sanders told me.

The Zero's domination of the skies over the Pacific ended with Sanders' test flights. No one knows how many pilots' lives were saved by the knowledge gained from Koga's Zero. Bill Thies summed it up very well when he told me, "If having Koga's Zero saved even one American pilot's life, it was well worth the effort of retrieving, rebuilding, and test-flying it."

THE JAPANESE BATTLE CRUISER

In December 1941, Bill Thies was a U.S. Navy ensign and a pilot assigned to VP-41 at Kodiak, which flew the long-range PBY patrol plane. "We

A PBY-5 Catalina amphibian, May, 1944, somewhere in the Aleutians. The crew is hand-turning the props before startup to prevent "hydraulicking"—damage to engines when oil has seeped into lower cylinders while shut down. Intended primarily for patrolling, PBYs attacked the Japanese carrier force that raided Dutch Harbor, and even dropped bombs on the enemy fleet in Kiska Harbor. NATIONAL ARCHIVES

were all green and didn't know what was going on. The sneak attack at Pearl Harbor had us all deeply concerned. We worried that they would attack Alaska," he remembered.

"A few days after Pearl Harbor, my first wartime assignment was to fly a patrol with another PBY southwest of Kodiak into the North Pacific. I almost ended my navy career on that flight. We were watching for approaching Japanese ships, and had flown about 200 miles, when I spotted the biggest warship I had ever seen. It was steaming north toward Kodiak at high speed."

Thies didn't go to the Naval Academy, and had almost no experience with the fleet. "I hardly knew a sub chaser from a battleship," he laughed.

"I got binoculars on it. Then I sent an Aldis lamp signal to the ship requesting identification. No answer. I tried all the radio frequencies we knew for our ships. No answer."

"That guy *has* to be part of the Jap fleet," I told myself.

He then studied his book of Japanese ship silhouettes. "My crew and I agreed it was a Japanese battle cruiser. I sent a CW (dot-dash) message to Kodiak. 'Sighted Japanese battle cruiser, course 030, speed 35 knots, 200 miles southwest of Kodiak.' "

The wives and families of VP-41, including Bill's wife, Vivian, were at Kodiak. At receipt of his message,

The downed Japanese Zero (Koga's Zero) where it was found on Akutan Island by Bill Thies and his crew on July 10, 1942. That's Thies, without jacket, hand and fingers outstretched. Bob Larson, his copilot is second from left, with cap. U.S. NAVY

Kodiak went on full alert. Wives and children were herded into the concrete power house. Soldiers ran into the hills to man guns.

"About then the pilot of a Navy Duck (amphibious float plane) landed on Woman's Bay with his wheels down—and the plane sank. With my message on hand, everyone decided the plane had been hit by anti-aircraft fire.

"With me was a first class ordnanceman who was the master bomber of my squadron. "I told him 'We're going up to 10,000 feet and get that bastard.' "

Thies' plane was equipped with a Norden bomb sight, designed for high level bombing, and his plane carried four 500-pound general purpose bombs. As he climbed, the "Japanese battle cruiser" started zig-zagging.

Thies continued to query the speeding ship with his Aldis lamp. No reply.

Ensign Jep Jonson, flying the companion PBY with Thies, had been unable to raise his wingtip floats. That, with the ton of bombs he carried, made it difficult for him to climb. Otherwise he'd have joined Thies. Jonson was a Naval Academy graduate who knew his ships. He had picked up Thies' message to Kodiak.

"Bill, I'll stay low and observe results," he radioed Thies.

Thies armed his bombs, reached 10,000 feet and started a bombing run. The ship increased speed and zig-zagged wildly.

"About a minute from drop point, Jonson frantically radioed, 'Bill, don't drop. The ship is a United States destroyer.'"

The ship was the *USS Gillis*, originally a World War I four-stack destroyer. One engine room had been converted to hold aviation gas, bombs, and other material support for PBYs. The conversion

Koga's Zero on July 17, 1942, at Dutch Harbor, being prepared for shipment to North Island, San Diego, for rebuilding. When flown by Lt. Commander Eddie Sanders in September, 1942, it revealed weaknesses our pilots could exploit. After that, the Zero no longer dominated the skies in the Pacific as it had. U.S. NAVY

removed two of the four stacks. Now it was a seaplane tender designed to support PBY's distant from land bases.

"Talk about being embarrassed. We were at war, and I had nearly bombed one of our own ships," Thies said.

Thies sent a three-letter Z signal to Kodiak that meant "Cancel my last message."

The Kodiak Command didn't believe it, suspecting the Japanese had sent it. They queried, "What is patrol commander's first name?"

"William," Thies radioed.

The Kodiak brass decided the Japs knew that half the guys in the American fleet were named William. They discounted the message.

"What is patrol commander's middle name?" they queried.

When Thies replied, "Nouris," they were satisfied.

The women and children went home and the Army gunners came out of the hills.

"I saw Commander Norm Garton, skipper of the *Gillis* that night, and we had a few martinis together. He had hurriedly left Pearl Harbor a couple days before the Japanese attack on Dutch Harbor, and had forgotten to take current identification codes," Thies explained.

"He told me 'I was damn near ready to shoot at you, but I knew if I did you would be convinced I was Japanese,'" he said.

Garton's radioman had heard the radio traffic between Thies and Kodiak, so Garton was braced for a bombing.

"Commander Gehres, the wing commander, had me on the carpet. He was a strict officer who rose through the ranks from an enlisted man, a pioneer of naval aviation. He had flown from the first U.S. aircraft carrier, the *Langley*.

"For a time, I spent a lot of hours studying ship identification," Thies remembered with a smile.

BOMBING KISKA HARBOR

THE JAPANESE seized Kiska Island on June 7. Reports that had been coming to Dutch every three hours from the ten-man Kiska Navy weather crew, ended abruptly. Ensign Jim Bowers, patrolling in a PBY, reported seeing unidentified ships in Kiska Harbor.

"Paul Foley, my squadron commander, came to me and said 'I know its not your turn to go on patrol again, but we'd like you to fly out to Kiska and see what's going on. We haven't heard from the weather crew for several days. We're not sure what Bowers saw,' " Thies told me.

"We loaded four, 500-pound, general purpose bombs and flew to Kiska Harbor. We were under a fog bank as we approached the island and when we were about five miles away saw what appeared to us to be about half the Jap fleet in the harbor.

"I flew on top of the clouds, and for about an hour we peered through holes to see what was in the harbor. As we flew through thin spots in the clouds we drew anti-aircraft fire, but weren't hit.

"It was our first experience with anti-aircraft fire, and none of us liked it," said Thies, in a typical understatement.

"Al Knack, one of my crewmen, sketched the harbor, and the location in it of two cruisers, a submarine, four destroyers, four transports, and four four-engine flying boats tied to our buoys there," said Thies.

The light aircraft carrier *Ryujo*, flagship of the fleet that attacked the U.S. Naval Base at Dutch Harbor on June 3 and 4, 1942. She carried forty-two planes and had no superstructure above the flight deck. This is the carrier from which Petty Officer Koga flew the Zero that he crashed on Akutan Island. Planes from the *USS Saratoga* sank the *Ryujo* in the eastern Solomon Islands in August, 1942. NATIONAL ARCHIVES

"I sent my contact and amplifying messages to Dutch, and said 'Let's get the hell out of here.' We then headed east, toward home.

"We were near Amchitka, forty or fifty miles from Kiska, when we received a message I'll never forget. I had a little radioman named Harvey. I've never seen Harvey to this day; nobody knows what happened to him. PBY pilot and copilot seats are pretty high, and there's a walkway into the cockpit. Harvey's head came to just below my shoulders when he walked into the cockpit. I looked down to see him with a .45 in one hand, pointed at me. In his other hand he had a radio message.

"Harvey, what's the gun for?" I asked.

"He handed me the message and said, 'You aren't going to do this are you?'"

"Do what? Put the damned gun away."

"I'll never forget that message. It was to my personal call sign, which was the number of the plane—42V5 or something—from OOV, Commander Gehres, the Wing Commander at Kodiak. He had intercepted my message to Dutch."

"Bomb enemy shipping in Kiska Harbor," read the message in plain language.

"Put the damned gun away and let's think about this," I told Harvey. "I don't know if he was serious. I know he was scared to death. He was probably *half* serious.

"He put the gun away, and I circled. Bob Larson was the navigator. 'I don't know, Bob. We can head back over there and drop the bombs but we'll be awfully vulnerable with this low ceiling,'" Thies said, worriedly.

"I felt cold sweat pouring off my arm pits—and we wore super warm, leather flying suits," Thies remembered.

It was his first close encounter with the enemy.

"Bob Larson had an idea. We had some of the very first airborne radar. It was pretty primitive, with a little green scope that showed the targets as pips at various points on a line across it," said Thies.

Koga's Zero in September 1942, in U.S. Navy markings, landing, with wheels and flaps down and canopy open. The pilot was Lt. Commander Eddie Sanders. The short radio mast behind the canopy identifies photos of Koga's Zero from those of other Zeros captured later in the war. Others had much longer masts. NATIONAL AIR AND SPACE MUSEUM

Larson studied a chart of Kiska Harbor. It showed a prominent spit on the northeast side, at the west end of Little Kiska Island.

"He suggested, 'Why don't we stay in the fog, and when the radar shows we're over that spit, I'll time how long it should take for us to be over the ships. They're concentrated in less than a quarter mile. I'll let you know when we're above them and you can dive down, drop the bombs, and climb back into the fog.' "

"Sounds good to me," Thies agreed.

"We set the intervalometer (a timer that drops bombs at pre-set intervals) to release the bombs in a run across the concentration of ships," Thies remembers. "But we weren't exactly up to speed when it came to bombing the Jap fleet," he laughed.

"Larson timed us, and when he figured we were over the ships, I dived out of the fog. Lohse, my copilot, was at the bomb release switch. I wanted to get rid of the bombs quickly and duck back into the clouds—flack was exploding all around us with loud bangs. It was hard to converse.

"I guess this is as good a place as any to drop," I told Lohse.

"What?" asked Lohse

"I said drop the bombs."

"You want me to drop the bombs now?" Lohse asked.

"I was a bit steamed by then," Thies laughed.

"Yes! Yes! Drop the goddamned bombs," I told him.

"He did, but one hung up and we released it manually. I climbed back into the clouds, circled briefly, then dropped below the clouds to see if we had hit anything. A huge column of smoke poured from one of the transports, and it was being maneuvered away from the other ships," Thies remembered.

"That was the first radar bombing run I've ever heard of. We did that, and we think we hit a ship. We were never sure to this day."

He described the new use of radar when he returned to Dutch, and other PBY pilots who bombed Jap ships at Kiska Harbor adopted the technique.

"Early next morning we flew back to Kiska with four more 500-pound bombs," Thies said. "Near Kiska, flying beneath the clouds, we encountered a Japanese Mavis (Kawanishi H6K) patrol plane—a huge four-engine seaplane. It started after us, but we ducked into the clouds and lost her. We climbed on top of the clouds and ran into a Jake, an armed twin-float reconnaissance plane (Aichi E13A).

"Back into the clouds we flew to shake the Jake. It wasn't very aggressive. The top of Kiska volcano stuck through the clouds, which helped me to know where I was. We headed for Kiska Harbor, seven nautical miles from the top of the volcano.

"We found a hole in the clouds, located the harbor, flew over the Japanese ships, and again dropped bombs. And again, one bomb failed to drop. I left it there, dangling from a wing, and climbed back into the clouds to avoid the flack that seemed to be getting closer. I needed to locate another target.

"Through a hole in the clouds I saw a Japanese cruiser. I shoved the yoke ahead and put the PBY into a steep dive, aimed for the cruiser and released the hung-up bomb manually just before we zoomed up. My engineer, sitting in his high seat, said the bomb headed right for the middle of the ship.

"Wall, a gunner in one of the waist bubbles, briefly strafed the ship with a .50 caliber machine gun.

"We headed back into the clouds and home. We had made a dive bomber out of our PBY!" remembered Thies.

TORPEDO & BOMBS

Thies recalls when a flight of six PBYs took off from Nazan Bay, Atka Island, with torpedoes and bombs. "We were to fly air support for cruisers and destroyers that were scheduled to bombard Kiska.

"We had two 500-pound general purpose bombs under one wing and a torpedo (2,000 pounds) under the other.

"It was a big deal—even Commander Foley was along. At first we flew in formation. However, there was a catch. It was the God-awfullest weather I've ever seen. It's almost always bad in the Aleutians, but this was just impossible. As we started out in formation we could practically reach out and touch the other guys' planes. The fog was thick and dark, even though it was daytime. It was simply too dangerous to fly in formation. Everybody broke off and the flight scattered. At Kiska, dense fog was all the way down to the water.

"No one dropped bombs or tried to torpedo Jap ships at Kiska that day," he recalled.

"It was dark that night when I got back to Nazan Bay, our base at the time. I located the narrow harbor entrance on radar. I still carried a torpedo and two bombs. I thought they were going to make us repeat the flight the next day. My crew was worn out, tired. We were operating on a continuous turn around with no rest breaks.

"I decided if we could save the torpedo and bombs we wouldn't have to take three or four hours to load them again, and we could get some sleep.

"Bob Larson was copilot that day. 'You aren't going to land in the open sea with the torpedo are you?' " he asked.

"Why not?" Thies asked.

"I set her down. We bounced a couple of times, but the torpedo and bombs stayed on," Thies told me.

"I didn't know it, but the *Casco*, from which we were operating, had taken a Japanese submarine torpedo that day.[3] Her bow had been run up on the beach to keep her from sinking.

"I slowly taxied about, searching for a buoy where I could tie up, or one of the two tenders (the *Casco* and *Gillis* were both there). I couldn't find a ship or a buoy. It was black dark, and I was, literally, blind. I knew if I kept poking around I'd hit a rock, beach the plane, or run into a ship.

"I finally lost my nerve and voice radioed, 'Will somebody please turn a searchlight on for me?'"

"No answer. No light.

"Finally, I got a little upset. 'Will some sonofabitch turn a god damned searchlight on so I can see where the hell I'm going?'" I radioed.

"I learned later that Norm Garton, the *Gillis* skipper, turned to his exec and asked, 'Do you think we ought to help this guy?'

'You're taking a big chance,' he answered.

'I know it,' Norm said.

"Norm turned on his searchlight anyway, and for about thirty seconds lit up the *Casco* so we could tie up astern of her. At the time I never got to thank him. I did thank him at our reunion in 1987."

Garton's *Gillis*, of course, was the "Japanese battle cruiser" Thies had almost bombed six months earlier.

"Captain Gehres was so delighted that I had saved the torpedo (the other guys all dumped theirs before landing), that he gave me a box of cigars, autographed, 'For Lt. Bill Thies, my personal decoration for bringing back the torpedo and bombs. L. Gehres. Capt. USN, CPW-4.'

"I've saved that cigar box cover all these years," Thies told me.

---

3. The Japanese torpedo that slammed into the *Casco* in Nazan Bay caught Captain Gehres sitting in the wardroom having a cup of coffee. It knocked his chair into the wardroom table and he grabbed the table to hang on. He cut his hand slightly on a projecting screw. As a result he gave himself a Purple Heart, the medal awarded to servicemen who were wounded by enemy action. He said that was the closest he expected he would ever get to enemy action.

His prediction was wrong. On March 19, 1945, he was the captain of the huge aircraft carrier *USS Franklin* sixty miles from the shore of Kyushu, Japan. Kamikaze planes struck the Big Ben (the name her crews had given her), killing 836 of her crew of 3500.

The burning *Franklin*'s condition became so desperate that Rear Admiral Ralph Davison, also on the *Franklin*, ordered Gehres to abandon ship. He refused, and despite the odds, he and his crew managed to save the ship. A board of investigation debated whether to court martial Gehres for disobeying Davison's orders, or to award him the Navy Cross for saving the ship.

He got the cross.

DODGING A ZERO

One rare clear day in the Aleutians, a short way east of Kiska, a float-equipped Zero fighter plane got on the tail of Thies' lumbering PBY. The fighter was about twice as fast as the PBY.

"There's a very small island there—it can't be more than a quarter or half mile in diameter. Probably an old volcanic peak, around 200 or 300 feet high," he told me.

"There were no clouds for us to hide in. We saw tracers streak by and I pushed the control yoke forward and dived for the water. I got my wing tip ten or fifteen feet from that little island and stayed there, just above the water, and circled.

"Each time the Zero got within shooting range, he had to break off because he couldn't fly into the island, and he couldn't fly under us because we were so close to the surface.

"We'd see a few tracers, then he'd have to break off. We never got hit. I kept flying around and around that island until he ran out of gas or ammunition. When he went back to Kiska we flew home," Thies recounted.

DISOBEYING ORDERS

The radar installed in the PBYs early in the war was primitive, but it proved invaluable. However, it required so much current that the plane's generators wouldn't run the radar and the radios at the same time. A pilot had a choice—run the radar, or the radio—not both.

When PBYs returned to Dutch after a patrol, pilots were required to radio an "in" report, saying who and where they were, and that they were coming in. This was so the Army wouldn't sound an air raid alarm and man anti-aircraft guns.

"When I came in, it always seemed to be foggy. I could never see where we were going. But we could find our way with radar.

"If we turned the radar off to use the radio to send an "in" report, we were in trouble. At least two PBY pilots did this, and crashed. Ensign Jules Raven was one of these.

"I refused to turn the radar off. I would just tool right on into Dutch Harbor," Thies remembered.

Lt. Commander Bill Thies, 8 March, 1945, at Moffett Field, California. U.S. NAVY

"The Army radar picked us up as an incoming unidentified aircraft. They would sound the air raid warning, and everybody dashed to foxholes and anti-aircraft guns. Then I'd show up. The general got angry and chewed on my skipper, and my skipper got angry and chewed on me.

"Why didn't you send in a report?" he'd ask me.

I told him flat out, "I'm not going to turn the radar off to turn the radio on."

"If you do that one more time, I'm going to send you back to the states," he warned.

"Great!" I said.

"All of us wanted to get away from the Aleutians. It would have been a reward," Thies remembered.

"I'm convinced that disobeying those orders saved my life several times," Thies said.

Shortly, the IFF system (identification friend or foe) was installed on U.S. planes flying in war zones. This is a simple pulse that displays with the airplane pip on a radar screen. That solved the problem at Dutch.

WILD BILL THIES

Thies was an aggressive pilot who sometimes pushed the airplanes he flew to, and sometimes, beyond, their limit. After leaving the Aleutians, he became the Commanding Officer of VPB-144, and flew combat missions in the Lockheed PV-1 and PV-2 in the Central and Western Pacific.

He once tore the wing skin off a PV2 (Ventura), a twin engine medium bomber, while making a strafing run on a water tower on the island of Ponape. He thought he was going to knock out a water system, but when he got within range, the "water tower" started firing at him. He was making about 300 knots.

"When I saw tracers coming at me from that tower, I hauled back on the controls and banked. One whole side of the left wing skin simply peeled back," he told me.

"On our return home, we threw everything loose out of the plane to lighten it and had to remain down on the water for around 350 miles. We barely stayed airborne, with the yoke held way over to keep one wing up. When we landed we junked that plane. It wasn't worth saving."

On another occasion when he was stationed at Whidbey Island, near Seattle, he told his wife, Vivian, that he would give her an aerial show. He got his hands on a Grumman Hellcat (F6F), a red hot fighter plane, and flew to where Vivian could see him from their home.

"After doing everything I knew how to do with an airplane, I decided to lose altitude by spinning. I put it into a left hand spin and after about three turns, at an altitude of about 1,500 feet, I tried to recover. The plane didn't respond. I later learned that the book warned not to spin it to the left.

"I opened the canopy, unbuckled the seat belt, and stood on the seat to jump. Evidently the shift in the center of gravity helped to straighten the plane out. I reached for the stick, pulled back hard, and leveled off about 50 feet above Puget Sound.

"My wife said it was a thrilling exhibition. Little did she know," Thies recounted for me in a letter.

As a Navy pilot, Thies was rebellious. While a student pilot, he disobeyed a direct order not to attempt to loop a single float seaplane after a catapult shot (his only catapult). He tried it anyway at 5,000 feet. At the top of the loop a loose gas tank cap came off and gasoline poured out, blinding Thies and his companion student in the rear cockpit of the open cockpit two-seater.

The plane fell into an inverted spin. Thies was lucky to pull it out at about 200 feet.

His instructor watched the entire action, and for some reason didn't court martial Thies.

His companion on that flight was Carl Rinehart who flew the American PBYs on loan to Great Britain that found the huge, fleeing German battleship *Bismark*. This allowed the British fleet to corner and sink the *Bismark* after days of cat-and-mouse maneuvering across the Atlantic.

Thus, both student pilots were destined to be involved in momentous World War II events—sinking of the *Bismark*, and discovery of Koga's Zero.

Soon after Thies earned his Navy wings of gold in 1940, he married Vivian, the love of his life, ignoring the rule that junior officers couldn't marry without permission.

Bill Thies, in 1987. He retired from the Navy as a Captain, operated a glass business briefly, and retired. He lives to catch steelhead trout. JOE RYCHETNIK

He refused to accept "no" from Commander Paul Foley when he asked to be freed to examine the Akutan Zero; he almost *demanded* permission to examine the plane.

Even during his encounter with a "Japanese battle cruiser," he was prepared to attack single-handed. And there was his gutsy refusal to turn off his plane's radar to return through fog to Dutch Harbor.

Thies' bold combat flying in the Aleutians earned him the Navy Cross, two Distinguished Flying Crosses, and six Air Medals. He told me, "We were at the Cold Bay Navy base and were told that Secretary of the Navy Frank Knox was there to see us. We we were ordered to put on our greens. We were standing in a line in the Quonset hut chow hall, and I didn't know if we were going to eat first or what, when I was called out of line to stand at attention and have Knox pin a Navy Cross on me. The other members of the crew got Distinguished Flying Crosses, and the enlisted men received Air Medals. It was rather informal.

The citation for the Navy Cross that Thies received reads: "The president of the United states takes pleasure in presenting the Navy Cross to William N. Thies, United States Navy Reserve, for service as set forth in the following citation:

"For extraordinary heroism and distinguished service as a pilot in action with enemy Japanese forces during the Aleutians Islands Campaign June

1 to 15, 1942. Despite the hazards of severe weather conditions, Lieutenant Thies constantly sought out and engaged the enemy, inspiring other members of his squadron to supreme efforts by his example of zealous aggressiveness.

"Boldly defying continuous and heavy antiaircraft fire, he participated in all night aerial patrols and bombing attacks on enemy Japanese ships in Kiska Harbor and succeeded in scoring a hit on an enemy transport. His fine spirit of determination in accomplishing difficult and dangerous missions and his outstanding devotion to duty were in keeping with the highest traditions of the U.S. Naval Service."

For his combat flying in the Central and Western Pacific he was awarded a seventh Air Medal. The Navy Cross is the Navy's second highest award, ranked just below the Medal of Honor. The Distinguished Flying Cross falls just below the Navy Cross.

Bill Thies deserves another commendation, for his loyalty and devotion were not only for the Navy. It should go something like this: "To William N. Thies: You are hereby elected to the Husbands' Hall of Honor With Five Stars, for a lifetime of love and devotion to your wife Vivian. Your loyalty and unswerving belief in the 'in health and sickness' phrase of the marriage vow was clearly demonstrated by your daily ministrations of hands-on care and love for Vivian during her decade of decline with Alzheimer's disease."

"What do you think was your most significant contribution to World War II?" I once asked Thies.

"My crew and I finding Koga's Zero, and convincing Paul Foley that we should examine it to see if it could be salvaged," he replied.

[AUTHOR'S NOTE: *The Japanese landed on Kiska June 7, 1942. On June 8 Captain Robert Speers, flying an LB30 [bomber] from Umnak, at Kiska circled a cruiser he took to be American, although he received an incorrect response from a flashed recognition signal. He spotted other vessels, which fired at him. On his return to Umnak he passed a PBY heading toward Kiska. Next he heard the PBY radio a report that it was being fired on as it attempted to land in Kiska Harbor. When Speers landed at Umnak he learned for certain the Japanese had occupied Kiska.*

The PBY Speers passed was flown by Lieut.(jg) Milton Dahl, who reported from Kiska that there were two transports lying at the harbor mouth. Shortly, Ensign William (Jim) Bowers, flying another PBY over Kiska, confirmed the presence of the Japanese in Kiska Harbor. Thus one Air Force bomber and two Navy PBYs "found" the Japs at Kiska on June 8, 1942.

Bill Thies and Bob Larson's PBY arrived over Kiska June 10.

On the same day, seaplane tenders Gillis, Hulbert, *and* Casco *were ordered to Nazan Bay Atka, to support PBYs in a bombing blitz against the Japs at Kiska. On June 10, any PBY with a search sector anywhere near Kiska had standing orders to unload bombs on the Japs before returning to base or tender.*

Casualties mounted; Ensign James T. Hildebrand disappeared on patrol. Ensign Leland L. Davis crashed on the side of Kiska Volcano—his aircraft was found after the reoccupation.

By June 14, Patrol Air Wing Four (VP-41, VP-42, VP-43, VP-51) PBY crews had flown continuous attacks, exhausting the stocks of bombs and aviation fuel on the seaplane tender Gillis. *On June 14 Patrol Wing Four resumed its normal duies of reconnaissance, and search and rescue, and the Air Force took over the sole honor of bombing Kiska.*

A postwar report by Admiral James Russell concluded that during the so-called PBY "blitz" of Kiska, only the destroyer Hibiki *had been damaged.*

SOURCES: Ransohoff, History of the Eleventh Air Force: History of Air Wing Four; Campaigns of the Pacific. All from notes provided the author by John Cloe, Chief of History, Office of History, Eleventh Air Force, Elmenforf Air Force Base, Alaska.]

REFERENCES

Larson, Robert R. "From Notes Made in Summer, 1942," and [Larson's] flight log.

Rearden, Jim. Tape-recorded interview with Thies, 1987. Seventeen pages, typewritten. Also, various letters from Thies to the author.

Rearden, Jim. *Koga's Zero; The Fighter that Changed World War II*. Pictorial Histories Publishing Company, Missoula, Montana.

6 MISTAKEN IDENTITY

DURING AN EVENING I spent with Admiral James Russell at Adak he told me the following heart-wrenching story:

Ensign Albert E. Mitchell was one of the PBY pilots of VP-42 under command of Russell, then a Lt. Commander. Like all PBYs in the Aleutians in early June, 1942, Mitchell's plane flew long patrols seeking the Jap task force that was expected to arrive in Alaska's waters.

On the night of June 1, Mitchell had difficulty keeping his PBY aloft because of contaminated gasoline. His plane captain was Aviation Machinist Mate Noel Hanson. Hanson's two brothers, Ray and Melvin, were also Aviation Machinist Mates. They too were with VP-42 stationed at Kodiak.

On June 2, Mitchell's PBY was refueled from a launch of the seaplane tender *Williamson*. The tank on the launch had been over-pressurized. When Noel Hanson started to refuel the plane, high-octane gasoline blew into his face.

He checked into the *Williamson*'s sick bay. Aboard the *Williamson*, he arranged for W. H. ("Rebel") Rawls, Aviation Machinist's Mate First Class, to temporarily take over as plane captain of Mitchell's plane.

Rawls was short on clothing, so Hanson loaned him some of his, including a skivvie shirt stenciled "Noel Hanson."

Mitchell and crew, including Rawls, still struggling with dirty fuel and misfiring engines, flew to Cold Bay. There Mitchell reported to his commanding officer, Lt. Commander Russell.

Russell had mechanics clean and flush the right wing tank, but the self-sealing tank in the left wing had too many nooks and crannies for the equipment at Cold Bay to clean.

"I ordered Mitchell to fly to Kodiak where there was better equipment for cleaning wing tanks," Russell told me. "Don't come back until both tanks are clean," he cautioned Mitchell.

Mitchell flew the sputtering PBY to Kodiak. There Wing Commander Captain Leslie Gehres ordered him to fly immediately back to Cold Bay, Dutch Harbor, and Umnak Island, with dispatches—dirty tank and all.

He landed at Cold Bay June 4 and reported back to Russell.

"I was burned up at having my orders countermanded, and forcing my pilot to risk his crew and his plane," Russell told me, shaking his head. "But I could do nothing about it. Gehres was an ogre, and we all hated him. He had little regard for the lives of our pilots," he told me.

When Mitchell, following Gehres' orders, took off from Cold Bay heading for Dutch, Russell warned, "Be sure to call Dutch before you go in."

Dutch had been bombed by the Japs the previous day, and could be attacked again.

Mitchell did call ahead, and was informed that another attack on Dutch was expected momentarily. Instead of flying north over the Bering Sea as he probably would have done with a safe airplane, Mitchell circled over Beaver Inlet, near Dutch, where he could land on calm water and drift ashore if his engines quit.

Ensign Albert "Bud" Mitchell, USNR, patrol plane commander of the PBY shot down by three Zeros in Beaver Inlet, Unalaska Island, on 4 June, 1942. Survivors who escaped to a raft were machine-gunned to death by the Zeros. CURVIN H. GREENE AND ADM. JAMES RUSSELL, U.S.N. RET.

Admiral James Sargent Russell. He was a Lt. Commander in the Aleutians during the early part of that campaign, and the Commanding Officer of Ensign Mitchell. Russell ordered Mitchell to fly to Kodiak to have his plane's tanks cleaned. Russell believed Mitchell's plane was shot down because of Mitchell's choice of where to circle while awaiting the end of the second Jap raid on Dutch. U.S. NAVY

"I think his decision to circle over Beaver Inlet was based on the uncertainty of his engine performance, as well as the safety of his crew," said Russell.

Soldiers at an outpost watched as three Zero fighters shot Mitchell's PBY down in flames. Mitchell managed to land it intact. As the plane started to sink, the crew climbed into a rubber raft and began paddling toward shore.

As the horrified soldiers watched, the three Zeros strafed the paddling crew until all were killed.

The soldiers radioed the news to Dutch, and the seaplane tender *Gillis* rushed to the spot at flank speed.

An extract from the war log of the *Gillis* for 4 June 1942 reads: "At 1948 [7:48 P.M.] received a dispatch from Dutch Harbor that a PBY had been shot down off Beaver Inlet near Egg Island and that the survivors were afloat in a life raft. Proceeded there at eighteen knots and just east of Unalga Island, between that island and Egg Island, a wingtip float with approximately eight feet of wing attached was found. Further searching revealed a life raft unfolded and uninflated, with several bullet holes through it, minor debris including a parachute bag, and a mattress and a body that was later identified as W. H. Rawls, Aviation Machinist's Mate First Class, USN.

"On the body was found the daily flight inspection form showing the airplane to be 42-P-4 and the senior pilot to be Ensign Mitchell.

"Just prior to dark, gave up the search for more evidence and returned to Dutch Harbor."

Unfortunately, at first, based on the name stenciled on his skivvie shirt, Rawls was identified as Noel Hanson.

Word reached Melvin and Ray Hanson at Kodiak that their brother had been killed.

A few days later Noel Hanson was aboard a PBY that landed at Kodiak. The PBY was a true seaplane, and when it approached the landing ramp, a crew, including Melvin Hanson, arrived to attach wheels so it could be pulled from the water.

Melvin momentarily fumbled as he tried to attach the side wheel. Noel, in one of the blisters, leaned out and kidded, "Man, you're clumsy. Where'd you learn how to rig PBY wheels?"

Melvin, shocked at seeing his supposedly dead brother, dropped the wheel, started crying, and swam to the plane to embrace him.

Noel didn't understand what the fuss was all about.

Fortunately, the mistake was discovered before Hanson's parents were informed of Noel's supposed death.

One of the Zeros believed to have helped shoot down Mitchell's PBY and strafe the crew, was that of Tadayoshi Koga, whose Zero fighter plane was found a month later on Akutan Island by Bill Thies and crew.

The *USS Gillis*, AVD-12, found, near Beaver Inlet, the debris of Ensign Albert Mitchell's PBY, and a body that at first was identified as that of Noel Hanson. This is also the ship mis-identified by Bill Thies as a Japanese battle cruiser shortly after December 7, 1942. He nearly dropped a bomb on it.

The *Gillis* was a World War I four-stack destroyer, converted to a seaplane tender by removal of two boilers and stacks to make room for fuel, parts and supplies for PBYs. NATIONAL ARCHIVES

An early model PBY at Dutch Harbor in 1942. This is a true seaplane, not an amphibian. To beach it, a crew had to wade into the water and attach wheels as seen here. It could then be pulled ashore. Later PBYs were amphibious, with wheels that folded into the hull in flight. They could be lowered for landing on airstrips. Note radar antennae under both wings—one of the earliest aircraft installations. White objects behind gun blister are canvas sea anchors. U.S NAVY

7

ALASKA IN A P-BOAT

By Robert R. Larson

[Author's Note: *When I was writing the book* Koga's Zero, *retired Admiral James Russell, who started me on the trail of that story, suggested I call on Bob Larson who had been involved in both the finding of, and the field investigation of, the downed plane. To my delight Larson had written a detailed account of the patrol flight of the PBY (P-Boat) on which the Zero was spotted. With his permission I used his fine account in my book. Part of that account also appears here.*

Larson received his Navy aviator training at Corpus Christi, Texas, graduating in March 1942. After the war he earned a degree in aeronautical engineering and had a long career with Boeing Aviation.

In a March 2003, letter, he told me that at the age of 82 he had returned to flying—taking the FAA test and receiving a seaplane rating. "The last time I landed a PBY on water was 60 years ago. It all comes back!" he wrote.

In compiling the present book of personal experiences of forgotten warriors of the Aleutian Campaign, I again called on Larson—and again, he generously provided detailed accounts of his flying experiences in the Aleutians. He wrote the following during and after the Aleutian Campaign. —JR]

Ensign Robert R. (Bob) Larson, in March 1942, at age 21, freshly graduated from Navy flight school. ROBERT LARSON

A PBY being serviced at a seaplane tender in 1943, probably at Attu. Crew members on the tender hold the plane off with bamboo poles. Note the fender under the stern of the tender, and the fenders hanging from the bow of the plane. A small bomb hangs beneath the left wing. Instead of the "hay rake" radar antennae first installed on PBYs early in the war, a more modern style can be seen under each wing. Wingtip floats fold up once the plane is airborne. A crew member (above the number 73) appears to be asleep. U.S. NAVY

NOTES AT DUTCH HARBOR SUMMER 1942

A MONTH AGO I was in Tongue Point, Oregon, on dull patrol duty. Suddenly we (Patrol Squadron VP-41) were ordered to move to Alaska. Just before leaving, I was transferred to Lt.(jg) Bill Thies' crew.

"Wild man" Bill Thies, he is justly called. I am glad to be on his crew. I think he can fly the pants off anyone else in the squadron. He's not the kind to sit around waiting for something to happen. He scared me silly the first time I flew with him by doing steep turns at 90 knots in a heavily loaded PBY-5A. That was ok; what bothered me was, we were below the level of radio station NGH's 400-feet-high towers.

On our way to Alaska we stopped overnight at the Sand Point Naval Air Station, Seattle, called "The Sand Point Country Club," because of its luxurious facilities.

Next morning, because of extra passengers, and full loads of gas, we barely made it off the Seattle runway. We flew several hundred yards a few feet above Lake Washington before we managed to climb out. With us was Captain Leslie Gehres, Commander of Patrol Wing Four.

We flew up the coast in a five-plane formation led by Lt. Commander Paul Foley, the squadron skipper, and landed to refuel at Sitka in fog and rain. We next arrived at Kodiak Island under blue skies and big lazy cumulus clouds.

At a VP-41 officers meeting that evening, the skipper told us we were going on to Dutch Harbor, and he hinted at the seriousness of our mission. Our trip had been conducted with so much secrecy that my curiosity was at a bursting point.

Captain Gehres satisfied that curiosity at a second meeting that evening when he told us a Japanese force of two, possibly three, aircraft carriers, three or more cruisers, a dozen destroyers, and about eight submarines was headed toward the Aleutian Islands for an attack on Dutch Harbor.

To meet this force, we had three cruisers (two lights and a heavy), six submarines, and about sixteen destroyers, new and old. Consequently, the success of resisting the invasion depended heavily on our use of the radar-equipped PBY-5A. A gloomy outlook. Even Bill Thies admitted his misgivings.

It was a wary formation that flew to Dutch the next day, following the chain of islands to Unalaska Island. Dutch Harbor (location of the navy base near Unalaska Island) and the village of Unalaska are in such a natural hiding place that we were practically on top of them before they came into view. We arrived May 28, 1942, a date I will long remember.

All houses, oil tanks, quonset huts, and wooden buildings were camouflaged with dark green paint. The Army's Fort Mears was on the far side (southwest)of

Dutch Harbor navy base, March 23, 1942. The stern half of the grounded ship *Northwestern* can be seen on the right. The old ship, used as a power plant and dormitory, caught a bomb during The June 4 Japanese air raid. NATIONAL ARCHIVES

Dutch Harbor under Jap attack June 4, 1942. Smoke and flames from exploded fuel tanks leap into the air twice as high as the radio towers, which are 150 feet high. NATIONAL ARCHIVES

the small island, while the Navy installation was next to the natural breakwater and Dutch Harbor on the northeast end. The two main hills of the island were honeycombed with trenches, foxholes and anti-aircraft gun emplacements. When the Japanese air raids came, it didn't take long for personnel to find the foxholes.

We started patrolling next day by flying to Otter Point on Umnak Island where the Army had a 4,000-foot Marston mat metal runway. Earth moving equipment was digging aircraft revetments, magazines, and ditches. The only planes there were a dozen P-40 Warhawks. Those to arrive later included B-26 Marauders, B-24 Liberators, B-17 Flying Fortresses, and P-38 Lockheed Lightnings.

From Umnak we patrolled to the west and returned to land at Akutan, about 30 miles east of Dutch, where we remained at the whaling station overnight.

BOMBS AT DUTCH

ON JUNE 3, at Dutch Harbor, an enlisted man woke me. "The four o'clock alert is on," he said. It was an experiment of the station, adopted by our squadron. I dressed and went to the PBY ramp, where I remained until about 0510, when I returned to my quarters, undressed, and went back to bed.

At 0553, a reverberating boom woke me. Then 20mm, 37mm, and three-inch anti-aircraft guns pounded away from a nearby hill. Air raid! The Japs had come.

I was frightened and excited. Grabbing my pants,

flying coveralls, jacket, shoes, socks, and gas mask, I hotfooted it to a concrete shelter overlooking the ramp. From there I watched the raid.

The Jap's timing was perfect; there was a 15,000-foot ceiling over the base, while all around the island clouds hung low to the sea. I learned after the war their timing was happenstance.

Two groups of four planes each dropped bombs, each group making two runs. Only one of the four sticks of bombs that were dropped did serious damage—it landed on barracks on the southwestern part of the island, killing or wounding soldiers, some of whom had arrived the previous night.

The Nakajima B5N Type 97, code-named "Kate," a three-man monoplane bomber, could also carry torpedoes. Kates, flown from carriers, attacked Dutch Harbor, as well as Pearl Harbor. NATIONAL ARCHIVES

Two Navy men were killed when a Zero fighter plane strafed a mail-carrying PBY piloted by Jack Litsey as he attempted to take off. Litsey ran the shot-up airplane up on the beach. Altogether twenty-five Americans died; another twenty-five were wounded.

The Jap bombers were low wing, single radial engine monoplanes with retractable landing gear (Kates). They seemed to fly slowly; I don't think they were going over 120 knots.

I stood in the entrance to the shelter and saw most of the raid. I saw the bombs the instant they fell from the planes, and could guess where they would hit. Even if I knew they were going to fall distant from me, I ducked; I had no helmet to protect me from fragments.

Anti-aircraft fire was tremendous; I don't see how the Japs came through as well as they did. Apparently no raiders were shot down at Dutch. At Otter Point a Japanese scout plane was shot down by a P-40.

At about the time of the raid, Ensign Jim Hildebrand Jr. was out on patrol, apparently fairly close to the Japanese fleet. He encountered two enemy cruiser catapult type scout planes.

The starboard waist gunner called on the intercom, "There's an enemy plane trying to fly formation with us!"

"Well, shoot him!" Hildebrand ordered.

The gunner fired. The Jap saw the tracers and crossed to the port side of the PBY. There the waist gunner finished him off. Hildebrand's crew also crippled another plane of the same type on that patrol.

JUNE 6, 1942
SUPER LOW ALTITUDE BOMBING

Two days after the second Japanese raid on Dutch,[on June 4] our mission was to search for a reported lone Jap cruiser on which radio bearings had been taken. On that day, four PBYs, including Thies' plane, searched for the cruiser in different sectors. The plane that located it was to keep contact until the others arrived; then all were to make a bombing run in formation from 10,000 feet.

We had flown for several hours in a westward section along the Aleutians. A message came. "Torpedo an enemy group reported thirty-five miles north of Seguam Island."

We flew the lead plane and radioed the others to rendezvous over Seguam, then fly to the target for bombing. We didn't have torpedoes—we carried four, 500-pound armor-piercing bombs and didn't want to waste time returning to base for torpedoes.

We waited an hour over Seguam. None of the other ships appeared. We decided to go alone, and headed north. Chief Ordnanceman Anderson was to operate the Norden bomb sight; he remained in the bow compartment most of the flight.

We searched for a while at 10,000 feet, depending on radar to pierce the overcast. We then dropped below the overcast that hung about 300 feet above the water and searched. We finally gave up, climbed on top, and started home.

Shortly, Harvey, the first radioman, called, saying the radar scope showed an object about four miles away. We passed directly over it. During the day we had had several indications on the scope that had turned out to be rocks, so we weren't eager to lose altitude to investigate.

We turned 180 degrees and flew for several min-

Army guns atop Ulakta Head, facing the sea, north of Dutch Harbor in 1942. The guns would have been useless for stopping an enemy offshore on the day the photo was taken; the Head was above the fog, as were the snow covered mountains in the background. STAN DOUGHTY

utes, then resumed our original course, and again picked up a signal on radar. Dropping down to investigate, we found the cloud ceiling varied from 200 to 300 feet, with visibility one to two miles.

Suddenly we sighted a surfaced Japanese submarine, apparently charging batteries, accounting for the fact that we hadn't been heard.

We were practically unarmed—not at all prepared for a low-level attack. The fusing arrangement for our 500-pound bombs was 0.1 second delay, which meant we couldn't drop them from lower than 750 feet without endangering our airplane. The ceiling was so low we couldn't get up to 750 feet and still see the sub.

We headed for the sub anyway, intending to strafe. Suddenly there was a sharp and violent explosion. Holes appeared all over the airplane and the starboard engine caught fire.

Panic and confusion reigned. We thought we had been hit with anti-aircraft fire. If the sub could do that much damage with one shot it was not prudent to let him have a second, so we pulled up into the soup. The engine fire was put out with the CO2 system and the starboard prop feathered. We jettisoned the bombs to reduce weight.

Shortly before they were jettisoned, I noticed that only three bombs were on the racks. There should have been four.

When we calmed down, we concluded we had dropped one of our bombs from low altitude and we had caught the blast. Anderson, excited, had selected a bomb to drop and must have later accidentally pressed a bomb release switch, dropping it at a dangerously low altitude.

We flew back to Dutch on one engine. The hull was full of holes of varying sizes that we repaired in flight as best we could. We plugged the large ones with rags and boards, while the small ones were stuffed with pencils and bits of wood.

One piece of shrapnel had passed between the pilot and copilot; another fragment had flown between the arms of the tunnel gunner while he was holding the spade grips of his gun. It was his last trip with our crew.

The largest hole was in the hull near the port side wheel well and measured about a foot long.

We made a water landing at Dutch and quickly taxied to the ramp, with water flowing in here and there; by the time we got on the ramp we had several inches of water in the bilge.

We probably missed the sub.

JUNE 10, 1942
BOMBING MISSION

That morning we were loaded up with four 500-pound demolition bombs and went over to Kiska Harbor to investigate. Ens. Jim Bowers had reported unidentified ships in the harbor, but that was all the information we had. The weather was pretty much in our favor. A dense blanket of clouds hung over the area around Kiska approximately 1,000 feet high and two or three thousand feet thick in spots. Between Umnak and sixty miles east of Kiska the clouds were broken and fairly good visibility prevailed.

When we neared our objective we climbed on top of the clouds and flew the rest of the way on top. We let down about five miles east of the harbor and took a look. It looked like half the Jap fleet was anchored in the harbor, taunting anybody to come near! Two heavy cruisers, one light cruiser, five or six transports and about eight destroyers patrolling the nearby area, all peacefully lying in Uncle Sam's territory.

We studied them carefully from that distance through the glasses and sent in a contact report on the regular contact pad. Then Bill Thies got that wild look in his eyes and climbed up into the soup. We spent a good part of one hour looking the situation over. There were still several clear areas directly above the harbor and we kept skirting the edge of the hole, occasionally drawing anti-aircraft fire from the ships below. It kept clouding over and finally we lost the hole.

Bill kept flying around and finally decided to come down to a point a few miles east of the harbor and look them over some more. We hit the clouds and went on instruments. When we broke through we found ourselves right over the north end of the harbor with anti-aircraft really breaking loose. We got a good look at the harbor then,

Three of four PBYs route to bomb and torpedo enemy ships in Kiska Harbor. Photo was taken from the fourth. Fog prevented the attack. ROBERT R. LARSON

close range! In addition to the ships what looked like PBYs were down in the harbor, proving to be four-engine patrol boats of the Japanese, four of them. Bill poured on the coal and we went back into the soup again, trying to figure a way to drop our bombs.

We finally decided to get a radar fix on an island east of Kiska and set a course to take us over the middle of the harbor. The plan was to set the intervalometer (bomb release), go across the bay and push the "pickle" (bomb release switch) on the chance of hitting something. We flew across the bay, again breaking into the clear and the A/A breaking around us worse then ever.

Bill Lohse was the copilot at that time and held the bomb release switch. Said Bill Thies to Bill Lohse, "Well, I guess this is a good place to drop them as any."

Lohse, "What?"

Thies, "I said drop the bombs!"

Lohse, "You mean you want me to drop the bombs?"

Thies, thoroughly exasperated, "Yes!"

And so he did.

We went below the clouds to investigate. We had hit one of the transports. Smoke was issuing from it in great amounts, and the Japs were maneuvering it away from the other ships.

After much insistence and pleadings from the crew, Bill finally headed for home.

[For more details on this event, see chapter five.]

WEATHER CREW RESCUE

RETURNING FROM our first day of bombing of Kiska Harbor, we were nearly to our mooring base at Atka Island when radioed orders came for us to fly to Kanaga Island to pick up a crew of navy weather personnel. Kanaga had reportedly been captured by the Japs, which didn't make us keen to go there.

We found the harbor, circled, and landed. To our relief the Japs hadn't captured the place, but we did panic the weathermen who thought for a time *we* were the enemy. We loaded weather instruments and other gear into the plane and took off near dark. At the last minute we set the dock afire with two gunnery runs, igniting gasoline drums stored there.

Though the weathermen were extremely happy to be evacuated, they had a miserable ride due to rough air. Not accustomed to flying, they all became airsick. One spent the entire flight near my navigation table leaning over a pail.

I saw him a few years later at Adak. He was still expressing his gratitude.

We arrived at Nazan Bay near midnight. So many PBYs were in the bay we had difficulty finding a mooring buoy. We finally found one and were taken aboard the seaplane tender *Gillis* to get some rest.

FINDING KOGA'S ZERO

Six weeks after the Jap raid on Dutch, we were back on routine patrols looking for enemy ships. Takeoff was at dusk and we flew all night to be at the extreme end of our search area at dawn. The Japanese liked to start their raids at first light, so we would be in the best position to find them if they were to attack.

On cloudy nights (most of the time) we couldn't get a celestial fix and we had to depend primarily on dead reckoning, which required that we determine wind velocity and direction.

In daytime, if we could see the water below, we could estimate wind from the state of the sea and check with drift sights. At night we could find the drift angle by dropping a smoke float out of the tunnel hatch. When the float hit the water a flare ignited and we measured drift angle by sighting on the flare with a pelorus. For some reason, however, which seems strange to me now, we were ordered not to use smoke floats for fear it would reveal our position to the enemy. As if the noise of the two 1,200 hp engines of the PBY weren't enough.

On the night of July 9, 1942, the sky was overcast, making celestial navigation impossible. We flew into a deep low pressure system south of Dutch. This produced strong and shifting winds. Bill Lohse was the navigator that night, and I was the copilot.

Lohse made a wind estimate just before dark. The wind was from the east, so we corrected our heading to the east to compensate for drift. The night was dark and the air was rough. When dawn came, the wind had shifted and now blew strongly from the west. We didn't know when the shift had occurred. We corrected the heading on the return leg to allow for the changed wind—and wondered how far off course we were.

After several hours we should have sighted land if we were on course. But we saw no land. We flew another hour, and still saw no land. With land sighting long overdue, Thies became worried.

At the time our radar wasn't very reliable. There was a possibility we had flown across the Aleutian chain without detecting it. If that were the case we were heading northward over the Bering Sea, with the next land several hundred miles ahead.

The sun finally rose, and though the angle was too low for good accuracy, I took a sight through the copilot's side window. My calculations showed us to be 240 nautical miles east of our intended course. Such an extreme error was suspicious, so I recalculated. It worked out ok and gave us reason to believe we were still south of land.

Thies decided to continue north for another fifteen minutes. Then, if land wasn't sighted, he would turn south and try to find an island. The next island to the south would have been one of the Hawaiians.

To our great relief, distant mountains appeared. They proved to be the Shumagin Islands. Weather improved, and we climbed to fly over the islands on our return home to Dutch.

While passing over Akutan Island, about twenty five-miles east of Dutch, Al Knack, on lookout at the starboard blister, reported, "Skipper, there's an airplane on the ground down there."

Thies banked and descended to have a look.

The upside down airplane had a red "meatball" (Japanese rising sun) insignia on the wing, and didn't appear to be badly damaged. We marked the position on the chart and returned to Dutch.

After considerable discussion with our Commanding officer, Lt. Commander Foley, Thies convinced him to allow us to go to Akutan Island to investigate the downed plane. We traveled there aboard a converted fishing boat used for patrol. We were warned to approach cautiously—the plane's crew might still be around.

We hiked in from the beach, all armed. I carried a Thompson sub-machine gun. We walked slowly in about a foot of water through which grass grew. From the air the valley looked like a smooth meadow. This probably convinced the pilot he could land his plane with the wheels down. That proved to be a fatal mistake. The wheels dug into the water and flipped the plane onto its back.

We found the pilot upside down, strapped in, his head submerged.

We took pictures and made notes, then attempted to tip the airplane right side up. It was more than we could handle. About all we could do was to hold the tail up enough to get the pilot and his gear out.

We also removed the two Oerlikon 20mm cannons from the wings. The Chief gunner's mate in the party had no trouble field stripping them; we accused him of getting his early training with the Japanese navy.

We were surprised at the details of the plane. It was well built. We could see only one bullet hole, and that was in the vicinity of the oil cooler. The pilot wore a parachute and had a life raft, somewhat discrediting the then-popular theory that Japanese pilots weren't interested in survival.

The plane had simple, unique features. Inspection plates could be opened by pushing on a black dot with a finger. A latch opened and one could pull the plate out. I kept one for a souvenir, figuring the Navy could build a replacement if needed. The wing tips folded by unlatching them and pushing up by hand.

It was a Model A6M-2, Serial Number 4593, manufactured February 19, 1942 by Mitsubishi Heavy Industry Company, Nagoya Aircraft Factory.

Our report on the Zero resulted in a salvage crew barging the plane to Dutch. From there it was shipped to North Island Naval Station, San Diego, where it was made airworthy.

A number of vulnerable features of the Zero were discovered during test flights. This information was radioed to all military pilots in the Pacific war theater. As a result, the Zero no longer held a total advantage over allied combat planes.

It was the first Japanese Zero fighter test flown in the U.S. during the war.

If we hadn't become lost that night we may not have found that Zero. It couldn't be seen from the usual PBY routes, nor from a ship's deck offshore.

The plane got good press. *Life* magazine featured it in an article, and that airplane has been written about in many books and magazines about World War II, the Aleutian Campaign, and aviation.

For the record, Thies' crew on the day of discovery was Bill Thies, PPC (Patrol Plane Commander); Bill Lohse, copilot/ navigator; Bob Larson, navigator/copilot; George Raptis, relief pilot and bow gunner; ARM Harvey, radio/radar operator; ARM Dan Maddox, second radioman; AMM Al Knack, plane captain; AOM Wall, ordnanceman and gunner.

THE PBY AS A TORPEDO PLANE

THE TYPE OF mission we feared most was a torpedo attack. The PBY was so slow that to make a successful drop, it would necessarily be within range of a ship's anti-aircraft fire for a considerable time. Chances of even reaching the release point were slim.

Bad news travels fast, and we soon heard of the disastrous attempts to torpedo Jap ships in the Battle of Midway. Torpedo Squadron Eight lost every single torpedo bomber in their attempted torpedo runs. The only survivor of the squadron was Ensign George H. Gay who was picked up in a life raft the day after his plane was shot down.

A similar attempt by six TBFs (Grumman Avenger Navy torpedo bomber) based at Midway resulted in four being shot down.

If the faster, smaller, more maneuverable TBFs couldn't pull it off, the PBY would probably do even worse. When there was talk of a torpedo attack, our crew morale sank to its lowest level.

Once, in a joint operation with our surface fleet, a group of six PBYs was formed to conduct a torpedo attack on Japanese warships in Kiska Harbor. Our fleet was to steam along the Kiska coast and shell the harbor, hopefully driving the Japanese vessels out—to our waiting torpedo-equipped PBYs.

Our crew and most others in our squadron had never dropped a live torpedo. Aircraft torpedoes are smaller than those used by submarines and destroyers, and have less range.

We were instructed to fly within 400 yards of the target, estimate the lead required, and drop the torpedo from an altitude of 100 feet. Speed and altitude were critical. If the PBY was too fast or too low, the torpedo wouldn't enter the water properly and would skip back into the air. If the plane was too high or too slow, the torpedo nose would dig in and tumble.

Instrumentation for a torpedo drop was "seaman's eye" and a rather unreliable pressure altimeter.

We were assigned a different airplane than usual. I was the navigator for the flight, and to my horror the previous crew had stripped the airplane of all navigation charts. I told Bill Thies I had to run back to the operations hut to get charts. "There's no time—the planes are in formation and ready to go," he said. "We'll follow them and hope for the best."

I kept a careful log, but without charts we were in trouble.

The torpedo-and-bomb-laden PBY cruised very slowly—about 105 knots. In the several hours required to reach the target area, I mulled over the stories we had heard about the poor survivability of our planes in torpedo attacks. My worry increased as the flight droned on. To help pass time, I picked up a book and stared at it. After about ten minutes, the radioman sitting next to me asked if I always read books upside down.

That was when I really looked at the page, and, sure enough, it was upside down. I then recalled the 23rd Psalm, "Yea though I walk through the valley of the shadow of death, I will fear no evil, for Thou art with me . . ."

It was a perfect line, and I started to feel better, giving me some deep-down courage. That Psalm has been favorite ever since.

A message "The show is on," came as we neared Kiska. The five planes formed a tight echelon to get set up to attack. Our Commanding Officer, Lt. Commander Paul Foley, was in the lead plane. We had Kiska on radar, but we couldn't see the island. Then the formation flew into a thick, low, cloud bank. Visibility dropped to practically zero, and we couldn't even see the airplane flying formation next to us.

Thies turned away to avoid hitting another plane, and everyone else did the same. Within moments we were six individual airplanes, each on our own. We couldn't see the shoreline—or, almost, our wingtips.

After milling around in the soup for a time, it was apparent conditions weren't right for a torpedo attack that day.

Now my problems really began. We had no charts and no other plane to follow. I searched that plane from end to end for a chart. Finally, I found a book describing the Aleutian chain, and it had a foldout map. The map was small, and the entire chain as illustrated was only about eight inches long—equivalent to 1,000 miles.

It was better than nothing and I laid a course for Nazan Bay at Atka Island, where our seaplane tender was anchored. Luck was with us, and we flew right to the desired landmark and were within five minutes of our estimated time of arrival.

It was near midnight when we landed in the bay. We had kept our torpedo, and returned it in operational condition—as well as two bombs. The other planes had jettisoned theirs as they made their individual ways back to various sheltered waters. Wing Commander Captain Gehres was so pleased that we had returned with our torpedo that he gave Thies a box of cigars. Bill loved cigars; it was an appropriate gift.

I guess our management changed their mind about torpedo attacks by PBYs. We never carried a torpedo after that.

PBY CAMOUFLAGE PAINT AND LUCK

One of our submarines had run aground on the southwest coast of Amchitka Island. This island is within forty-five miles of Kiska, then held by the Japanese and it was feared they might try to salvage it, once they knew it was there.

The sub crew was found, and picked up by PBYs.

Our mission was to take a volunteer Army demolition crew to Constantine harbor at Amchitka and get them and their explosives ashore in a rubber raft. They were to hike to the sub and blow it up. Another PBY was to pick them up later.

We were assigned a PBY that should have been in the shop for repairs. The electric starter of the starboard engine refused to work. The engine had to be started the old fashioned way—with a mechanic hand-cranking it with the inertia starter while standing on the wing.

The flight to Amchitka was uneventful, but since Amchitka was so close to Jap-held Kiska, we were apprehensive. We were within easy range of the float-equipped Zero fighters ("Rufes") and the four-engine sea planes ("Mavis") based at Kiska.

We didn't have the vaguest idea when their patrols could be expected.

Thies approached Constantine Harbor cautiously, circling the harbor and the abandoned Aleut village. There were no signs of life. We landed and tied to a buoy the Navy had installed, and Bill cut the engines.

The life raft was inflated. Half the explosives were put in it and the demolition crew started to row ashore. We moved the remaining half of the explosives to the waist hatch for loading when the raft returned. I was at the navigator's position, sorting charts and planning the return trip when I heard the unmistakable sound of a multi-engine airplane.

Mavis was on patrol!

I have heard the expression "frozen with fear." Prior to that I thought it a quaint figure of speech. Now I am convinced it is a very real physiological phenomenon.

We were sitting ducks, nicely set up for a strafing attack with no way to defend ourselves or escape. Some of the crew were half way to shore in an explosive-laden life raft; we had one cranky engine that would take several minutes to start manually; our waist guns were stowed; explosives were piled at the base of the port gun.

I saw the Mavis half a mile away flying east, off the mouth of the harbor. If we could see him, he certainly could have seen us. I imagined what was going on with the Mavis crew. "Battle stations. Prepare to attack."

But Mavis remained on course and flew out of sight.

The Navy blue camouflage paint on our PBY apparently did its job. Either that or the crew of that Mavis had bad eyesight.

Despite the fear that the mission might be compromised, the demolition crew decided to remain and continue their assignment. While the life raft made another trip, we went through the painful process of starting the starboard engine. It took two tries.

Our crewmen returned with the life raft and climbed aboard, swiftly dragging the raft inside. Thies didn't wait for the usual engine warm up. As soon as the engines were warm enough to take full throttle without coughing, he took off. We were a half hour on our way home before the panic level subsided.

LOSSES OF VP-41

VP-41 HAD ITS share of losses during the campaign. On June 3, 1942 Lieutenant (jg) Jean Cusick's airplane was shot down while on patrol. Ensign Wylie Hunt, crewmen Carl Creamer, AOM3c, and Joseph R. Brown, S1c, survived and were picked up by a Japanese cruiser. They spent the rest of the war as prisoners of war in Japan.

On June 4, Ensign James T. Hildebrand Jr.'s plane and crew were lost when their plane was probably shot down while trailing the Jap fleet.

On August 4, 1942, Jules Raven's plane and crew were lost during a search for a missing PBY.

Jep Jonson ran into a mountain in bad weather and was killed. Some of his crew survived, however.

AN AFTER-WAR SALUTE TO VPB-136

IN EARLY 1943, we traded our slow, vulnerable PBYs for hot new PV-1 Venturas at Seattle's Whidby Island Naval Air Station.

The U.S. Navy Ventura was developed from Lockheed's Hudson medium bomber. It entered service in 1942 as part of a program to supply the Navy with fast, well-armed patrol planes for use in ocean areas where enemy fighters could be expected and flying boats were too vulnerable.

I was lucky to get my ex-Patrol Plane Commander Bill Thies as an instructor in transitioning to PV's. He had barely checked out in them himself, but he had explored the plane's flight characteristics.

During our first demonstration flight, he said, "Let me show you how nicely this recovers from a spin." He then pulled the wheel way back and kicked full right rudder. I hadn't been in a spin since primary training, and never in a multi-engine plane. I was pretty puckered as the airplane responded with a sharp roll-off to the right and the nose pitched down sharply. We did about a half turn and Bill recovered it smartly. Aileron control was effective at all times due to the wing slots ahead of the ailerons. It was a good confidence builder.

Robert R. (Bob) Larson and his crew with his first PV-1 Ventura bomber. ROBERT LARSON

The PV had two 2,000 hp Pratt & Whitney engines compared with the 1,200 hp engines of the PBY, giving it a top speed of around 320 mph—about 150 mph faster than top speed of the PBY-5. Acceleration and rate of climb were impressive to ex-PBY pilots.

There was a two-speed supercharger, a new factor which became useful in all-out escapes from Zero fighters. The power turret with twin fifties which didn't immediately run out of ammunition was also welcome (our PBYs were early models with canister fed ammunition. After fifteen seconds or so of firing, it was necessary to remove the empty canister and replace it with a full one. Later models had Air Corps style belt-feed models which had considerably more firing time).

Intimidating to PBY pilots was a complicated fuel system. Instead of the two tanks of the PBY, we were faced with eleven tanks and a maze of valves and fuel transfer possibilities that defied understanding.

After three months of training, VB-136 was ordered to the Aleutians. There we patrolled from Adak Island. Having flown in the Aleutians for so long in PBYs, we tried to operate the PV in a similar fashion—flying low to the water. That proved to be hazardous. We lost two planes and crews that way—(Lt (jg) Permenter and Lt.(jg) Malloy). We nearly lost another, flown by Patrol Plane Commander Lt. Bill King who made a very low approach to landing and hit the water but managed to pull the plane back into the air, with minor tail damage.

After that we tended to fly above the clouds, and we diligently practiced instrument letdown techniques. The PV could change altitude very fast, and flying it close to the water like a PBY was not the way to do it.

After a few months of uneventful patrols, our fearless wing commander, Commodore Gehres, decided to go after the enemy base at Paramushiru in the Kurile Islands. Half of the VB-136 crews were sent to train in Army Air Corp B-24s (Liberator bombers). They were to fly B-24s to Paramushiru from Attu, once the airfield there was completed.

While these men trained, we were short-handed and the rest of us had to fly nearly every day. I logged a lot of PV time during this period.

Several VB-136 Navy crews were checked out in Air Corps B-24s. However, when senior Air Corps generals got wind of the scheme, they declared that if Paramushiru was going to be bombed by B-24 Liberators, crews would be Air Corps, not Navy.

VB-136 was back up to strength for patrols.

In a sense, one crew and plane loss resulted from the B-24 training. It was "Throck" Throckmorton.

Throck had not flown a PV for a couple of months when he took one out to re-familiarize himself. His plane plunged into the bay shortly after becoming airborne. His elevator trim tab was found in the full nose-down position. At the time, the trim tab sense was not "natural,"—the direction one turned the knob was not oriented to the airplane response. We conjectured that he had forgotten which direction to turn the trim handle and had inadvertently cranked it to the full nose-down position when he meant to put in nose-up trim.

Shortly after VB-136 arrived back at Attu, the Japanese sent a welcoming committee of six Betty bombers (Mitsubishi G4M) to bomb the airfield. Our defenses sent up an impressive array of anti-aircraft fire, but made no hits.

Bettys patrolled toward Attu from Paramushiru, and it was inevitable we would meet one now and then. Pilot John Conners chased one, but the Betty was fast (270 mph), and Conners ended the chase when his fuel ran low. Pilot Sandy Dinsmore closed to extreme range on a Betty and fired his bow guns until they overheated. Some damage was noted on the Betty, but it escaped.

In December 1943, we returned to the states for leave, rest, and recreation.

We were deployed to Attu again in June, 1944, with new PV-1s, which had another cabin fuel tank, a better arrangement for the copilot, and another three .50 caliber machine guns in a "chin gun" installation. We also got a third pilot who acted as navigator.

With the extra fuel, missions to Paramushiru were more or less practical, and we were assigned to daylight bombing there, as well as long patrol missions.

Robert R.(Bob)Larson in 2003. After World War II Larson studied aeronautical engineering and had a distinguished career with Boeing Aircraft Company. Long retired, he took up flying again at age 82. "It all comes back," he wrote the author. ROBERT LARSON

Lt. Everett Price nearly didn't make it back from a bombing mission to Paramushiru. A push rod housing on one engine was hit by anti-aircraft fire. His engine lost oil, but slowly. He thought he could make it back to Attu. About half way, oil pressure got so low the propeller acted up, and he shut the engine down and feathered the prop. He flew the rest of the way on one engine. A rescue PBY met and escorted him on the last segment of his return.

Lt. Francis Littleton became the first PV-1 pilot to shoot down an enemy fighter with his bow guns. A "Tony" (Kawasaki Ki-61) made a head-on attack. Littleton raised his nose and gave the fighter a burst of his five fifties. He got a picture of the Tony going down trailing smoke.

Lt. Carl Lindell found that after some time maneuvering near Paramushiru, he didn't have enough fuel to return to Attu, so he became the first VB-136 pilot to land at nearby Petropavlovsk, Russia, on Russia's Kamchatka Peninsula. He and his crew were interned, as were all American airmen who were forced to land in Russia during WWII.

He was followed by Lt. (jg) John Dingle and our skipper Lieutenant Commander Charles Wayne, with planes damaged by ground fire and fighters. A fourth PV-1 plane piloted by Lt. (jg) John Cowles, made a crash landing on a Russian beach.

After this loss of four planes and crews to Russia, VPB-36 was relieved of bombing missions, and reverted to patrolling.

VPB-136 left the Aleutians in March 1945, never to return. One more airplane was lost on the way home. Lt. Al Moorehead, with passengers as well as his crew, became lost on the way to Kodiak—easy to do with false courses and swinging beams characteristic of the low frequency radio ranges of the time.

Moorehead ditched his airplane offshore from Karluk village on the southwest coast of Kodiak. All were rescued by a boat from the village. However, their baggage was lost.

One bright note: Most thought Moorehead had the worst looking aviation greens uniform in the Navy. He lost it in the ditching and was forced to buy a new, much more presentable set.

VPB-136 was decommissioned at war's end.

8 GEORGE HEROLD AND THE S-27

[The following is based on "The Loss of S-27," an article written by George Herold that appeared in The American Submariner, *as well as correspondence between Herold and the author. Herold was a quartermaster who served on that submarine.* —JR]

George Herold in September 1942, at the Royal Hawaiian Hotel on Waikiki Beach. At the time he was a crew member of the fleet submarine *USS Finback*. He also served on the submarine *Picuda*. While a crew member of these two submarines he helped sink eighteen enemy ships in the Central and far Pacific. GEORGE HEROLD

IN 1941, HITLER was rampaging through Europe. Japs were brutally slaughtering and raping Chinese. World War I (the war to end all wars) had ended only two decades earlier. Its horrors were still a fresh memory, and most Americans didn't want any part of a new war.

Nevertheless, on May 27, 1941, three days after his 17th birthday, George Herold of Hasbrouck Heights, New Jersey, enlisted in the U.S. Navy. As he trained at boot camp at Newport, Rhode Island, he could see an anchored submarine offshore. This attracted him, and he wrote home that his ambition was to enter submarine service.

About that time an early model submarine, the USS O-9, was lost with all hands.

Not an auspicious omen for Herold.

His parents tried, futilely, to persuade him to forgo submarine service. After boot camp he qualified for and attended submarine school at New London, Connecticut, training in 475-ton displacement, 175-feet-long, O model boats. (WWI and II submariners called their vessels "boats"; other Navy vessels are "ships.")

He next reported aboard the USS S-27, an 854-

The S-26, sister boat of George Herold's S-27, and identical in appearance, at launching 22 October, 1922, at Quincy, Massachusetts. This boat was rammed by friendly escort and sank 24 January, 1942. U.S. NAVY/GEORGE HEROLD

ton-displacement 219-feet-long submarine at San Diego, California. Built at Quincy Massachusetts, and commissioned in 1924, S-27 had a maximum surface speed of thirteen knots; submerged maximum was nine knots.

The S-27 was one of fifty-one S-boats that came off the ways shortly after World War I.

"Boats of the S class, ". . . proved to be too slow, short-legged, and fragile for extended operations with the fleet," wrote Clay Blair, Jr., in *Silent Victory*, his encyclopedic work on World War II submarines. He said, ". . . the S class . . . was consigned to coastal defense roles guarding Manila, Hawaii, Panama, and the east and west coasts of the United States."

While remaining attached to the S-27, Herold was sent to quartermaster/signalman school at Pearl Harbor.

On December 7, he watched with horror as Jap war planes destroyed our battleship fleet in their infamous sneak attack. As he peered, unbelieving, at the rising sun emblems, enemy planes flew a couple of hundred feet overhead while plunging to attack Ford Island.

Herold completed quartermaster school in late February 1942, and returned to the S-27, which had just completed overhaul at Mare Island Navy yard at Vallejo, California.

The two-decades-old, outmoded *S-27*, commanded by Lieutenant Herbert Jukes, was then assigned to the Aleutian Islands.

While northbound for Alaska along the west coast, ". . . around 300 miles south of Seattle we ran into a heap of trouble with the propulsion system, and limped into the Bremerton, Washington, Navy Yard for repairs," Herold wrote.

Repairs took several weeks. Travel time from Puget Sound to Dutch took another nearly three weeks. The S-27 arrived at the naval base at Dutch

Harbor shortly after the Jap carrier plane raids of June 3 and 4.

Herold and his fellow crew members must have looked uneasily at the fresh bomb damage to the dock where they tied up.

"Nearby Unalaska was a real small town with lots of mud and boards as sidewalks for walking. Some Aleut kids had set up a wooden roller rink to skate on," Herold remembered.

With fuel topped off and fresh stores, S-27 embarked on what could have been a sixty-day patrol.

"The Japs were on Attu, Aggatu (a small temporary camp), Kiska, and maybe some other islands," Herold wrote. "I don't think anyone knew for certain where they were."

During wartime, while in enemy waters, submarines commonly remained submerged during daylight and surfaced at dark to recharge batteries and air. There are few dark hours in the Aleutians during June, so daylight submergences were unusually long. This required extended surface time to recharge batteries.

In a profound understatement Herold wrote, "On an S-boat, you darn sure knew when you were submerged more than twelve hours."

Trapped air inside the submerged S-27 got low on oxygen from the crew of fifty repeatedly breathing it. Diesel fumes, cooking odors, human body odors, damp clothing and bedding, and constant condensation on the inside of the steel hull, didn't sweeten the stale air.

"We were patrolling the area south of Tanaga Island and with the periscope saw plenty of enemy aircraft, but little shipping.

"The weather was bad—nothing but rain and overcast. Occasionally we tried to get a decent tangential fix [from land]. Sun lines and star sights were impossible.

"After surfacing shortly after sunset June 16, we received a message instructing us to proceed to an assigned area at Kiska via Amchitka Pass. Prior to leaving Dutch, the Skipper had received verbal orders to inspect Constantine Harbor on Amchitka Island for enemy activity.

"We set course to clear five miles northward of the islands. We were able to obtain fixes until we rounded Gareloi Island. We headed across Amchitka Pass on course 245 true. At 2345, the captain went to the bridge to see if Amchitka Island had been sighted, and to be present if landfall was made.

"At 2400, when nothing could be seen ahead, we changed course to 270 true in order to make certain of landfall in case the current, on which we had no data, had set us to the south and east during the passage.

"After steaming for one hour at two-thirds speed (eight knots) on this course, without sighting anything, the decision was made to circle with ten-degree rudder until light was better.

"The skipper was concerned about not being able to see land because the *U.S.Coast Pilot* and a confidential chart we had aboard showed the entire [Amchitka] island was low and we might not see it in time to prevent grounding. This was done even knowing that our 0100 dead reckoning position still gave us seven-and-a-half miles of open water.

"We picked up the island and obtained a fix, then patrolled until 1200, and started rounding the southern end before it was time to surface and charge batteries. It was deemed advisable to remain submerged during daylight because of the earlier periscope observations of enemy air activities.

"The decision to round the island to the south was made, among other reasons, because a northern route might disclose our presence—we wanted to reach our area north of Kiska Harbor undetected.

"After rounding East Cape on Amchitka, tangential fixes were obtained, and it was determined a current of about two knots set us to the north. Such currents had been encountered in other Aleutian passes.

"At 1735, we increased speed to about six knots and adjusted course in order to round St. Makarius Point and be at least five miles from the island before 2000. It would be necessary to lie to for about four hours to charge batteries. We thought this position would remove us from the influence of the pass's currents. No data were available on currents of the area.

"We surfaced at 1920. Visibility was about 1500 yards and the island wasn't in sight because of fog.

To close the line to steer for our assigned area we came to course 315 true at eight knots, then stopped at 2005 to start the battery charge.

"Dead reckoning put the boat five miles west of St. Makarius Point, which provided the least chance of detection by radar or visual search because of our blending with the shore background.

"The battery charge was started at 2010. Visibility was less than a mile. It was overcast, the sea was calm, and the island was not in sight. The bridge watch was ordered to be especially alert for land.

"At 2200, the night order book was given to the officer of the deck. It included instructions to set course 305 true, speed six knots, when one engine was released from the charge; and to keep a careful watch for land, breakers, or any indication of land in event the boat could be set towards shore.

"Upon sighting any vessel we were to dive immediately. The captain was to be called when the charge was completed.

"At 0027 the Officer of the Deck went ahead six knots on the starboard engine on course 305 true, and informed the captain. At 0043 he reported he was coming left to 225 true with full left rudder, as he had spotted land on the starboard bow.

"The captain was on his way to the bridge when the boat went aground with a terrible jolt.

"I had the four to eight watch, and was in my sack in the forward battery compartment, where forty-two men slept. All of us were suddenly and rudely awakened by the sound of the hull going aground.

"A dark object, believed to be land, loomed suddenly one point on the starboard bow and was sighted at the same time by the OOD (officer of the deck), Boatswain T.E. Krueger, Quartermaster Dick Lister, and starboard lookout Seaman 1st class Stan Jorgesen.

"Krueger immediately yelled, "Left full rudder. Come to 225 true. Call the captain.

"Immediately thereafter the OOD saw breakers dead ahead and rang all back emergency on both engines and sounded the collision alarm.

"The boat grounded before we had sternway. The captain arrived on the bridge, followed by Lieutenant Smith, the executive officer.

"The skipper relieved the OOD. The port screw was backing and the starboard screw started backing in a few seconds and the boat was reported rigged for collision.

"The boat started bumping violently on rocks and rolling ten to fifteen degrees. Both motors continued backing at full power, but to no avail.

"Nelly (Roe D. Nelson), fireman second class, the ship's comedian, yelled, "What the hell are we doing on the railroad tracks?"

"Orders were given to blow fuel from number three main B tank, the after fuel group, and all variable tanks. We kept trying to back clear as the boat became lighter.

"However, as we became lighter, the stern began to swing to starboard and bang against rocks. Then the starboard screw hit rocks and became disabled. We had to move the boat in order to clear the stern. We found the boat could be moved only about twenty feet forward or aft before it became held fast. We sounded with a lead line for a possible passage through which the boat could be warped, but found none.

"At 0115, we sent our first message (in code). "ANY OR ALL USN SHIPS x AGROUND SOUTHEAST SIDE AMCHITKA ISLAND."

"The rocks on the starboard side were almost as high as the bridge. When we backed down, the stern went onto a reef and rode up a little, then it sheared to starboard.

"It was starting to become light and we could see another group of rocks just off the starboard quarter, and on several occasions the stern got close against them. We then kicked ahead. This maneuver did no good with only one screw operational, so we stopped and took soundings all around the boat. All depths were shallow except ahead where there was one spot twenty or thirty feet deep. However, there was apparently another reef beyond.

"Bilge plating in the motor room was buckled, and it could be noticed coming in as she pounded. We secured the motor room and put air pressure in this compartment.

"At this time Lieutenant Butler was busy encoding messages. Amchitka is thirty-four miles long, averages about three miles in width. We weren't sure if it was free of the enemy. We were aground on the southeast corner. Earlier, with the periscope we had seen a small village of several houses on the north side. They appeared uninhabited, but we were unsure of this.

"At 0145 we sent our second message, a repeat of the first.

"The pounding was increasing and we thought the tanks might give at any moment. Our one rubber life raft was brought topside and made ready. An officer and an enlisted man, both capable swimmers, took the raft, with a line, to the beach.

"At 0200, daybreak, this place looked like a calendar picture of the Maine coast, with rocks, fog, and breakers. The two swimmers returned, reporting that conditions were favorable beyond the rocks closest to the boat.

"A ferry system was organized between the beach and the boat, with the line tied to S-27 as well as to the beach.

"We sent our third message at 0440. CANCEL MY 19140 x WEDGED SOLIDLY ST. MARKARIUS PT. AMCHITKA x PORT SCREW WORKING ON MOTOR BUT MOTOR ROOM FLOODING x ALL TANKS DRY x UNABLE TO BACK OVER ROCKS x POUNDING IS BAD x AM PREPARING TO ABANDON X HEAVY FOG.

"Provisions, dry and warm clothing, small arms, medical supplies, and crew were safely transferred to the beach using the rubber raft. By 1100, all but six men and the captain were landed.

"Those remaining aboard destroyed the ECM (coding machine) for which all wheels were broken and scattered in deep water. The typewriter of the ECM was destroyed by hammer. Sonar equipment was demolished with a hammer—the QC (sonar) head was run out (below the bottom of the boat) when we grounded.

"The JK listening device (topside soundhead) in the torpedo room was demolished, and all torpedo approach data and tables were burned. The Mark eight torpedo angle solver was thrown overboard seaward as far as possible, and all confidential and secret publications, codes, ciphers and crypto aids were taken ashore and burned. Unburnable items were smashed and thrown into deep water.

"At 1345 another message was sent: HEAVY POUNDING CONTINUES x HELPLESS x ALL ASHORE EXCEPT SIX x ALL COMPARTMENTS DRY EXCEPT TORPEDO ROOM x WILL STAY UNTIL UNTENABLE x ALL CRYPTO AIDES DESTROYED BUT THIS x WHEN ABANDONED WILL WALK TO CONSTANTINE IF FREE OF ENEMY ON EIGHTEENTH.

"At 1330 three of the remaining men came ashore. A motorman first class, a radioman first class, and the captain remained aboard.

"The heavy pounding had loosened the side plating, for it could be heard rattling with each jar. The torpedo room was slowly flooding, even though air pressure had been built up in this compartment. An angle of about six degrees down by the bow was now noticed. The screws were both clear of the water.

"At 1513 we sent our last message: DUE TO SEA CONDITIONS I AM ABANDONING SHIP x IF POSSIBLE WILL RETURN TOMORROW OTHERWISE CONSTANTINE MY 200145.

"At 1550, since nothing further could be done to help the boat and with the torpedo room half flooded, the two remaining men and the captain came ashore.

"We were in sort of an unsheltered cove with everything we could get off the boat—a goodly supply of food, some small arms and medical supplies. I made sure I saved my $30 set of tailor-mades I had bought in San Diego before being sent to Pearl. Our boat was now a goner, resting on rocks and generating chlorine [gas] from both batteries.

"All of us were wet and the temperature was a cool sixty degrees, so we built driftwood fires and changed into warm dry clothing. Coffee with an ounce or so of grog perked us up. No injuries were reported. A cliff overlooked the cove, and at dark we doused the fires and stationed a man on top with a .45 [pistol]. We set two-hour watches. By then we were pretty sure there were no Japs on the island, but we took no chances."

"I had to relieve Seaman 1st class Scott Horton on watch that night, and when I crawled to the top of the cliff-like hill it was black dark. I can't say I wasn't nervous because I was. I called out,

'Horton', but not too loud. He heard me and said at first he thought it was a Jap trick.

"I didn't move around much while on watch. I was relieved in two hours.

"Next day we decided there were no Japs on the island so all fifty of us put everything we took off the boat on our backs and headed to the little village to the north. It was tough going on the mushy tundra with our loads, but we made it by 2030.

"At the village, there were six small houses, a little church, and a few storage bunkers. The Japs had dropped a string of bombs and three of the houses were destroyed.

"We moved right in. It had been a Russian fishing settlement, and they probably pulled out when the war began. They left lots of good stuff, tin dishware, working stove, kerosene and books, but all in Russian."[1]

"We didn't know it at the time, but only one of our messages had been received, and it didn't give our position.

"Food rationing started, two meals a day. There was a bell on the church-top and we had a man standing watch next to it with orders to ring it if anything was seen. We saw aircraft but they were never closer than six or seven miles. Theirs or ours, we never knew. We didn't make any changes that would be noticeable from the air. We had roll call every morning and joked about it.

"On the fifth day (June 24), the church bell rang and all hands scrambled for cover. An airplane flew straight for our little camp. As it neared, we saw it was a PBY, and everybody began waving and jumping. We laid out the flag. The pilot circled a few times at about 300 feet and sent a message with an Aldis lamp. WILL SEND POSIT x WILL LAND. He then made a nice landing in the harbor.

"The residents of the village had left an old weather-beaten but serviceable dory. We rowed out to the PBY and introduced ourselves. The PBY crew threw equipment overboard to lighten the plane so fifteen of us could fly out with them.

"Food rationing was abandoned and we stuffed ourselves with whatever food was left. Next morning three beautiful big Navy PBY birds landed in the harbor and in about an hour we were all airborne. The PBY I rode circled as it climbed and we all waved farewell to our little retreat.

"After a flight of around three hours, we sat down in Chernofsky Bay. Launches took us to the *USS Hulbert*, a WWI four-stack destroyer converted to a seaplane tender. There we had a quick medical checkup and hot showers. Next day we were flown to Dutch and issued a complete new sea bag. We had lost everything, including my tailor-made dress blues, having to discard weight for our flight.

"At S-27 reunions over the years since, we have chatted about the loss of the boat and our adventures on Amchitka. However more than fifty years passed before we learned anything about the pilot of the PBY who found us.

"Sadly, that pilot, his crew, and his plane were reported missing on a routine patrol a couple of weeks after our adventure. I can still see him standing in his cockpit with the hatch open, waving.

"In the mid-1990s, I learned of a reunion of PBY airmen, and called the telephone contact in Satellite Beach, Florida. He promised to make inquiries at the PBY crew get-together.

"A month or so later, he called to tell me that the plane was from VP41, and the pilot had been Ensign Jules Raven. With Raven that day as copilot was Ensign R. ("Rock") Bannister—a replacement for the day.

In later years Rock Bannister described the rescue, a copy of which Herold provided me:

Bannister wrote, "I was flying co-pilot for Ensign Jules Raven, VP-41, on this patrol out of Dutch Harbor to Attu. We were told to be on lookout for a U.S. submarine S-27, as it was reported lost and overdue.

"After a search, and taking pictures of Attu and Kiska, which were occupied by Japs, we came back via Amchitka to discover many men running from the beach. As we circled with manned fifty-caliber waist guns, the men returned to the beach with a U.S. flag, many white cloths, and cut a sign, 'U.S.

1. The village was that of native Aleuts. The early Russian influence and use of the Cyrillic or Russian language was still common in the Aleutians of 1942, even though Alaska had been part of the United States for 75 years. The U.S. had bombed the village to prevent its use by the Japs.

Submarine Veterans' World War II memorial for the submarine S-27, dedicated May 29, 2004, at Arco, Idaho. The reverse side lists the names of the crew of the S-27.
GEORGE HEROLD

SS-27,' in the sand. We landed in the bay and tied to an old buoy. An officer and men rowed out in an old boat they had found.

"They reported the submarine was making a beach search when it ran aground. We agreed to take fifteen men with us to Dutch. This, with our crew, made twenty-three men aboard the PBY.

"It was a long trip home with lousy weather and the most unstable plane I have flown. We made a night landing in open water at Dutch. After a couple of big bounces, the PBY stayed on the water. The submariners thanked us and said they would never get in another plane.

"The sad ending to this story is that two weeks later, Ensign Raven and his crew were reported missing on a routine patrol."

Rock Bannister survived the war, but died in 2001.

George Herold, searching with his computer, located Art (Jake) Jacobson, another of the PBY pilot's who flew the stranded crew from Amchitka. Here is Jacobson's 2003 e-mail response to Herold:

"What a surprise after all of these years! You are the first person in exactly sixty-two years, yesterday, to bring up that rescue event. My flight log book shows I flew PBY Serial Number 04427 for 12.3 hours to and from Amchitka Island to rescue eleven men from the S-27. I was in charge of the three plane section of planes and to this day remember the foul weather and low ceilings we had to deal with. I received the Air Medal for that rescue.

"Do you think you were one of the eleven men in my airplane?"

Earlier, George Herold was on the other end of an e-mail search. He wrote me:

"Fifty-nine years after loss of the S-27 I received an e-mail from a young man at Fort Collins, Colorado, who was researching the career of Jules Raven. His grandmother was married to Raven in 1942, and at Raven's loss she had been left a young, newlywed, widow.

"So, in time, perhaps we'll learn more about the guy for whom we have raised our glasses to at reunions over the years."

AUTHOR'S NOTES

AFTER THE LOSS of the S-27, Herold served aboard some of the most famous of the fleet submarines of WWII. He did five patrols in the *Finback*, five in the *Picuda*, and served on the *Pike* and *Amberjack*. While on the *Finback* and *Picuda* he helped sink eighteen enemy vessels in the China, Philippine, Celebes, and Yellow seas, as well as in the Central Pacific around the Marshall, Caroline, and Mariana Islands.

His Navy career was cut short after eight years by a leg injury. He raised three children on Long Island, New York, and retired from the U. S. Postal Service in 1986. In 1987 he moved to Florida where he still lives.

Herold's submarine career places him high on the list of those valiant warriors who served in the most hazardous branch of the U.S. Navy during World War II. Exploits of the submarine service, sometimes called "The Silent Service," did more to bring the Japs to their knees than most Americans will ever know.

The PBY pilot who flew Captain Jukes from Amchitka said that Jukes was terribly upset over loss of his boat. He was also despondent over loss of his good dress uniform, "Because I don't have anything to wear to my court martial," he told the pilot, quite seriously.

A court martial was planned for Jukes, but sanity prevailed, and it was canceled. The Aleutian weather, strong currents of the violent, unpredictable seas, and the ungainly, aged, S-boat, which was clearly unsuited for Aleutian waters, did Jukes in. He really couldn't be blamed. To his credit, his entire crew was saved without an injury or illness.

Command of the fleet submarine *Kingfish* went to Jukes in 1944, and he ". . . turned in a splendid first patrol off Indochina," according to Clay Blair, who described the action, ". . . the night of January 3, 1944 in a brilliant and dogged attack, Jukes sank two tankers from a convoy off Indochina. Four nights later, off northwest Borneo, Jukes sank a third tanker."

Two of his later patrols in *Kingfish* were unsuccessful in sinking any ships, and Jukes was relieved of his command and ordered to commission a new boat, *Cutlass*.

A few other postscripts seem appropriate to Herold's story. The S-27 had no radar or fathometer, both considered essential for navigation in the U.S. Navy after about 1943.

Samuel Eliot Morison, the respected naval historian, wrote that the Washington Treaty of 1936 declared the life expectancy of a submarine to be thirteen years, but, he said, ". . . these boats [the Navy's S-boats] were twenty years old in 1943."

The S-27, lying like a stranded whale on Amchitka Island, was bound to be discovered by the Japanese on nearby Kiska. It certainly provided some tense moments for PBY pilot Bill Thies, his copilot Bob Larson, and their crew, when they flew demolition experts to Amchitka to destroy the stranded boat.

George Herold's modest account conceals a gutsy warrior. It required men of outstanding valor to fight submarines in WWII. To man an antiquated S-boat, and in Alaskan waters at that, and write about it with no complaints on the dangers, discomforts and hardships, as he has done, reveals a lot about the writer.

Dates, times, speed changes, courses listed for the last two days of the S-27's cruise are based on microfilms from the ship's log obtained by Herold.

REFERENCES

Blair, Clay, Jr., *Silent Victory; The U.S. Submarine War Against Japan.* Vols I and II. J.B. Lippincott Company, 1974.

Harold, George, "The Loss of S 27," *American Submariner* Number 2001–04. October–December.

Harold, George. Personal correspondence with the author. 2004.

Morison, Samuel Eliot, *History of United States Naval Operations in World War II. Vol. 7, Aleutians, Gilberts and Marshalls.* Little, Brown and Company. 1962.

9

TROOP TRANSPORT AT SEA; ADAK

UP RELEASE BY RUSSELL ANNABEL
AT SEA WITH AN ARMY TASK FORCE
AUGUST 29, 1942

THIS ANCIENT, CREAKING slattern among transports has had a lurid past. Built in Holland as a luxury liner, she was taken over by the Germans during the First World War and used as a blockade runner and a raider. She was later recaptured by the allies and became successively a transport, a cannery tender, and a derelict piled up disastrously on an uncharted rock in the North Pacific. So the old girl's been around and seen her full share of high adventure—but probably nothing to equal the deal that now lies ahead of her.

We're somewhere in the Aleutian fog belt, plowing at top speed through the ghostly graybacked combers, with escorting warships sleuthing ahead and behind us. We're combat-loaded and headed west, but nobody, save the master of the ship, and the commanding troop army officer knows precisely where we are going. It isn't difficult to guess, though, that this is the army's initial move toward kicking the Japs out of the Aleutians.

Word has spread that we will make a landing at daybreak tomorrow morning, and probably this is true because tense conferences are being held tonight in every stateroom along officers' row. The engineers are checking blueprints and lists of material. Signal corps men are going over the abstruse details of setting up radio receivers and transmitters, of establishing telephone lines and aircraft warning systems and codes. The quartermaster outfit is sweating over the plan for unloading and storage of cargo. The gun crews are happily loading clips. Everyone is working at top speed and anticipating twenty-four-hour shifts after we land, because it is no secret that the success of this movement depends almost wholly on taking advantage of the element of surprise.

We've got to reach wherever it is we are going and get ashore and dig in before the enemy discovers our presence.

We have so many troops aboard that the boys are eating and sleeping in shifts. There are tiers of bunks in the holds, in the rococo saloons, in the recreation rooms, and even in the passageways. Some of the boys, needing more fresh air than is available at night in most of these places, have spread their bedrolls on deck. Yet despite the close crowding, most of the outfits have managed, like soldiers the world over, to bring their mascots aboard. Thus far, at least four dogs have appeared on deck, two bulldogs, a black shepherd, and a giant, hard-boiled Airedale who stands guard night and day with the forward gun crews.

Bits of conversation overhead on deck reveal the morale:

"So I says to the Sarge, 'Let me land with the first wave. If there's any Japs there I want a crack at 'em before they all get mowed down' ";

"The first Jap I see I'm gonna shoot, and the second one I see I'm gonna make him carry my pack";

Aboard the UST *Zeilin*, May 1943. Alaska Scout Clyde K. Peters (in buckskin shirt) and Sgt. Robert E. Morgan cut a good luck cake from Lieutenant Colonel Howell, G-4 of the Attu landing force. NATIONAL ARCHIVES

"When we started up here a guy told me there was a girl under every tree in the Aleutians. Only he didn't say there wasn't any trees."

The tactical difficulties our forces have encountered in the battle of the Aleutians offer the best clue as to why we are moving westward. The distances between our bases and the Jap-held islands are so great that our bombers have been forced to fly missions without fighter escorts, with the result that their effectiveness has been decreased. Bombers alone not being sufficient to gain control of the air, we need a base close enough to the Japs so that fighter squadrons and observation planes can go in with the bombardment groups.

Then, too, sending planes great distances in these areas involve terrific weather hazards. A flight may take off in good weather, with unlimited visibility and every expectation of a perfect view of the target, only to be completely souped in before reaching its objective. Moreover, time and again pilots return from these long flights to find their own field closed in, so the ground crew has had to "talk them down," a desperate, nerve-racking business no matter how good the equipment and personnel involved.

So we are plowing westward, loaded as probably this venerable hooker never was loaded before. And this time the much-maligned Aleutian fog is our friend. The Jap sub commander or bomber pilot who spots us in this all-enveloping

Seabees laying steel Marston mats for an aircraft runway on Adak, fall 1943. U.S. NAVY

Air Corp P-40 fighters parked in a revetment at Adak, June 8, 1943. NATIONAL ARCHIVES

murk will have to be a genius. If the thick weather holds, and if we make a successful landing tomorrow morning, we'll have a surprise for the next enemy patrol that flies the Aleutian chain. It'll be a surprise that will cause Tojo to take a long, thoughtful look at his hole card. Because, if the indications mean anything, we'll be right in the enemy's back yard, getting set to give him a monumental shellacking.

AUTHOR'S NOTE

Censorship of war correspondents' copy was strict during the Aleutian Campaign. Annabel may have known the destination of the transport, but couldn't reveal it. Today, the dateline is a giveaway—destination of Annabel's "creaking slattern among transports" was Adak, where troops started landing August 30, 1942. For months after Adak

Sweeper Cove at fortress Adak, June 14, 1943. By this date Adak could support 90,000 troops, mostly in tents. Some quonset or Pacific Hunts have been erected, along with other buildings and docks. NATIONAL ARCHIVES

was an established base, correspondents were not permitted to mention the word "Adak."

The first American war plane to land on Adak was a B-18, on September 10, flown by Colonel Willian O. Eareckson. Two days later Marston matting was in place, and the runway, though sloppy, was ready for use; water flew, nearly concealing planes, as they took off and landed.

REFERENCES

Cloe, John, *The Aleutian Warriors; a History of the 11th Air Force & Fleet Air Wing 4*, Anchorage Chapter Air Force Association and Pictorial Histories Publishing Company, inc., Missoula, Montana 59801, 1991.

10 AMCHITKA

IN MY COLLECTION of materials relating to the Aleutian Campaign is a nine-page single-spaced typewritten report by Benjamin B. Talley, Colonel, Corp of Engineers, titled "Reconnaissance, Amchitka Island, December 1942." It was labeled S-E-C-R-E-T and addressed to The Commanding General, Alaska Defense Command, Fort Richardson, who, of course, was Lt. General Simon Bolivar Buckner.

It describes a December 17–19, 1942, ground reconnaissance of Amchitka. Jap-fortified Kiska lay a mere 45 miles away.

It takes little imagination to speculate on the response of the Japs at Kiska if they had discovered the reconnaissance party that resulted in this memo—or the earlier party of Alaska Scouts which, in September 1942, also explored Amchitka, seeking a suitable location for aircraft runways. Both were exceedingly dangerous ventures into enemy-controlled territory.

The September survey party of Alaska Scouts was made up of Major William Verbeck, Captain Bob Thompson, and Sergeants Ed Walker, and Joe Kelly.

Accompanying Corp of Engineers Colonel Ben Talley on the second reconnaissance were Talley's assistant, Major Leon DeLong, Alaska Scouts Captain Bob Thompson and Sergeant Ed Walker, and a small party of unidentified Army personnel.

The following is a condensation of Colonel Talley's report to General Buckner.

> The party landed in Constantine Harbor in two PBYs at ten thirty a. m. December 17 and went ashore in life rafts. A security party was dispatched to St. Makarius Bay and remained there until the following afternoon. Except for arms,

The December 1942, search on Amchitka Island for aircraft runway sites by (l. to r.) Alaska Scout Bob Thompson, Colonel Ben Talley, Major Leon DeLong, and Alaska Scout Ed Walker. U.S. ARMY

the remainder of the party cached the gear in a barabara (native sod house) at the ruined village at the head of Constantine Harbor, left it under guard, and proceeded along the beach, across the shallow lagoon and up the small stream for approximately a mile.

Approximately twenty feet from the stream was a rectangular test hole about three by five feet and approximately four feet deep. Spoil from the hole was apparently thrown into the stream and washed away. This test hole was dug to good material.

Adjacent to the 200-foot contour was a second test hole. It was about twenty inches by two-and-a-half feet and eighteen-inches deep. The spoil was beside the hole and was still slick from shovel marks which seem to indicate its recent origin.

Tracks of a party of four were found. Our party was unable to determine whether tracks were Jap or American. Colonel Verbeck (of the Alaska Scouts) was on the island in September, and stated that the holes were not made by his party.

It is the opinion of this office [Corp of Engineers] that the purpose of this test hole was to determine the feasibility by the enemy of this area as a site for a fighter field. If I should guess when the hole was dug I should say probably during November by the enemy, probably prompted by the same intention underlying the present reconnaissance.

At four p.m., December 17, while the party was on the hilltop south of Constantine Harbor, a single radial engine, twin float Jap monoplane flew almost overhead at about 400 feet, from east to west. The party fell to the ground and remained motionless until it passed; it is believed we were unseen.

P-40 Warhawk fighters on parking strip at Amchitka, April 1943. Although Americans landed on Amchitka in January, some troops still lived in tents in April, which can be seen atop ridge behind the runway. NATIONAL ARCHIVES

A PBY-5 refueling at Amchitka on a Marston-mat parking area. April 1943. NATIONAL ARCHIVES

This plane returned at three fifty-five December 18 and flew the same course. Our party was at the ruined village that day and was not detected.

It was expected the party would be picked up on the afternoon of December 18; it is considered fortunate that the planes did not return at that time because of the appearance of the enemy plane.

The two PBYs returned at 10:30, December 19, in very cloudy weather and landed under extremely hazardous conditions in Constantine Harbor. In embarking, one life raft overturned and four men went into the water. They were saved, but a considerable quantity of equipment was lost, and more than half the film was ruined.

The party returned to Adak without further incident.

Sites exist on the island for the construction of airfields with runways in excess of 5,000 feet. Utilizing an Engineer Aviation Battalion, it is estimated that a runway 200 feet by 5,000 feet could be constructed in from ninety to one hundred twenty days. [A 4,000-foot fighter strip was completed in less than a month; a 15,000-foot bomber strip took several months. —JR] Practically unlimited folds, valleys and hillsides exist for the dispersed and protected construction of a garrison.

On the basis of constructing a major airfield suitable for the operation of all types of aircraft and a defensive garrison of more than 5,000 men, the following major facilities are required:

a. Fighter field
b. Lighterage docks
c. Access roads (probably eventually 100 miles)
d. Ocean dock
e. Main airfield (for bombers)
f. Aviation gasoline storage
g. Garrison housing
h. North jetty
i. Fuel oil storage
j. Utilities not already constructed
k. Essential field fortifications should be built by tactic troops immediately upon the occupation, and camouflage of all installations should be immediate.

AMCHITKA WAS TO BE the new base from which to attack the entrenched Japs on Kiska. By February 16, a 4,000-foot fighter runway was complete enough for the P-40K Warhawk fighter plane of Lieutenant Kenneth Saxhaug to land there; other P-40s and P-38 Lockheed Lightning fighters followed.

The presence of our fighters on Amchitka ended the frequent harassment of bomb-dropping by Jap floatplane fighters. They discovered the American presence on January 18, and had made frequent light bombing attacks that resulted in the deaths of several men, but no significant material damage.

A 10,000-foot bomber runway, a seventy-by-eighty-foot wharf protected by a 2,400-foot breakwater, hangars, storage for one-and-a-half-million gallons of aviation fuel, a 500-bed hospital, and huts for almost 15,000 men, were put in place—a $21 million project.

I was on Amchitka for a couple of weeks in September 1967. The main (bomber) runway was still good and used by Reeve Aleutian Airway planes. Hundreds of weathered Pacific huts—Quonset-type half-round things—were gradually mouldering into the ground. Gun emplacements and barbed wire entanglements were everywhere.

The letters IHTFP were prominent on crude signs on power poles, written on an old hangar, and elsewhere. At first I assumed it was some arcane military abbreviation, but after a week I managed to translate it. Some lonely and unhappy G.I. had expressed his deeply-felt view of Amchitka.

It had to mean "I hate this 'f—ing'? place."

Retired Brigadier General Benjamin Talley, October 1989, at the age of 86. Talley's efficient work in building aircraft runways in the Aleutians was a key to providing air power during the campaign. AUTHOR

AMCHITKA LANDING
UP RELEASE BY RUSSELL ANNABEL.
AN ARMY BASE IN THE ALEUTIANS.
JANUARY 25, 1943.

IN A SURPRISE move which caught the Japanese totally unaware, United States troops led by Brigadier General Lloyd E. Jones have occupied an island in the Rat group, forty-five miles east of the Kiska garrison, it was announced today by army authorities.

The occupation was carried out successfully on schedule, despite a howling Bering Sea storm which shrouded the island in blown snow and hurled mountainous surf onto the icy beach. One troopship was blown aground and landing barges were overturned by hammering waves.

There was no opposition from the enemy until ten days after the landing, when two float Zeros attacked the shipping harbor, dropping four bombs, causing slight damage.

The following day two Zeros [Rufes—JR] returned and dropped four more bombs, three falling into the water, and one on the beach. There was no reported damage or casualties.

As a result of a troopship going aground, the landing was necessarily lighter by a considerable part of the men and their equipment. Barges were under increased difficulties as men worked night and day digging in on the frozen ground, unloading supplies on the snowy tundra beach. They were often soaked to the skin by the wind-whipped surf. The force was made up largely of men hardened to Aleutian weather, and their commanding officers

October, 1944. Wind at Amchitka rolled this heavy steel Marston matting into an eight-ton ball—about 3,500 square feet of the stuff. U.S. ARMY, COURTESY COMMAND HISTORIAN'S OFFICE, ALASKAN COMMAND

praised their fortitude in carrying out "one of the most difficult operations of its kind our troops have ever been called on to perform."

Within a week, communication lines were established to all units and adequate tentage, stoves, fuel, cots, food, guns and ammunition were brought ashore, and an airfield was under construction.

Troops were preceded by a unit of combat scouts famous in the north as Castner's Cutthroats, under Lieutenant Colonel William J. Verbeck. All were heavily armed. These arctic woodsmen, trappers, and dog mushers went ashore in rubber boats, bucking offshore gales and made certain there was no opposing force, and occupied strategic points, including a Russian Aleut village, one of the oldest in the island chain, which our bombers had previously partially destroyed to prevent Japanese use.

The occupation convoy was protected by naval vessels, and an umbrella of army bombers and fighters from the Andreanof base. The fact that the Japs failed to discover the move is believed due in part to the extreme secrecy maintained on our part, and partly on the fact that Japanese planes were largely destroyed by the storm of our fighter bomber attacks on the Japanese garrisons.

The new base, when completed, will make it possible for our airmen to attack the enemy garrisons at well as the terrific hazard of long overwater flights in foul Aleutian weather will be largely eliminated, army authorities said.

Remains of a P-40 fighter at Amchitka in 1968. Parts of World War II warplanes, now valuable relics, are scattered widely throughout the Aleutians. An agreement with the U.S. Fish and Wildlife Service, which administers the Aleutians as a wildlife refuge, allows such parts to go to the Alaska Aviation Heritage Museum in Anchorage. AUTHOR

AMCHITKA CELEBRATION UP RELEASE BY RUSSELL ANNABEL. ALASKA DEFENSE COMMAND, FEBRUARY 27, 1943.

ARMY AIR FORCES Alaska celebrated the first birthday of the outfit on February 18 in a manner eminently satisfactory to everybody from the newest member to Major General W. O. Butler, Commanding General, Air Forces, Alaska.

It was a bad day for the Japs in the Aleutians, and that made everybody happy.

On February 15, six Japanese Zeros [Rufes] attacked the new army base in the Rat Islands [Amchitka], killing two men and wounding one. The following day, the landing strip on this base was completed and the first fighter planes landed. The Japs had been making almost daily raids over this base and Air Corp members had sworn to pay them off with interest.

When the Japs returned February 18th, the outfit's birthday, our fighters rose to meet them. In the first few seconds of the action, Major Harold C. Larson, of Salt Lake City, Utah, shot down one Zero, and a moment later a second Jap plane caught cross-fire from several of our fighters and plunged into the sea. There was no damage to our planes or pilots.

The Japs haven't returned since. They apparently have no taste for raiding the base now that it has fighter protection.

The new field was completed in thirty-four days, and gives us a base for our planes that is within forty-five miles of the Kiska garrison.

11

CASTNER'S CUTTHROATS

Officially, they were the Alaska Combat Intelligence Platoon. Most of the military called them the Alaska Scouts. The Press and the public called them Castner's Cutthroats.

With authorization from Lieut. General Simon Bolivar Buckner, Commander of the Alaska Defense Command, Col. Lawrence V. Castner, G-2 (intelligence) officer of the Command, formed the unit in November, 1941. At first he personally hand-picked the expert and rugged outdoorsmen that made up the platoon.

Castner was bald, with a scarred face from an X-ray accident. He disliked being photographed. He was not strongly built, even had skinny legs. But he made up for physical strength with his personal drive.

Most of the Scouts he chose for his intelligence platoon were Alaskans. Included were big game guides, trappers, prospectors, miners, commercial fishermen, Indians, Eskimos, Aleuts. All had teethed on firearms. They had hunted everything from whales to the great hump-shouldered coastal brown bears.

Included were small-boat men from the Bering Sea, arctic-wise sourdoughs, and sled dog mushers. All were tough, and all were capable of living from the land.

Their nicknames give a clue to their character; Bad Whiskey Red, Quicksilver, Bucko, Trader Joe, Quill, Indian Joe, and Aleut Pete, were a few. Their wilderness experience made them better scouts than the Army could have created with years of training.

Castner's assistant, Japanese speaking Major William Verbeck, hardened the scouts in field training, taught them how to collect military intelligence, and how to fight like commandos.

"I really gave those boys hell," Verbeck once said, "There were fifteen hours a day of marches through snow in the woods. And day after day they

Five Alaska Scouts (Castner's Cutthroats) on a successful moose hunt between missions. They are (l. to r.) Jack Heinan, Jim Radford, Pete Trefon, Tom Sandford, Joe ("Trader Joe") Mello. JACK HEINAN, ALASKA SCOUT

Alaska's Natives were included in Castner's Cutthroats for their survival, hunting, and fishing skills. Pete Trefon (left) and Nels Hedlund are hardly recognizable in uniform. In the field they, like other members of the unit, wore civilian garb they had used in the bush. JACK HEINAN, ALASKA SCOUT

learned to shoot every weapon a man could carry on his back or over his shoulder."

Eventually, there were sixty-nine members. [A payroll provided to me by the Army listed sixty-two members in August, 1943, and sixty-five in December, 1943. —JR] Today (2005) probably fewer than fifteen survive. During my fifty-five years in Alaska, I have known twelve of the former Alaska Scouts.

One I knew well was George Bishop. At age 37 he was the oldest Scout, and the others called him Pop. He was 20 in 1925 when he arrived in Alaska. For the next sixteen years he trapped and traded furs, and guided big game hunters. He mushed dog teams, poled riverboats, and roamed the mountains, forests, and tundra of our last frontier.

Unmarried, living near Fairbanks, he was drafted into the Army in February, 1942, and was sent to Fort Richardson, near Anchorage.

Bishop and the other scouts learned map-making, hand-to-hand combat, and how to evaluate potential aircraft runways as well as beaches for amphibious landings.

Alaska Scouts did not operate as a single unit, except at Adak and Amchitka Islands. Usually, Castner sent them out in small detachments on specific assignments. They used civilian Trapper Nelson packboards, belt knives, tin (canvas) pants and jackets, rubber-bottomed leather-topped shoepacks, and other non-GI equipment. Some carried their personal .30-06 hunting rifles.

LANDING-STRIP SEARCH

ON A TYPICAL assignment, in April, 1942, Castner sent four of his scouts—Buck Delketti, an Athabascan Indian from Iliamna, long-time Army sergeant Joe Kelly, Arnold Akers, and Jimmy Radford—to Ugashik to search the Bering Sea coast of the Alaska Peninsula for possible emergency landing strips for Air Corp planes being flown to the Aleutians. Bush pilot Art Woodley flew them there, probably in one of his Travel Air 6000 monoplanes.

Each scout carried his Springfield rifle, and had a pack consisting of grub, blankets, ammunition, extra socks. They returned to Ugashik May 3 (the day of the first Jap bombing of Dutch Harbor), and by happenstance met General Buckner, and a group of other officers who had flown there in two airplanes on a familiarization flight. The Scouts showed Buckner the map they had prepared.

The Scouts had been eating fish they had caught, and bear meat from a brown (grizzly) bear they had shot. They had greased their shoepacks with seal oil from a seal they also shot. Their clothing was saturated with smoke from wet wood fires, and the underwear they wore was practically rotted.

They smelled terrible.

When it was time to fly back to Fort Richardson, one of the new-from-the-States Colonels complained to another about the prospects of "... riding in the same plane with those stinking scouts."

Buckner overheard. "You're damned right you won't ride with them. They're riding with me," he growled.

Buckner was fond of Castner's Scouts.

COOL, CORRECT, AND IMPARTIAL

On June 3 and 4, 1942, Jap Zeros screamed out of the sky to shoot up ships, buildings, and soldiers at Dutch Harbor, an American base 150 miles from the tip of the Alaska Peninsula. While the Zeros sprayed with their two 7.7mm machine guns and their two 20mm cannons slammed explosive shells into various targets, from high overhead Jap bombers dropped their lethal loads.

Seventy-eight Americans died. During the raids, Alaska Scout, Sgt. Donald Spaulding, camped on Ballyhoo Mountain above Dutch Harbor, radioed a bomb-by-bomb account to Castner at Fort Richardson, near Anchorage.

"Those reports were cool, impartial, correct, and the best received on that raid by the Alaska Defense Command," Castner said later.

Don Spaulding, shown here, was regular Army, and one of the original members of Castner's band. He was an expert rifleman, according to Jack Heinan who took this photo. He was also the Scout at Dutch Harbor, who, during the Japanese bombing raids, transmitted a report directly to Castner at Fort Richardson, Anchorage. JACK HEINAN, ALASKA SCOUT

That raid and the exploding bombs marked the beginning of the fifteen-month-long Aleutian Campaign. After bombing Dutch, the Japs landed on and fortified Attu and Kiska Islands in the western Aleutians. Soon after, detachments of four or five Alaska Scouts started slipping ashore on lonely, remote, Aleutian Islands. They penetrated Jap-held territory by Navy PBYs, battered bush planes, fleet submarines, and storm-tossed fishing boats. They sought sites for airstrips, looked for beaches suitable for amphibious landings, and mapped previously unmapped islands, while keeping a sharp eye out for Jap invaders.

The Aleutian Islands stretch from mainland Alaska 1,000 miles across the North Pacific toward Japan. Attu Island, 1,500 miles from Hokkaido, is the westernmost; Kiska lies 175 miles closer to mainland Alaska. To drive the Japanese from these American islands, the U.S. started to leapfrog islands.

DRAIN THAT, GENERAL

First leap came shortly after the attack on Dutch. General Buckner wanted an aircraft runway on Adak Island, 450 miles west of Dutch. Buckner flew to Adak in a Navy PBY, accompanied by several Alaska Scouts. Six-foot-four, brawny, regular Army, Ed "Hiram" Walker was one of those Scouts.

Adak, treeless like all of the Aleutians, rises abruptly from the sea in a jumble of sharp peaks, with narrow valleys. In summer, flapping seabirds, eagles, and ravens swarm the island. Seals, sea otters, and roaring sea lions squirm on the beaches. No human lived there. Were Japs there? Nobody knew.

Walker described for me his trip to Adak with Buckner. For most of a day, the general, silver-haired, husky, broad-shouldered and sturdy, fruitlessly searched for a level site for his runway. As he impatiently strode about, the alert Scouts kept to high ground, guarding the general against any possible Japanese patrol. Finally, one of the Scouts pointed to a coastal lagoon.

"Drain that, and it'll make your runway, General," he suggested.

Buckner seized on the idea, and the lagoon became the Adak runway.

First, however, the U.S. had to fortify Adak. On the moonlit night of August 27, 1942, the fleet submarine *USS Tuna* quietly surfaced near Adak. Led by Castner, twenty-three ready-to-fight Alaska Scouts paddled five rubber rafts ashore.

A burly Scout, being helpful, slung Castner's pack over his shoulder with his own. Castner, searching for it, worked the action on his .45 handgun, snarled, "Who the hell has my pack?" At the answer he growled, "Don't ever touch my pack."

The chastened Scout handed it over silently. All nerves were on edge. Were there Japs on Adak? No one knew.

Ed Walker told me, "Wilbur Church and I had paddled our raft about 300 yards when one of its compartments exploded, accidently punctured by Wilbur's belt knife. Fortunately a lookout on the *Tuna* saw us sinking. They steered our way and pulled us from the deflating raft."

Castner led his men to a low hill. "We'll sleep until daylight," he ordered. He posted Sgt. Leonard Peterson "Quill" as guard (so nicknamed because he once put porcupine quills in a rear pants pocket. Unfortunately, they worked their way into his posterior. His buddies had to use pliers and iodine). "Wake someone in an hour to relieve you," Castner ordered.

After an hour of listening to the restless sea, the wind, and his snoring comrades, Peterson planted a shoepack on the nearest body.

"Shake your duff out of that sack and take over guard duty," he growled.

The figure groaned, but arose. To Peterson's dismay, it was Castner.

"I'm sorry, Colonel, I didn't know that was you," Peterson stuttered.

In later years Castner related, "So what did I do? I got my duff out of the sack and stood guard."

Shortly, a burly Scout loomed. He gruffed, "Who do you think you are, Colonel, George Washington at Valley Forge? Go get some sleep. I'll stand watch."

If Castner had told one of his Scouts to go to Hell, the man would have looked forward to the trip; they respected, admired, even loved him.

Next night, the submarine *USS Triton* eased her bow onto a sandy Adak beach, and another twenty-two Alaska Scouts silently slipped ashore.

Scout Bob Garr described for me his experience on Adak: "Three of us hiked forty-five miles around Mount Moffett as fast as we could. Our orders were to kill any Japs we found before they could send a radio message.

"I got back to the beach at three o'clock in the morning and reported my sector clear. I flopped on the tundra and was instantly asleep. I didn't notice the rain. I awoke two hours later, soaked. The bay was full of ships. Castner had heard from all the Scouts, and had given the landing fleet the all-clear."

THEY'RE . . . CUTTHROATS

According to Ed Walker, one of Castner's original Scouts, after the Scouts' Adak Jap-clearing patrols, they camped at a beach-side trapper's shack. Two Scouts stripped and dived twenty feet into the icy water to catch half a dozen ten-pound king crab. Others caught Dungeness crab and dug clams. One Scout used a grenade to kill a mess of Dolly Varden in a nearby creek. Another head-shot a seal. Driftwood fires smoked, and the tired men cooked ate, snoozed, and relaxed.

A soldier from a just-ashore outfit wandered near and saw the scruffy-looking scouts.

"What outfit is this?" he asked an insignia-free Castner, who was kneeling over a fire, cooking his own meal.

Castner, a West Point graduate, looked at his scouts. For a moment he must have seen them through the eyes of the curious soldier. Most wore a mix of army and rough civilian woodsmen's garb. A couple wore fringed buckskin jackets. All wore belt knives. Some had beards. Spit-and-polish military they weren't.

"Why, they're Castner's . . . uh, cutthroats," he replied, with a grin.

"He was tickled with himself for that crack," Walker told me.

The name stuck. The press especially liked the colorful title, although *Time* magazine (Aug. 9, 1943) called them "Tundra Troopers." *Yank* (July 6, 1942) called them "The Alaska Scouts," reporting that none of the Scouts liked the cutthroat title. *Collier's* (July 3, 1943) called them "Castner's Cutthroats." Alaska's newspapers and the *Alaska Sportsman* magazine commonly used "Castner's Cutthroats."

Within weeks, Adak was a U.S. stronghold. Its steel Marston-mat runway was serviceable, although water flew with every take-off and landing. Bombers flew from Adak to attack Japanese-held Kiska and Attu.

Pilots of our war planes needed weather forecasts to plan raids. The Navy weather stations planned for Adak and Attu were never established. The Kiska station was silenced by the June 7 Jap landing on that island. The personnel at the Atka station were pulled out after the Jap invasion of Kiska and Attu. Other arrangements for weather forecasting had to be made.

THE LONELIEST PLACE

In September 1942, the Navy gunboat *Charleston* deposited a ten-man weather detachment on treeless St. Matthew, an uninhabited thirty-five-mile-long four-mile-wide island in the Bering Sea, 225 miles from mainland Alaska. It is perhaps the loneliest uninhabited place in Alaska, even today. A freighter accompanying the *Charleston* carried fifty tons of freight for the detachment's use, including two Quonset huts, food, 400 sacks of coal, and other living necessities.

Soft-spoken, modest, Alaska Scout Bob Garr was in charge of the St. Matthew detachment. With him were Alaska Scouts Harry Lyons, George Ruef, and Jacob Stalker. Included were two weathermen, two radiomen, a medic, and a camp roustabout. In November, 1983, I talked with Garr about his time on St. Matthew.

"Our stuff was lightered ashore at low tide on a calm sunshiny day and dumped on the beach. Within two hours, as the tide flooded, a ten-foot sea started washing our supplies away. We lost food, coal, and other items," he told me. "We had to rustle driftwood for fuel all winter. It was scarce, for the only driftwood on St. Matthew is from the 300-mile-distant Yukon River."

He went on, "In October, Bering Sea pack ice locked the island in, isolating us. Because of our losses to the sea, we had to live partly from the land."

Garr praised Scout Jake Stalker, an Eskimo hunter from northern Alaska. "Jake kept us supplied with trout, codfish, seal meat and a variety of ducks, cranes and geese," he said.

Garr himself was no slouch at collecting food. "One day I saw five and six-pound arctic char in a creek. Eskimos had taught me how to catch fish by easing a hand down and flipping them out. I got four or five of them that day," he told me.

"We made a twenty-foot seine from camouflage screen by nailing a pole on each end. When the weather was cold enough to freeze them, we seined hundreds of pounds of arctic char and stored them out of reach of the foxes—a nice addition to our slim food supply."

"Colonel Verbeck loaned me his shotgun to help with the food supply. I got a case of #4 shells for it, and killed a lot of ducks. There was a little, black,

Alaska Scout Tom Sandford with a fresh-caught salmon. Scout in background is unidentified. JACK HEINAN, ALASKA SCOUT

short-billed fast-flying duck that was sweet tasting that all of us liked. I learned to lead it about ten feet, and got so I could kill on the wing about three of them out of every five shots," Garr told me.

He remembered, "Arctic foxes were a terrible nuisance. They came ashore by the dozen from the sea ice and ate and chewed anything they could reach. We had to get up at two a.m. one morning to reset antenna poles after foxes chewed through the guy lines.

"We had no salt, so we boiled sea water to produce it. A metal drum was our bathtub; we'd fill it, heat it with a fire underneath, and run through the snow and jump in."

When ice went out, the first boat the detachment saw from their lookout was the U.S. Fish and Wildlife Service *Brown Bear*. It was manned by Navy personnel, some of whom came ashore to check on Garr and his men.

"What do you need?" they asked.

"Reading material," was the response.

"A box of classic books had been among our supplies, and we all had read every one of them several times," Garr told me.

Not long after the visit of the *Brown Bear*, a PBY came winging over the island. "It flew low, and out tumbled a huge box holding about every kind of magazine imaginable," Garr grinned.

"The box busted and magazines were scattered to hell and gone. We picked them up for two weeks.

"Our favorite entertainment was the weekly Lux Theater of the Air—a radio program we picked up with a short wave radio," Garr remembered.

In June 1943, after they had been ten months on St. Matthew, the Coast Guard cutter *Clover* arrived with a relief crew, supplies, and two letters. One of these was a Christmas card from his home town church to Scout Sergeant Harry Lyons. "The only letter I received in ten months," Lyons wryly commented.

He kept the card as a reminder of his time on St. Matthew.

Similar detachments, supported by Alaska Scouts, were landed on the two Pribilof islands and St. Lawrence Island—all three also in the Bering Sea. During critical aerial raid months of the campaign, daily weather reports arrived from these four stations.

Alaska Scout Jack Heinan. Photo was taken by a *Time* magazine photographer, but never used. "I didn't look mean enough," Heinan, tongue in cheek, wrote the author. He was called "The Brain," by the other Scouts because he held a college degree in forestry and taught the others map-making, and was skilled at math. "I could figure how much each would receive for his share of muskrat furs we caught while training in the field," he told the author. JACK HEINAN, ALASKA SCOUT

Colonel Lawrence V. Castner (second from left, holding binocular case) in August 1972 aboard the yacht *Cavanaugh*. To Castner's right is Brigadier General Eugene M. Landrum, in charge of landing troops on Adak.

The *Cavanaugh* took Castner and his scouts to Dutch Harbor where they boarded the submarines *Tuna* and *Triton* for the journey to Adak, where they were the first ashore as they swept the island for possible Jap patrols.

JOE KELLY, ALASKA SCOUT. COURTESY OF COLONEL LYMAN L. WOODMAN

UNDER JAPS' NOSES

Next major landing was on Amchitka Island, 175 miles from Adak. But first, on September 23, 1942, four Alaska Scouts—Castner's assistant Major William Verbeck, Captain Bob Thompson, Ed Walker, and Joe Kelly—with P-38 fighters buzzing protectively overhead, were flown to Amchitka in a Navy PBY. Virtually under the noses of the Japanese on nearby (45 miles) Kiska, they searched for a site for an aircraft runway.

A second foray to Amchitka was made December 17–19 by engineers Colonel Ben Talley and his assistant Lt. Col. Leon DeLong, accompanied by Scouts Ed Walker and Captain Bob Thompson.

In 1990, then-retired Brigadier General Ben Talley told me that while he and the Scouts were on Amchitka, a twin-float Japanese patrol plane flew over them.

"It was so low I could see the pilot's eyes," he claimed.

He and the Scouts hid in beach grass and escaped discovery.

Amidst a howling Aleutian storm, on Jan. 11, 1943, thirty-four Alaska Scouts went ashore on Amchitka from the new destroyer, *USS Worden*. They had nine two-man boats—four of which were flipped by the white-capping sea. Nevertheless, all made it ashore. A whaleboat from the *Worden* landed the others. Soon after, the *Worden*, plunging on huge waves in Amchitka's Constantine Harbor, was pierced by a pinnacle rock. It started to sink, and the Captain, Lt. Commander William Pogue, ordered the ship abandoned. Those still aboard

The *USS Triton* at Dutch Harbor, July 16, 1942. This submarine and the submarine *Tuna* transported Castner's Cutthroats to Adak Island from Dutch Harbor. NATIONAL ARCHIVES

leaped into the stormy and icy water. Fourteen Navy crewmen drowned. (See chapter thirteen.)

Small boats were smashed as they attempted to land on Amchitka's beaches, and supplies were scattered. With snow flying horizontally in the screaming wind, Alaska Scout Fuller "Bucko" Thompson saw a boat approach shore to land, only to capsize in the breakers. He waded up to his shoulders in the wild seas (soaking his fringed buckskin jacket) and, one at a time, pulled twelve men from the surf. The men were so chilled by the frigid water they could hardly move. Thompson had barely enough energy left to change into dry clothing from his pack.

The next day, with moderating weather, the rest of the 2,100-man landing force reached shore.

Scouts helped troops cope with the January chill of treeless wind-blasted Amchitka. They piled sod around tents to hold them in the shrieking wind. They coaxed cold-stiffened oil to flow into reluctant stoves for heating, and cooked meals for exhausted and chilled GIs.

"Much of the food was lost during the landing, and we had to live partially off the land," George Bishop told me. "For a time every soldier on Amchitka lived on one or two cans of C rations a day."

Joe Kelly and a couple of other scouts salvaged supplies that drifted ashore from the wreck of the *Worden*. In his diary he also recorded, "Picked up ninety-seven cans of smokes at the sunken sub." (See chapter eight.)

As engineers built the airstrip, six Alaska Scouts, including Lieut. Earl Acuff, Bishop, John Heinan, and Pete Trefon, were taken by destroyer to the northern tip of Amchitka. There they built an observation post of driftwood covered with grass and sod. From it, with binoculars, they could occasionally spot Japanese planes high over Kiska. They could also see approaching Rufes after the Japanese discovered the American presence on the island.

The astounded Japanese on Kiska could hardly believe that Americans had landed on nearby Amchitka. They were certain the constant winter storms made a landing impossible. Eventually, a Jap plane discovered the American presence. Soon after, pontoon-equipped Zero fighter planes (Rufes) bombed and strafed. Some Americans were killed.

After establishment of the observation post, Alaska Scouts, who constantly scanned the skies toward Kiska, radioed warnings when Rufes approached.

A decision was made to establish a radar site at the observation post. Scout Jack Heinan was assigned to lead the radar equipment to the site. He walked from the post across the island to the main camp, and, with a bulldozer towing the radar equipment, started back. They didn't get far. The

Alaska Scouts building the observation post (OP) at the north end of Amchitka Island, January 1943. It was concealed with grass, and, from the air it was indistinguishable from the surroundings. From this OP they observed air activity of the Japanese on 45-mile-distant Kiska. JACK HEINAN, ALASKA SCOUT

tundra wouldn't support the dozer, and the plan to install radar was abandoned.

The Alaska Scouts were relieved of the observation post assignment by a small detachment of regular soldiers.

Talley's engineers completed a fighter runway by February 16. A squadron of Curtiss P-40 Warhawk fighters arrived. When, on Feb. 18, Alaska Scouts radioed that Rufes were approaching from Kiska, a flight of P-40 fighters snarled into the air and climbed high. When the Rufes arrived, the P-40s plunged to shoot two of them down. Jap air raids to Amchitka almost ceased.

Flying from Amchitka, American bombers dropped tons of bombs on the dug-in Japanese on Kiska and Attu.

TIME FOR ATTU

WITH DUTCH HARBOR, Adak, and Amchitka as bases for support, it was time to meet the Japanese invaders on the ground. On May 11, 1943, Americans stormed beaches of rugged 40-mile-long Attu. Alaska Scouts were assigned to various army units as guides, map readers, scouts, messengers, snipers, and advisers on how to live in the hostile environment.

Alaskan experience paid off on Attu. California-trained soldiers waded streams, heedless of getting wet. Not the Alaska Scouts; they were careful to stay dry, knowing how long it takes to get dry in that damp country without sunshine.

Through experience they instinctively chose hard ground while climbing the rugged, steep, mountains, recognizing it by the color of the vegetation, and by the slope above.

They knew how to stay clear of innocent-looking but dangerous snowbanks under which streams flowed—snowbanks that could cave under your weight and drop you to your armpits in icy water. They knew how to climb without dislodging rocks that could roll downslope and kill or injure someone.

Pop Bishop guided the 165-man 7th Cavalry Recon Troop, which sailed to Attu from Dutch Harbor aboard the destroyer *Kane* and two gigantic submarines, *Nautilus*, and *Narwhal*.

Bishop remained in action during the entire three week Battle of Attu. He didn't get a scratch. (See chapter twelve.)

FOR THE HELL OF IT

ON THE LAST DAY of the Battle of Attu Island, May 30, 1943, Alaska Scouts Raymond Conrad and Edward R. Bagby were with a patrol of infantry descending a rocky, steep ridge. They were gunning for Japanese stragglers not already killed by their own grenades (in defeat, many Japanese on Attu committed suicide).

"Our job, which was to locate the enemy for the infantry, was finished," Conrad said later. "Bagby and I went along for the hell of it.

"We almost stumbled over the first Jap we saw. Wrapped in a blanket, he peeked at us, then covered his head. He wouldn't surrender and he wouldn't fight. After we shot at him, he killed himself with a grenade.

"We dumped grenades into a smoking stove pipe at a half-buried Jap hut. Ammunition was stored there. The resulting explosion made it look as if a bomb had hit. We didn't stop to count the Japs that had been hiding there. There was at least one.

"On a low mound near the beach we saw five Japs dive into a cave. Infantrymen took them out." Next, through binoculars Bagby spotted a Jap crawling toward a big boulder with a hollow behind it. He fired at him with his Springfield. Wounded, the Jap killed himself with a grenade. Another ran toward the rock. "I shot him. He dropped and didn't move.

"We figured there couldn't be more than four or five Japs behind that rock, and decided to smoke 'em out. They'd killed a lot of Americans, and now it was our turn."

The two alternated sliding toward the hollow on their stomachs, one covering while the other moved. One at a time, four Japs peeked out of the hollow to shoot at the Scouts. Each was killed by the sharpshooting Scouts.

They covered the rock, waiting for the infantry patrol to catch up. Every time they decided it was safe to advance, another Jap bullet zinged past.

Alaska Scouts aboard a landing barge going to Alaid Island in the Semichi group, May 28, 1943, for the first American landing there of the Aleutian Campaign. No one knew if it held Japanese troops. Captain Robert Thompson is third from left. Former Alaska Scout Al Brattain told the author, "Bob Thompson was one of those rare men who, in addition to being an excellent officer, could gain the complete confidence and loyalty of men under his command. He would do anything for his men, and the men for him." Tragically, after the war Thompson was killed in a truck accident near Anchorage. CHARLES A. O'LEARY, ALASKA SCOUT

When the patrol arrived, the two Scouts bellied within grenade-tossing range.

"I had never thrown a grenade," Conrad admitted. "Personally, they scare the wadding out of me, but I hated to admit to Bagby I was a coward. So I let one go. I even held it a few seconds after pulling the pin. It cleared the rock by six inches."

A Jap soldier ran out, his clothing afire. He had been visible and Conrad and Bagby thought he was dead. The grenade had set dry grass afire. The first man in the infantry patrol shot him as he ran. The infantryman then raised up to look into the hollow. He fell dead from a Jap bullet.

Conrad and Bagby continued to inch forward, and enemy riflemen kept popping up to fire at them. By the time the patrol finally arrived in force, the Scouts were close enough to see four live Japs still in the hollow. They left them for the patrol.

The two Scouts had killed eight enemy riflemen in the ninety-minute point-blank duel.

Colonel Castner had ordered his Scouts to avoid combat—that was the job of the infantry. He gave Conrad and Bagby hell for disobeying orders, then congratulated them for their courage, and recommended them for the Silver Stars each received.

Finally, the guns were still. A few remaining Jap

snipers roamed the high ridges. Some were hunted down like wolves. The last one surrendered in September. Others lay dead in the mountains with rust forming on the long barrels of their rifles. The hungry big shiny black Aleutian ravens no doubt found them.

In June, blue forget-me-nots, purple shooting stars, and other colorful flowers bloomed in the shell-pocked fields. Peace had once again settled on this lovely island.

Proportionately, the Battle of Attu was the second bloodiest in the Pacific. For every 100 Japs who died, seventy-one Americans died or were wounded; 1,700 Americans were hit by Japanese gunfire; 549 died. In the Pacific, only the Battle of Iwo Jima had a higher ratio.

Afterward, Americans buried 2,351 Japanese. Twenty-eight Japs were taken prisoner.

Bad Whiskey Red (Willis Cruden), one of Castner's Scouts, was killed in action at Attu; Kenton Hill, Leonard (Quill) Peterson, and Clyde Peters were wounded. Raymond Conrad, Edward Bagby, and Al Brattain received Silver Stars for heroism and gallantry in action.

KISKA

In August 1943, American and Canadian troops landed on Kiska Island. As usual, Alaska Scouts, including Leonard (Quill) Peterson, Ed Walker, Stanley Dayo, Billy Buck, and Chuck O'Leary were the first ashore. They were pleasantly surprised. Weeks earlier, in a concealing fog the 5,000 Japs had fled.

That ended the Aleutian Campaign. During the remainder of the war, Alaska Scouts mapped and

Pete Trefon (left) and Al Brattain, Alaska Scouts. "Pete was a good man to run the ridges with," said Brattain. AL BRATTAIN

Alaska Scouts hamming it up on Attu with captured Jap items. In the rear, standing, left to right, are Don Spaulding, Dale Sims, and Joe Kelly. The two men on ends of front row are G-2-assigned American interpreters: interpreter on right is Ben Moriwaki. The two scouts bottom center and interpreter on the left are unidentified. Japanese items held are: .30-caliber machine-gun clip, sake bottle, infantry cap, belt of 1,000 stitches, shakuhachi (flute), helmet, gloves, folding water bucket, three flags, port and starboard lanterns, 20mm high explosive shells, .25 caliber rifle with bayonet, and a pistol. U.S. ARMY/ COURTESY AL BRATTAIN, ALASKA SCOUT

explored the far places of unknown Alaska. They field-tested military equipment, and functioned heroically as search and rescue teams.

For leading the Alaska Scouts, Col. Lawrence Varsi Castner received the Distinguished Service Medal. Castner died in 1949 and his body was interred at San Francisco's Presidio.

The Alaska Combat Intelligence Platoon, otherwise known as the Alaska Scouts, or Castner's Cutthroats, received the Presidential Unit Citation for its leadership and performance in action during the Aleutian Campaign.

Thus did Alaska's woodsmen-sourdoughs respond in time of war, as have American woodsmen in so many other wars.

An abbreviated version of this article appeared in the December 1991, *Alaska Magazine*. It received a silver award in the Historical Feature category at the 1992 Regional Publishers Association awards competition.

Charles O'Leary, Alaska Scout, with mascot on Nizki Island, June, 1943. Nizki is one of the Semichi group, near Attu. Alaska Scouts were sent there to search for Japanese. "We found one dead Jap pilot on the beach," O'Leary told the author. CHARLES A. O'LEARY, ALASKA SCOUT

[AUTHOR'S NOTE: I found this letter (next page) in the National Archives. It is the only official military communication of any kind in which I have found the term "Castner's Cutthroats." The letter verifies Scout George Bishop's account (chapter 12) that eight scope-sighted Springfields were issued to the Alaska Scouts. It also appears that General Buckner, Commanding Officer of the Alaska Defense Command, decided he'd like to have a scope-sighted Springfield for himself. –JR]

Alaska Scout Simeon Pletnikoff ("Aleut Pete") aboard the transport taking him to Attu island for the invasion. The Trapper Nelson packboard and sack on his back was a commercially made item popular with Alaska's woodsmen of the time. It was standard issue to Alaska Scouts, who used a mixture of military and civilian clothing and equipment. NATIONAL ARCHIVES

Headquarters Alaska Defense Command
OFFICE OF THE ORDNANCE OFFICER
c/o POSTMASTER, SEATTLE, WASHINGTON
May 21, 1943

Lt. Gen. S. B. Buckner, Jr.,
A.P.O. 980
United States Army.

Dear General Buckner:

The G-2 Section furnished this office with data on a telescopic sight of commercial manufacture, which could be readily adapted to the U.S. Rifle, caliber .30, M1903 without modification of the major item. It was intended to make this an item of issue for use by the snipers in "Castner's Cutthroats."

In reply to my inquiry to the Equipment Division, Field Service, they advised that an Ordnance Department modification was being applied to the "Springfield" to provide it with a telescopic sight. This sharp-shooter's weapon is designated M1903A4. Eight of these new rifles were shipped recently direct from SPOE to Adak for G-2.

I told General Hatcher of your interest in this weapon. He advises me that he is sending one to you by an Ordnance officer, who will visit this office in the near future.

I shall be pleased to have your instructions as to where you desire this rifle and sight directed upon its receipt at Fort Richardson.

Sincerely yours,

William I. Wilson
Colonel, Ordnance Department
Ordnance Officer

UP RELEASE BY RUSSELL ANNABEL. AN ARMY OUTPOST IN THE ALEUTIANS [AMCHITKA], MARCH 1, 1943.

City-raised troops in some cases have had a tough time adjusting themselves to outpost life on this wild, lonely sea frontier.

When Corporal Abe Slivovitz, Brooklyn, a company cook here, recently informed Lieutenant Colonel R. G. Emery that whale steaks would be served for supper, the colonel inquired as to how the whale had been bagged.

"One of the scouts killed it, sir," replied Corporal Slivovitz. "He grabbed it by the tail, heaved it out onto the beach, and stabbed it with his belt knife."

The colonel says that while he was aware the famous Alaska Scouts were capable of Paul Bunyan feats, he nevertheless didn't believe they were good enough to sling whales around by the tail. So he asked to see the carcass from which the steaks in question had been cut.

It was the carcass of a medium-size leopard seal (harbor seal).

When the difference between a seal and a whale had been explained to him, the crestfallen Corporal Slivovitz said, "I guess you might describe me as being just a fighting man, sir. I don't know nothing about those meat-bearing animals—but just you show me some Japs and I'd know what to do!"

REFERENCES

Acuff, Earl, Tape-recorded interview by author. October 16, 1989, 5 pp., plus correspondence.

Bishop, George. Alaska Scout. Tape-recorded interview by author. Typed, double-spaced, 36 pp. April, 1957.

Cloe, John, *The Aleutian Warriors; a History of the 11th Air Force & Fleet Air Wing 4,* Anchorage Chapter Air Force Association and Pictorial Histories Publishing Company, Inc., Missoula, Montana 59801, 1991.

Dept. of Army, Chief of Military History. *Alaskan Combat Intelligence Platoon.* Two-page summary. July 30, 1979.

Ford, Corey, and MacBain, Alastair, "Castner's Cutthroats," *Colliers*, p. 17, July 3, 1943.

Garr, Bob. Tape-recorded interview by author, November 18 and 20, 1983.

Heinan, John. Letter to author from Heinan, describing his experiences on Amchitka.

Land, Leo. Tape-recorded interview by author, 18 double-spaced typed pages. November 1983.

Meyers, Georg N., "The Alaska Scouts," *Yank*, pp. 1–3, July 6, 1942.

Rearden, Jim, "Castner's Cutthroats," *Alaska Magazine*, December 1991.

Rearden, Jim, *Castner's Cutthroats, Saga of the Alaska Scouts* (historical novel: end pages includes factual background); Pictorial Histories Publishing Company, Missoula, Montana, 2001.

Talley, Benjamin, personal interview. October, 1990.

Time (magazine), "Tundra Troopers" (no by-line), August 9, 1943.

Walker, Ed, Interview by author. Written notes. January, 1984.

Weiss, John, "Castner's Cutthroats," *Anchorage Daily News*, Sunday (magazine section), August 27, 1967.

12

GEORGE BISHOP: ALASKA SCOUT

George Bishop, born in 1905, grew up on a Wyoming ranch and arrived in Alaska in 1925. He trapped for fur and prospected for gold in the Takotna-McGrath region, then moved to the Richardson Highway about fifty miles from Fairbanks where he became a registered big game hunting guide, trapped, and had a fox farm.

After World War II he moved to Homer, near the tip of the Kenai Peninsula, where he homesteaded near Clam Gulch, briefly operated a sawmill and a fish processing business, then bought and operated the Inlet Trading Post, a general store.

I worked for Bishop as a clerk in the trading post in the winter of 1957–58. The following is based on my April 1957, tape-recorded interview of Bishop.

THE LETTER to me from the Fairbanks draft board opened with the usual draft board's humorous and ironic "greetings." I hardly had to read the rest of it, which informed me that I was going to join the Army.

It was February, 1942, and we had been at war with Japan for two months. I was single and 37 years old. The nearest thing I had to a family was my team of sled dogs.

I went to Fairbanks and reported to the draft board office. When I told the woman clerk there I had 100 miles of traps still in the hills, she informed me that only the U.S. Commissioner could grant me extra time to pick them up.

The Commissioner obliged, and I picked up my traps, and turned my cabin and dog team over to my friend Calvin (Doc) Cripe.

Back at Fairbanks, "The FBI is looking for you," the clerk at the draft board told me, kind of sharp-like. She thought I was a draft dodger. Bad stuff in 1942.

I high-tailed it to the Commissioner's office and asked, "What the hell is going on?"

He had forgotten to notify the draft board of my extension.

I was burned up even before I got into the Army.

SETTLING THINGS WITH WASHINGTON

THEY SENT ME to Fort Richardson, Anchorage, for training, where I completed a form that required me to list my occupation. I wrote "trapper."

Shortly, I was called into the company clerk's office. The form had returned from Washington, D.C. with a note: "Find out how this man made a living." They didn't understand "trapper" in Washington D.C. and somehow they were burned up about it.

The clerk and I talked it over. I admitted I had a small garden, and had sold two sacks of spuds the previous year.

"You might put 'farmer' as well as 'trapper' there if you think it would ease the tension any down there in Washington," I suggested.

That satisfied them.

I didn't have any idea of getting into the Alaska Scouts. I had never heard of them. When I got in the Army they didn't know what to do with me. I'd lived in the woods all of my life and that's all. After I passed the physical they sent me to school to become a medic.

With a net, food fish can be caught almost anywhere there are lakes or streams in Alaska. Nels Hedlund, one of the Alaska Scouts, taught the other Scouts how to make a gill net from a ball of twine. Here Hedlund makes a net with a shuttle he carved. Twine is between his feet. Net floats can be made from small pieces of wood. Rocks serve as sinkers. The net could be carried in a large pocket. Hedlund, from the Iliamna area, was a legendary dog sled builder. When you ordered a sled from him you had to be prepared to wait about five years for delivery—he was never without a waiting list. JACK HEINAN, ALASKA SCOUT

WANTED BY G-2

I HAD JUST about finished medic school, with only a few days until graduation, and we were training in the field several miles from base. One evening a sergeant arrived in a Jeep, saying I was wanted at G2 (intelligence) headquarters.

I worried as the sergeant and I drove to the base. What had I done to get crosswise with G2? What crime had I committed? I thought of everything I'd done, all the mischief I thought I'd gotten away with, and still I couldn't think of anything. I was about half scared, figuring I was about to be court martialed, as you do when you first get in the Army.

I was directed to an office where a major sat behind a desk. I pitched him a highball (salute) very military-like, thinking maybe that would ease things. He kind of raised his hand in response, hardly looking at me. He was reading from an old musty book—it was all discolored. I couldn't figure out what the book was, and never did know.

He asked my name, and I told him.

"Do you know how to backpack?" he asked.

I thought it a stupid question, but answered, "That's what I've been doing for nearly twenty years."

"Can you pole a boat up a river?" he asked.

"Yeah, I've done that and I've also run motorboats upriver," I told him, figuring maybe I could ease out of poling, which I wasn't too crazy about.

"Can you drive a dog team?" he asked.

"Yeah, I've done that too—about as long as I've back-packed."

"Could you survive off the country, living in the woods?" he asked.

Puzzled by his questions I answered, "That's all I've done for almost twenty years."

"All right," he said. "Go get your duffel. We have a place for you."

That's how I was transferred to the Alaska Scouts, popularly known as Castner's Cutthroats. You didn't apply to become an Alaska Scout—they came for you.

Authorized strength for the Alaska Scouts was eighty. Qualification requirements were fairly stringent, and the highest number of members ever reached was sixty-nine.

Colonel Lawrence V. Castner, the leader and originator, preferred older, more experienced men, and, of course, all were outdoorsmen. He chose trappers (the form I had filled out somehow got back to him), hunters, guides, commercial fishermen—men familiar with the out-of-doors. Usually a commercial fisherman knows woods lore, especially those from Alaska's bush. They hunt, trap, and fish for a living, and they are good with boats, so they fit the pattern.

Members of the Scouts had to be reliable as well as otherwise qualified; you couldn't have a bunch of goof-offs working on military intelligence. And, early on, before you were accepted as a qualified member you took six months of special training. If a Scout in training didn't measure up, the permanent Scouts tipped Castner off, and the man was quietly transferred. Lots of guys came and went.

Later, when the need was greater, members were chosen from obviously competent outdoorsmen and the six months of training was skipped.

We were probably the most independent, and the least GI, of any outfit in the Alaska Defense Command of World War II.

We used clothing and outdoor equipment we were familiar with as civilians, bought with a special fund. Included were Trapper Nelson packboards, little single-bit camp axes, top quality sheath (hunting) knives, Swede saw blades, tin (canvas) pants and jackets, shoepacks (rubber bottom, leather top, boots), tarpaulins for our beds and tent flies.

We commonly wore a combination of government issue and civilian clothing. Some of the Scouts wore buckskin jackets and western hats. Many sported beards and mustaches. In the field, every Scout wore a belt knife.

Most of us used issue sleeping bags, but some carried those they had used as civilians. We were issued 6 x 30 binoculars, and some 30X spotting scopes.

At the time the Army (at Fort Richardson, at least) didn't issue 100 percent wool underwear. Some of us used our own underwear, preferring 100 percent wool. Army rain gear was fairly good and we used it. After we became known, various companies sent us clothing for trial.

We carried fishhooks and fishing line whenever we were in the field. Each squad was issued a .22 pistol for potting ptarmigan, rabbits, and whatever, for food while on the trail. I carried my own .22 Hi-Standard handgun.

I trained with other scouts at what we called the "Fish Camp" outside of Fort Richardson. A little stream ran nearby where we caught salmon which we often smoked or dried.

LEARNING FROM EACH OTHER

A LOT OF our training was a pooling of knowledge. Members came from the arctic, the panhandle, the interior, the Aleutians, and the southwest coast. We

Alaska Scout Pete Trefon with emperor geese he shot near the observation post on the north end of Amchitka. George Bishop also shot many of these fine eating geese on Amchitka. JACK HEINAN, ALASKA SCOUT

learned from each other and it was pretty basic survival stuff.

For example, Scout Nels Hedlund, from the Iliamna area, was an expert at making a gillnet from a ball of twine. He taught the rest of us how to do this, and the nets became a regular piece of equipment for each patrol. The shuttle or needle for knitting the net can be whittled out of almost any piece of wood. Floats can be made from dry wood, and stones make good weights.

Fish are everywhere in Alaska, in freshwater and salt. With a little gillnet we found food almost everywhere we went.

Some of the Scouts were good at building boats. They taught others some of their tricks—how to build a boat frame—keel and ribs—from natural-shaped roots found along the banks of streams. It can then be covered with canvas—or moose or caribou skin.

We compared notes on edible wild foods—mushrooms, wild rhubarb, celery, peas, kernels of rye grass common along salt water, roots of willows, Hudson Bay tea leaves as a drink. And blueberries, wild strawberries, currents, lowbush cranberries or lingon berries, highbush cranberries, salmon berries, crowberries also called blackberries.

Almost every kind of animal life is edible. When you are on the seashore, with a sandy or muddy beach, when the tide goes out the table is set with a wide variety of clams, crabs, and fish.

We learned how to make skis and snowshoes from material found in the woods. We taught Scouts from the arctic how to blaze trails in timber—there is little timber in far north Alaska.

We learned how to crawl through woods and grass without moving grass or brush, and to keep our feet sideways while crawling—otherwise heels show above your body. You cradle your rifle in the hollow of your arms while you crawl.

Those of us from the woods taught others how to use spruce logs laid atop each other four or five high to reflect heat when a fire is built, and to cut spruce bough tips to make a bed or put on the floor of a tent. And to cut heavy green logs to lay a floor on deep snow on which to build a fire so the fire won't thaw down through the snow and be lost; I've seen fires melt ten feet to the ground in deep snow.

What seemed simple to those of us from forested country was often new to Scouts from arctic Alaska, like which wood to use for campfires. Wood should be dry if possible, although green alder will burn if you get it started. Wood from dead standing trees is best. Cottonwood is tops for a long-holding fire. Dry wood doesn't smoke like wet wood. Simple.

We taught others how to wade a deep, fast running river by using a solid pole, feeling ahead with the pole, and keeping the pole upstream on the bottom while you step forward. Hang your packboard by its strap on one shoulder—that way if you are swept off your feet you can shed it quickly.

We taught each other how to determine ice thickness on a river or lake. Wearing snowshoes, I once followed in the tracks of a moose and broke through ice. But for my rifle, which caught crossways on the hole, I'd have drowned. A four-footed animal can sometimes travel on ice where a man can't because their weight is more distributed.

We learned hand-to-hand commando-type fighting. For a silent kill from a short distance, some of the Scouts got pretty good at throwing a knife. We were trained and prepared to go behind enemy lines to gather information. We were at war, and no one really knew what to expect, so we were trained in various ways.

Map-making is an art, and we learned from fellow Scout Jack Heinan, a university-trained forester, how to develop reasonably accurate maps that could be useful in determining where troops could travel, where amphibious landings could be made, or where potential air strips were found.

In the field we carried twenty-five or thirty pounds that included rice, sugar, tea, flour, salt, pepper, and dried beans, usually with about five pounds of dried fish. We could stretch this to about thirty days with what we caught or shot.

Camp gear included, in addition to a short-handled light-weight axe, a ten-inch frying pan, a tea can, a boiling pot, and a sheath knife.

With a fishing line, hooks, and a fish net, snare wire for small animals, a sleeping bag, and a tarp, and a .22 handgun, we could survive almost anywhere in Alaska, save perhaps winter in the deep cold arctic.

The Aleutian Islands, where we fought the Japs, are blessed with abundant seafood and migratory birds, but land food is scarce. The ptarmigan, found on almost every island, is about the only food-quality upland bird.

TO ADAK

In August 1942, at Anchorage we boarded the *Cavanaugh*, a luxury yacht, which had belonged to Mr. Sorensen, Vice President of the Ford Motor Company. Like me, it had been drafted.

All of us knotheads from Alaska's bush got a kick out of that elaborate, plush boat. The skipper was a white-haired old guy. The multiple, tiled bathrooms had gold-plated fixtures; the extra-wide bunks were fancy with white sheets and super light blankets; woodwork was all teak.

At Dutch Harbor we transferred to two submarines; some of us went aboard the *Tuna*, others went aboard the *Triton*. We traveled submerged part of the way, a new experience for every Scout. Most took it in stride; a few were claustrophobic, but kept it under control.

The submarines landed us on Adak Island on August 26, where we searched for possible Jap patrols. Our orders were to immediately kill any Japs we found. No way did we want a Jap patrol to radio a warning that we were establishing a base on Adak before troops, supplies, and equipment were landed.

We found no Japs on Adak.

We remained on Adak for some time. While there we showed soldiers new to Alaska how to set up their tents, and how to care for themselves in the rain, fog, and wind. A lot of men were from big cities, with no experience in tent living.

We also pilfered their grub piles.

At Adak we were issued eight telescope-sight-mounted Springfield .30-06 sniper rifles. A shoot-off was held to determine who would use them. Using issue Springfields (no scopes) we shot at targets at 300, 400, and 500 yards. The highest scoring Scouts were issued the sniper rifles. I got lucky and came up with a high score, and was one of the eight to carry a scope-mounted Springfield into battle.

A few of the Scouts packed their own sporting-type .30-06 rifles, which, of course, chambered military .30-06 ammunition. Several of these were mounted with scopes.

AMCHITKA

On January 10, 1943, thirty-four of us were landed at Amchitka from the destroyer *Worden*. Since we were getting close to forty-five-mile-distant Jap-held Kiska we went light on grub and heavy on ammunition. Our packs weighed from 110 to 125 pounds.

We landed during a howling storm. The *Worden* was pierced by a rock and sank, and fourteen sailors drowned. After troops were ashore, the troop transport and supply ship *Middleton* dragged anchor and ran aground. Much of our food and a lot of other supplies were lost. Until more food arrived, all troops were limited to two cans of C rations a day.

We hunted and fished for additional food. With Lieutenant Earl Acuff, Jack Heinan, Pete Trefon and two other scouts, I was at an outpost on the west end of the island. From there we watched Kiska through binoculars. On rare days when weather cleared, we could occasionally see Jap planes over Kiska.

The Japs discovered our military presence on Amchitka, and with Rufe fighters started to bomb the airfield the engineers had under construction. After we had our observation post established, when Rufes approached to bomb, we radioed a warning to cat skinners and others working on the fighter strip so they could get under cover.

The fighter strip was barely finished when P-40 fighter planes arrived. When we warned of approaching Rufes, a flight of P-40s climbed high and shot down a couple of them. That mostly ended raids on Amchitka by the Japs.

The first time I hunted on Amchitka hoping to

get a seal or sea lion for food, I spotted a line of emperor geese strung out single file feeding across the tundra. I could hardly believe my eyes. I had never heard of such a thing. I crawled to within forty yards, picked one out, and shot it.

The others didn't fly, but stood honking. I shot two more before they flew off. They had probably never been hunted.

They learned fast. Every day, weather permitting, for the next three weeks I hunted geese and they became pretty wild. It got to where I was shooting at them from around 200 yards. The scoped Springfield gave me a big advantage.

We boiled them, and they were better eating than C rations—or nothing.

I also killed Amchitka ptarmigan with my .22—a tasty addition to our diet.

We caught and ate cod and halibut, and finally killed a sea lion about a week before we left March 15. By then the food supply had caught up with us, and we were back to eating Army food.

We returned to Adak where we studied maps of Attu, and trained. It was obvious that in battle Alaska Scouts would serve as guides and advisers, so we prepared for that.

ATTU

For the Battle of Attu I was assigned to the 165-man 7th Cavalry Recon Troop, which had trained in a California desert. At Dutch we boarded the submarines *Narwhal* and *Nautilus* and the destroyer *Kane*. I was on the destroyer.

The men all wore blucher-type all-leather boots, and their Captain, James Austin, couldn't understand why I was wearing shoepacks. He insisted I change to bluchers. I firmly refused. The argument went on for almost two days until we landed. He wasn't happy about it, but I had orders from the Alaska's Scouts' Captain Thompson: "You're old enough to not let 'em give you a bad time," he had warned me in advance, knowing the mindset of many officers.

Another mistake. Officers and noncommissioned officers were issued fur-trimmed parkas for the battle of Attu. It was only a short time before the Japs caught on, and selectively shot at those wearing fur-trimmed parkas. Loss of officers and noncoms was high.

About half of the Alaska Scouts were sent to Adak before the Attu landing, and from there they were taken to Agattu Island, just east of Attu, where they remained on standby during the battle of Attu.

Thus there were only thirty-odd Alaska Scouts involved in the battle. Six Alaska Scouts (including me) went with six different units as map readers, guides, and advisers.

Major amphibious landings were made at three different places on Attu. The 7th Recon Troop I was with landed on the northeast side of the island.

It was so foggy we couldn't see the beach from sea; we could barely see outlines of the mountain tops to get a general idea of where we were going. Our assignment was to climb the mountains that rose abruptly from the ocean so we could come down behind the Jap camp.

We spent all day climbing 4,000 feet almost straight up. I led, and did the map work. The men were greatly handicapped because they'd been on ships for two weeks with no exercise, and they were over-loaded with gear and ammunition. They couldn't keep up with me, and I got cussed out a few times.

I gave them every advantage possible by zigzagging and picking the easiest route. The leather soles of the blucher-type boots slid with virtually every step. Even though well-oiled, in that kind of snow, water soaked through the leather in about three hours. The men's feet got wet and very cold.

The issue socks they wore were cheap half-wool, half-cotton with insoles. They would have been fine if they could have been dried over a stove every night. And, of course, the boots could have worked too if they were dried over a stove daily, and re-greased.

I didn't have my shoepacks off except briefly for two solid weeks. My feet weren't dry, even with shoepacks because water penetrated the leather. I changed socks whenever I had a chance. When I

A common casualty on Attu was frozen feet, making it impossible for victims to walk.The leather blucher boots issued for Attu didn't protect from snow, ice, and wet tundra. The three other soldiers in the Jeep were probably also suffering from what the military called "immersion foot." Note chains on Jeep's tires. NATIONAL ARCHIVES

managed to crawl into a sleeping bag I'd take my socks with me to dry them. During the day I often dried damp socks next to my body inside my shirt. For two weeks about three hours a night is about all I ever slept; like the others, I kept going mostly on nerve.

We were in the line of fire most of the time, and I never pulled my clothes off. A lot of fellows did, but I wanted mine on just in case. The Japs were good at slipping through the lines. Whenever I snoozed, my rifle was handy, and my shoepacks were either on my feet, or where I could quickly jump into them.

We thought we were going to get the fight over quickly, in three days or so, therefore we didn't have any grub—just one K ration each. I had 300 rounds of ammunition, two grenades, no bedding—about seventy-five pounds.

The men tired quickly and had to sit and rest. I frequently dropped my pack and climbed ahead for a look around, accompanied by Gomez, a young soldier from Colorado who was in good physical shape.

When finally we broke over the top we saw the Jap encampment far below. I studied it with glasses, and went back and reported to the lieutenant in charge. He decided where we should locate for protection and for firing on the camp. We drew back a little and set up mortars and made ready.

We held off attacking; the force supposed to hit the Japs camp from the sea hadn't yet attacked. The Japs didn't even know we were there that night.

BISHOP'S PEEK HOLE

NEXT MORNING the firing started and continued on and off all day. Next day—the second day of fighting—the lieutenant wanted to move closer. He sent me to do some reconnaissance so he could decide where we could move. I went alone.

The slope facing the Jap camp was exposed and visible from their camp. To stay out of sight I followed down a draw. Snow drifts there were deep. I remained out of sight behind a big one and dug a hole through it for four or five feet. I shelled it out inside, making a fairly good size hole to peek through. I didn't dig straight, but at an angle, so it wouldn't show light from the Jap camp.

I watched for quite a while. I could hear the battle going on above and to our south, where another part of the 7th Reconnaissance had gone into another pass.

My unit had started lobbing mortar shells into the Jap encampment. In return, the Japs fired blindly up the mountain. I don't think they had seen any of

Medics massage legs and feet of 17-year-old Private Donald Lynch (left), who had to stand in a water-filled trench at the front line on Attu for more than twenty-four hours. He was credited with killing five Jap soldiers. Lynch was rescued by medics and taken to a hospital at Red Beach, Holtz Bay, for treatment. NATIONAL ARCHIVES

our outfit; they just figured the general direction and started firing mortars and some 70 mm stuff.

I returned to the unit just before dark and made my report.

Our forces were advancing from two sides. We were mostly just staying out of the way.

The Japs were disorganized. They didn't have enough men to cover all fronts. They were splitting into little groups.

The next day we had to pull out. We couldn't remain any longer without grub. Many of the men were sick. They drank water and tried to vomit. But they didn't have anything to throw up. Some were crippled from having their feet exposed to ice water for three days.

A SECOND LOOK—AND THREE JAPS

The lieutenant wanted me to take another look at the Jap encampment. The outfit was packing up to leave as I headed down the ravine to my peek hole of the previous day.

There was no change. The Japs still seemed confused.

After studying their encampment I was ready to return. The habits of a lifetime in the woods probably saved my life. I peered all around before standing—and saw three Jap soldiers walking toward me. They were between me and my outfit.

They had probably been trying to locate our mortars. They had likely seen our outfit pulling out, and were heading back to their encampment.

I hoped they would go around me, but they continued down the slope, ever closer. Two of them were about thirty yards apart, and the other fifty yards beyond.

They were bound to see me. I had no choice but to shoot my way out.

I shot the first Jap in the chest at about fifty yards. He dropped dead. The second and next closest was about seventy yards. He stopped when I shot his companion, and tried to locate me. I was partly concealed, with a low ridge between us. I fired at him and hit his shoulder. At that, the third Jap ran for cover. By this time the shoulder-hit Jap had seen me and was trying to get a shot at me.

I fired at the wounded Jap twice more before he dropped, then missed the one running for cover with my fifth shot. I had never shot at a man and was keyed up.

I jammed another clip into my Springfield.

The running Jap got into a washout in a draw. I couldn't see him. I fired two or three times into the hole. He didn't show himself.

I was up against it. If I tried to leave I would have been in the open—he could have nailed me.

He remained out of sight.

The washout was about 100 yards away—too far for me to throw a grenade. I studied it for a time. Smooth snow sloped toward the washout. I thought perhaps I could roll a grenade into it.

I pulled the pin and tossed one. It gathered speed and bounced over the washout before exploding.

I had one grenade left. Instead of tossing it as I had the first, I let it roll easy like—a lethal game of golf.

I was lucky. It dropped into the washout and exploded.

I dashed to the washout, rifle ready, peered, saw it wasn't needed, and went back to my outfit.

BACK TO THE BEACH

We then headed down the mountainside. I suggested to the lieutenant that rifles be slung and we walk into our lines single file. I didn't want a trigger-happy GI shooting at us thinking we were the enemy.

I led the long line and picked out a guy on a machine gun and hollered at him, "Friendly troops."

We didn't know the password because we'd been out of contact for three or four days, and the password had been for one day.

"What outfit?" the machine gunner called.

I told him.

"Come on. We figured you were all dead," he yelled back.

We arrived at the beach where there were piles of supplies. As we arrived I looked around and spotted an old friend, Colonel Leon DeLong, Corp of Engineers Colonel Ben Talley's assistant. I had known him briefly when I was at Cordova for a time. An engineer, before the war he had worked for the Morrison and Knutson construction company.

He didn't recognize me at first—I had whiskers, a grimy face, and wore a tinpot helmet. "Hello Leon," I said.

"Christ, it's Bishop. We thought all of you were dead. Where you been?"

"Never mind where we've been. Is there anything to eat around this damned place?"

"Follow me," he said.

He led us to a pile of K rations guarded by several soldiers. DeLong helped pry the boxes open and distribute the food.

We then rustled sleeping bags. It was about eleven at night, and we scattered out and bedded down.

At three a.m., just four hours later, we were called to return to action. In the semi-dark of May we re-climbed our mountain and dug in about half a mile from where we had been earlier.

We reorganized and had new reinforcements next day, and after that we moved on to other parts of the battle, including Holtz Bay.

Willis "Red" Cruden (Bad Whiskey Red), an Alaska Scout, was killed at Attu. Kenton Hill and Leonard "Quill" Peterson were wounded. The 7th Recon outfit had eleven fatalities while I was with them, including Captain James Austin.

I don't know how many were wounded from the 7th Recon. In battle you have little idea of the overall picture; you look out for yourself and maybe the fellow next to you.

SHOOTING AT JAPS

SHOOTING JAPS on Attu wasn't like shooting a caribou or a moose where you see it fall and can walk over and see where you hit it. A Jap would appear in the distance and maybe half a dozen guys would shoot at him. You can't tell who made hits, or sometimes, even if hits are made. Sometimes the Jap dropped into cover and perhaps no one hit him.

Whenever the Japs were near, or charging, they shouted, yelled, and screamed, apparently trying to confuse or excite us. It didn't work—it just made them better targets.

They could crawl along on open ground with the aid of their camouflage net and hardly be seen. This is where the Alaska Scouts had it over most other soldiers. Most of us had hunted a lot. Anyone who has hunted extensively learns to pick up slight movements readily, more quickly than a nonhunter.

Many times I have located moose, caribou, or bear by the flick of an ear or slight movement of a paw. Once, while guiding a nonresident hunter, I was lying on a knoll glassing a rocky ridge, a likely place for a bear. As I held the glasses steady, a huge paw and forearm of a grizzly reached up. That's the only part of the bear I saw until we got closer.

He soon became a trophy for my client.

It was the same way with a Jap on Attu. You could figure where he should be, or where you would be if you were in his place. And then with patience, study the area with binoculars. If he moved you could spot him.

Their favorite trick was to dig a hole beside a large rock and hang a camouflage net over it. There are no trees or high brush on Attu for cover, and the grass was all dead during the May battle.

The Japs sometimes covered up with beach grass and would remain still as our troops passed—they would then shoot our troops from behind.

Attu had an abundance of mossy hummocks where the blue foxes made their dens. The Japs liked to enlarge these and sit in them, well camouflaged, ready to shoot. Most Japs were only about five feet tall and small, so they could curl up into tiny places.

THE JAP SNIPER

ONE DAY DURING the battle I went to headquarters with a message from the lieutenant of the 7th Recon for Colonel Frank Culin, commander of the northern force.

While I was there, an artillery captain arrived, reporting that a sniper high on a mountainside had killed a man at his battery. He wanted the sniper wiped out, but he couldn't locate him to do it with his artillery. Another fellow, from Wisconsin, happened to be there. The Colonel looked at the two of us.

"Do you want to go after that sniper?" he asked us.

Hell no, we didn't want to go after that sniper, but he put it in such a way that there wasn't a choice.

I told the Colonel I'd take the answer to the message back to the lieutenant, and then see what I could do about the sniper.

The sniper was hidden between two draws. I suggested the Wisconsin fellow take one and I take the other and we'd climb to get closer. That way the sniper couldn't concentrate on both of us at the same time. Of course I didn't know as much as I knew a few minutes later—mainly that a Jap sniper could have someone protecting him.

I climbed my draw, keeping out of sight until I reached a big snowdrift. I couldn't get across it without crawling over or around it. It wasn't terribly high, so I tossed my rifle on top, then dug my fingers in to pull myself up. When I reached the top, a Jap machine gun cut loose at me.

Snow flew as bullets hammered all around me. I kicked my rifle forward and slid after it into the upper side of the drift. It was full of water—dammed by the drift.

When I skidded into that ice water it was kind of welcome; I was still alive.

One of the machine gun bullets had put a hole in my coat and shirt, and cut my underwear, but it didn't draw blood.

No purple heart.

I continued on and lay in some low willows from where I could see the sniper. It was like hunting, which requires patience. I waited and watched. Every once in a while he slowly raised his head to peer at the artillery unit.

Occasionally he'd send a shot their way—mostly harassing them. He had been lucky to hit a man, for the distance was 800 or 900 yards.

I was within 300 yards of him.

My scoped Springfield was just the ticket. I nestled down with it, held the crosshairs precisely where the sniper's helmet occasionally appeared, and waited.

Finally he moved into sight and my crosshairs were on his helmet. I squeezed the trigger. The bullet went into his head.

Some infantry units had started to move forward about then, and one of their mortars took care of the three-man crew of the machine gun that had sprayed bullets at me.

The Wisconsin guy and I returned to the artillery unit the sniper had been harassing. They were making cocoa, and every man in the crew wanted us to have his cup of the hot brew. It was a little embarrassing.

SCOUTING FOR JAPS

Later, I was sent to join the southern force to be closer to the general command headquarters. I did a lot of scouting with one or two of the other Alaska Scouts.

George Gray, another Alaska Scout, and I were trying to locate some Jap artillery from various observation points.

The Japs had had an observation point where they could overlook the Massacre Bay area. Gray and I spotted it, then covered each other as we slipped up on it. When we peeked in the door, we found a dead Jap lying on the bed.

It was a nice dry little hut and we decided to use it as our bivouac. For a few days we camped there at night. Each time we moved in we lifted the dead Jap out, then returned him to the hut in the morning. We treated him very carefully and with great respect.

No one attempted to move in. The hut was all ours. We weren't squeamish.

Later in the battle, three of us were patrolling along the beach—we preferred smaller units because they made less noise, and gave us more chance to spot things. We weren't supposed to pick a fight; our orders were to stay out of the fighting.

We were trying to spot some Jap artillery. They moved it at night, but they left tracks wherever they dragged it, and we were looking for the tracks.

We came to an American outpost—a holding position. Two of the officers there decided to attach

Alaska Scouts at Attu island with a captured Japanese flag. George Bishop, owner of the flag is on right. Scout on left is six-foot-four James F. (Big Jim) Picken. Center Scout is unidentified. After the war Bishop shared a Fairbanks home with famed Alaska hunting guide Slim Moore, who had a young daughter. Bishop was aghast when he returned home one day to find that Moore's daughter had snipped his treasured flag into pieces to make doll clothing. CHARLES O'LEARY, ALASKA SCOUT

themselves to us for the patrol—they hadn't had any combat experience and they were looking for excitement.

The five of us carefully moved along the beach. The guy in the lead walked a couple hundred feet while the others kept him covered. Someone else would then take the lead. We traveled several miles, alternating leads, and peering for Japs or their activities.

I had learned to smell Japs. It was a peculiar, specific odor I can't describe. Whether it was their clothing, their food, or what, I don't know. Probably a combination.

"I smell Japs," I told the others. Unconvinced, Gray laughed at me.

"I smell smoke, too," I whispered a few minutes later.

"We're getting close to something."

There was a little ridge ahead. Shoreline wave action helped cover any noise we made.

While the others waited, I crawled up the ridge, removed my helmet and put it down, then peeked down into an encampment of about twenty Japs. Two of them had a charcoal burner working, cooking something. The others were mostly sleeping.

I looked left and right and saw that I was on a trail where the Japs had been walking a beat.

Quietly, I slid down, forgetting my helmet, and hand-signaled for the others to go back.

We quickly retreated about half a mile.

"Ok, Bishop, what did you see?" Gray asked.

I told them. "I thought we'd just let 'em sleep," I said.Next day a platoon was sent to wipe them out. My helmet was gone. I've often wondered what the Japs' reaction had been when they found it.

LAST PATROL

After the battle ended, six of us Alaska Scouts were sent on a patrol from Massacre Bay. We were to map, look for Jap stragglers, and determine if the beaches could be walked all the way around the island.

Late the first day we came upon an outpost of about forty men with a lieutenant Fields in charge. It was raining, with a cold wind. The men were glum; chins were all but dragging the ground.

That was typical Attu weather. I think it rained every day of the battle, and there was always ground fog. The day after we finished mopping up, the sun came out and remained out for seven days. A tundra fire even started and burned several acres.

"We'd like to stay overnight with you," I told Fields, thinking of a nice dry tent to sleep in.

"We have no food," he said, and then he told me his tale of woe. They had been issued two gas-burning stoves, which had probably been made in a hurry and hadn't been tested.

When the cooks started to use them, solder in the joints had melted and rendered the stoves useless. The only food on hand consisted of A rations (food for cooking).

"Are there any gas drums lying around?" I asked.

"What about driftwood?"

One of the men had seen a drum on the beach. "Have it brought in," I suggested.

A couple other guys were delegated to bring in a pile of driftwood.

One of the other scouts had his camp axe with him, and I had mine. There was also an axe at the outpost.

With axes I cut the drum in half and stood each half on end, open end on the ground. In each I cut out a hole for a draft, and a place to fit stove pipe, which I took from their gas stoves.

"The driftwood is all wet. We tried, and even with oil on it it won't burn," one of the soldiers commented.

"Watch," I told him.

With my axe I split the wet outer layers off of the driftwood until I reached the center, dry wood. This I split into kindling with some larger pieces.

"Damn!" exploded Fields. "I didn't think there was any dry wood within a thousand miles."

Ed Bagby, one of the scouts, was a very good camp cook. He found all the necessary ingredients but baking powder to make hotcakes. However, he found some concentrated lemon powder which he used to make the cakes rise instead of baking powder (I later saw him make doughnuts the same way).

With a good fire under each "stove" and two griddles, in a couple of hours we cooked hotcakes and fed this hungry bunch.

By this time everyone in camp was treating us like brothers. They even put up a tent for us to sleep in.

The next night found us on a beach with a lot of driftwood, with an overhanging cliff which offered shelter for a camp.

We got our packs off and driftwood gathered for a fire. About then two drake Pacific eider ducks came sailing in and landed offshore. The others insisted I try to shoot them, since the only grub we had with us was some rice, flour, and salt.

I crawled to within about fifty yards of the ducks and killed one with a shot from the little .30 caliber carbine I was carrying at the time. The other duck flew out about a hundred yards and settled, being reluctant to leave his companion. I took careful aim and shot him too.

The next problem was how to retrieve them. The water in the Bering Sea is icy, so I was reluctant to swim to recover them. Instead, I took from my pack about fifty yards of fishing line I always carried, and for a weight tied a couple of cartridges on the end of the line. As the tide came in, the nearest duck floated toward shore. After several tries I succeeded in throwing the line over it, but the other was too far.

I had to go into the water after it.

I yelled to Ernie Shupert and Bagby, "Build up the fire," pulled off my clothes and dived into the cold water. The shock was so great I thought I would quit breathing, but I swam out and took the tip of a wing in my mouth, and swam ashore.

I hurried to the fire and in a few minutes was warm again. The other men soon had the ducks cleaned and in a pot hung from a stick over the open fire.

About then a flock of ravens flew in. They apparently roosted in the cliffs above where we were camped. Everyone opened fire on them. Three of them pitched to the ground, shot on the wing with rifles. They went into the pot with the ducks.

When they were almost done, we threw some rice into the pot, and in a short time we had a meal that I'll never forget, mostly probably because I was hungry. Those two big ducks [an adult male Pacific Eider can weigh six pounds] plus the ravens and rice, made a good meal for the six of us.

We had to give up on our beach hike around the island; there were too many high cliff headlands with no beach. We returned by the route we had already covered, and I reported to Captain Thompson with our map. We had been gone for a week.

"I knew you fellows could take care of yourselves—I wasn't worried about you," he said when I apologized for taking so long for the patrol.

George Bishop died at Homer on January 15, 1973. He was 67. He is buried at Homer's Hickerson Memorial cemetery.

13

LEO LAND: ALASKA SCOUT

The following is based on a November, 1983, tape-recorded interview by the author of Leo Land at Land's home in Haines, Alaska.

JOBS WERE SCARCE to nonexistent in the 1930s. In Washington state, young Leo Land joined the Civilian Conservation Corps (CCC) as the only steady work he could find. Born in 1917, he grew up on a farm near Walla Walla, Washington, so the CCC work wasn't unfamiliar. He built trails, upgraded parks, cleared brush, improved rural roads.

From his monthly check of $40 he kept $5 and sent $35 to his mother which largely supported her, his two brothers and two sisters. A dollar went a long way in the 1930s.

In 1938 Leo attempted to join the Navy, but the Navy wouldn't accept him because of a missing tooth. The Army wasn't so choosy—he enlisted in the Fourth Infantry at Fort George Wright at Spokane, Washington. A year later he read a notice that Army cooks were needed in Alaska and the Philippines. He applied for Alaska. That earned him a ride on the Alaska Steamship *Yukon* to Chilkoot Barracks at Haines, where he arrived August 19, 1939.

Chilkoot Barracks was the last of six goldrush military posts built in Alaska to maintain law and order during the goldrush. Originally named Fort William H. Seward, it was renamed in 1922. The other five, Fort Davis, Nome; Fort Egbert, Eagle; Fort Gibbon, Tanana; Fort St. Michael, Norton Sound; and Fort Liscum, Valdez, were all abandoned by 1925.

Chilkoot Barracks was an overlooked holdover from the previous century. The 200 Springfield-rifle-equipped soldiers stationed there was a forgotten legion that led a quiet, leisurely life.

Leo told me, "In January 1940, I married a beautiful Tlingit girl. That got me kicked out of the Army. In those days one had to get permission to marry, and even then, one had to be a staff sergeant or better; I was a Private First Class."

Out of the Army, and living in Haines, he joined the Army reserve and in February 1941 received a notice inviting him to rejoin. The country was readying for war.

He signed up and was sent to Sitka. He applied for a transfer back to Haines, where his wife was, but he didn't wait for a decision. The steamer *Aleutian*, headed for Juneau, stopped at Sitka. He bought a ticket to Juneau. From there he bummed a ride to Haines on a fishing boat.

He reported to the Chilkoot Barracks guard house telling the sergeant on guard, "I'm over the hill," (AWOL—absent without leave).

Leo spent eighteen days waiting for trial.

During those eighteen days he mowed the expansive lawns at Chilkoot Barracks ". . . with a little hand mower. I also drove a wagon, pulled by a mule, delivering ice to the officers' row. A rifle-carrying guard followed my every step."

He was court-martialed and fined five dollars.

At this point in Leo's story I knew I was listening to an independent thinker—and a man with nerve and a sense of humor.

Time passed, and in August 1942, he found himself a sergeant with the Fourth Infantry at Anchorage, preparing to go to the Aleutians. He and his wife had rented a log cabin at ninth and A street. She had a job at a laundry.

When Leo knew it was nearly time for departure to the Aleutians, he went AWOL again. He told his sergeant, "Come get me when it's time."

On his third day of AWOL his first sergeant drove a jeep to his cabin. "Leo, we're leaving on the train to Seward at one-thirty this afternoon. Do you want to go to the laundry and say goodbye to your wife?"

"Nope. Too many tears. I'll leave her a note. She knew I was about to leave and she's ready," Leo said.

"I'd have liked to have said goodbye to my daughter, but she was at school," he told me.

"Before we boarded the train to Seward a major told me I was in for another court martial, and that I'd be busted.

"It didn't happen.

"With others of the 4,500-man 4th Infantry Regiment, I went ashore on Adak Island on August 30, 1942 during a terrible Aleutian storm. There were no docks. A big old steamer with the masts cut off was beached and functioned as a landing dock. We off-loaded equipment and supplies from ships in the bay onto barges, and the barges tied up alongside that beached steamer to be unloaded.

"I was unloading steel Marston mats (used for airstrips) when the air raid sirens blew. Lights were turned off. In the dark a nineteen-year-old private working with me stepped through a hatch and fell about twenty feet onto steel mats in the hold of the ship.

"We discovered him when the lights went back on. I sent a shore boat for a doctor from a nearby submarine tender. The private's back was broken and he had internal injuries. He died that night. He was a nice guy, and I felt terrible about it.

"We had a big job turning the island into a base, and, at the same time, training for combat. We lived in tents. Rows and rows of tents."

MAPPING ADAK

"NOT ONE PERSON on the island knew anything about the topography of Adak outside of the immediate developing area. What if the Japs attacked? We didn't know which beaches could be used for landing, what weapons could be taken ashore at various places, even where troops could easily travel.

"Leslie J. Story, another 4th Infantry sergeant, and I, got permission from our company commander to explore the beaches, hills, and peaks of Adak to make a map.

"Story weighed 180 pounds and I weighed 140. I asked the first sergeant for a .22 rifle and ammo, so we could live partially off of ducks and ptarmigan.

"Our packs weighed about eighty pounds, but we were both in good physical condition. We circled the island in fourteen days and developed a map. We ate a lot of ptarmigan and ducks—they were tame and easily taken with the .22. Some of the brass were worried about us, and were amazed when we showed up in good shape and with leftover food.

"A few days later the Colonel asked me to take a platoon of infantry from New York around the route Story and I had followed. Each soldier packed the same food amounts we had taken.

"After three hours of hiking, I could see that platoon would never make it; they weren't physically fit. I off-loaded twelve to fifteen pounds from each and stored it under a rock. It's probably still there.

"We started again and hadn't gone far when an officer decided, 'Let's turn back. We'll never make it.'

"We went back to camp. That was the end of that expedition.

"Later the Colonel requested that I take a Lieutenant from headquarters around the island—just he and I. Within two hours the Lieutenant started to limp. He asked if we could stop and camp for the night. The next morning we returned to camp.

"We didn't know it then, but Story and I qualified ourselves for the Alaska Scouts by circling Adak, living off the country, and making that map.

A VOLUNTEER

"One day a runner came to my tent. 'The Captain wants to know if you'll volunteer.'

"Volunteer for what?" I asked.

"I don't know," the runner answered.

"I went to the Captain and asked what I was supposed to be volunteering for.

"I don't know," he answered. "It's top secret."

"He asked me and Story to choose another "volunteer." We chose Arthur Upickson, an Eskimo from northwest Alaska.

"We volunteers reported to a big tent at Regimental Headquarters. No officers, or anyone not volunteering, were allowed. Sergeant Joe Kelly, an Alaska Scout I had known at Chilkoot Barracks, told us we would be attached to the Alaska Scouts. About thirty-five Alaska Scouts were to go to Amchitka Island aboard a destroyer. They were to be first ashore.

Alaska Scouts had been to Amchitka twice; first in September to scout for Japs and to see if an aircraft runway was possible; and the second time to take Corp of Engineers Colonel Ben Talley to finalize a runway site.

"Story and I volunteered with several of the long-time Alaska Scouts to go to the north and high end of Amchitka to set up an observation post to watch for Jap planes from Kiska.

"The day we left, the Adak harbor was roaring with huge, frothing, whitecaps. We boarded a navy shoreboat and headed for the new destroyer *USS Worden*. We bounced up and down in the waves as they became higher and higher. Part way to the destroyer the boat's engine caught fire and quit.

"Wind blew us toward a cliff where breakers were pounding and spume was flying high. The troop ship *Middleton*, with troops aboard for the landing at Amchitka, was pulling out. Her skipper saw we were in trouble and turned toward us. Sailors on the *Middleton* readied a line to toss to us. About then the crew of the shoreboat got the fire out and the engine restarted. A couple more minutes and we'd have been slammed into that cliff.

"It was so rough in the outer harbor that waves lifted and dropped the anchored *Worden* eight or ten feet. The shore boat pulled alongside. On swells, it rose higher than the deck rail of the destroyer. When we topped each swell, we tossed a pack or a rifle aboard. Two sailors worked the tie-up lines to the shore boat—tightening and slacking them as we flew up and down.

"A tie-up line wrapped around a foot of one of the sailors as he slacked it. When it tightened it broke his foot. A crew member took his place as he was dragged off to sick bay.

"We got aboard, one at a time, by leaping *down* to the deck of the *Worden* when the shore boat was at its highest."

Lt. Colonel William Verbeck and thirty-five Alaska Scouts—including Land, Story, and Upickson, were aboard.

The *Worden* left Adak, plunging directly into the high westerly wind and mountainous seas. Green water rolled the length of the ship, sweeping overboard everything that was loose. Two securely fastened whaleboats remained.

Most aboard, including the crew, were seasick. After fighting the storm for a time, the Captain, Lt. Commander William G. Pogue, turned back toward Adak. Near Adak he broke radio silence to report the storm was too violent for him to get to Amchitka, much less land the Alaska Scouts.

"Proceed as ordered," he was told, "even if you land only one man on Amchitka."

"It was rough enough the first time we plowed into those seas; the second time was worse. We had to make up for time lost by turning back," Leo told me.

AMCHITKA

"On January 11 it was still the dark before dawn when the *Worden* pitched and rolled into Constantine Harbor at Amchitka. The water was, simply, boiling.

"We were all on deck to say goodbye to the Alaska Scouts who were first to go ashore. Nine two-man inflatable rafts were launched near the beach, and they all made it ashore, although four flipped in the surf.

"The *Worden*'s captain headed to the outer harbor. The *Worden* rose on a huge wave and descended on a pinnacle rock. It impaled the *Worden*. One sailor was knocked off the stern. I don't know how, but the crew managed to get him back aboard.

"The crew let go the anchor. The ship was tilting heavily to starboard. Each wave shook us to our teeth. I looked up and saw the mast swaying at least six feet.

"Day was just breaking when the troop ship *Middleton* cruised by heading into the harbor. Her skipper radioed Captain Pogue and asked what we were doing anchored so close to a reef.

"Another destroyer got a line to the *Worden*, but when it took up slack and pulled, the line broke.

"One of the two *Worden* whaleboats was launched and the crew tossed into it the ship's log, money in a seabag (I heard it was $87,000), and various papers.

"A Navy officer came to me. 'Jump aboard, we're taking the rest of you Scouts to shore. Then we're coming back to ferry the crew ashore,' he said.

"The crew of the *Worden* included a lot of young fellows—mostly teenagers. They were frightened—almost panicking.

"I suggested to the officer, 'Why don't you take some of those young guys? I can swim some if I have to. I'll go next trip.'

"'Ok,' he agreed, handing me his binoculars to put around my neck. 'Try to keep these dry for me,'" he requested.

The immobilized destroyer *Worden* in Amchitka's Constantine Harbor, its bottom pierced by a pinnacle rock. The Alaska Scouts had been put ashore. The destroyer *Dewey* (background) attempted to tow. The line broke. The aerial views don't show the steep waves and high wind. NATIONAL ARCHIVES

Swift current has swung the bow of the sinking *Worden* around and her starboard side is nearly under. Steam appears to be rising from the stern. The crew has abandoned ship, and are being hauled from the frigid January water by the four small boats in the foreground. Fourteen crew members drowned. Those rescued were taken to the transport *Middleton* to have their oil-soaked clothing cut off, and hot showers. NATIONAL ARCHIVES

ABANDON SHIP

"THAT BOAT didn't return. Orders came over the loudspeaker to abandon ship.

"I looked toward the beach. The tide was out, and reefs were showing between huge breakers. Waves were slamming against nearby cliffs, spume flying high. Swimming that direction would have been fatal.

"The life jackets were below decks under water. So were packs, rifles, and other equipment planned for the landing. All lost.

"An old Chief Petty Officer took empty cardboard canisters that had held five-inch ammunition and, as far as they would go, lashed two of them together for each man. He handed me a set of these. I left the binoculars I had been given on board, then, clinging to the canisters, leaped into the icy water. It instantly squeezed my chest and took my breath away.

"It was about a mile around a point and inside the harbor to the troop ship. There were no small boats in sight. Those who could swim headed for that point.

"There was a lot of confusion. Some of the sailors weren't very good swimmers. Waves washed over them and they'd disappear. The cold almost paralyzed me, and soon I could hardly move. Swimming was difficult in that raging sea, and I didn't seem to be making headway. It wasn't long before I was tempted to quit trying. But what would happen to my wife and daughter? With that thought I knew I couldn't quit.

"I saw a young sailor about fifteen feet away. He was frantically paddling, trying to stay afloat without anything to cling to. For a moment he looked me in the eye. I sensed his fear, his panic. Waves repeatedly broke over him. I paddled toward him, but before I could reach him he was gone. That memory still haunts me.

"I kept swimming. The waves were eight or ten feet high. I held my breath as they broke over me. Then I breathed deeply as I dropped into the trough between waves. Then did it all over again.

"Finally, as I topped several waves, I saw small boats approaching. They had landed Alaska Scouts, as well as some other soldiers in case there were Japs on the island, and now they were coming to save us.

"We were all covered with oil from the ruptured tanks of the sinking *Worden*. About all our rescuers could see of us were our white teeth and eyeballs.

"A boat reached me. A sailor grabbed my clothes and slid me over the side. With other oil-soaked survivors I lay in the bottom of that bounding boat, helpless, paralyzed by cold."

"The boats ran us to the *Middleton* where it was anchored in the inner harbor. A sailor jumped down from the *Middleton* with two-ounce bottles of brandy. I hadn't had a drink in months. He grabbed my head, tipped it back, and shoved this little bottle in my mouth. I gulped a couple of times, swallowing the stuff.

"A cargo net was lowered. Each helpless survivor was rolled into the net and lifted aboard. By the time I was rolled into a cargo net and swung aboard I was about half drunk. As I lay helpless on the deck the crew cut my oil-soaked clothes off and took my wallet and other items out of my pockets. They carried me to the showers.

"I managed to stand, clinging to the wall while under the hot shower. It burned like fire, but nothing ever felt so good.

"I was issued navy clothing—a little white cap, a blue shirt and pants, underwear, belt, black oxfords, socks, and a peacoat. They assigned me a bunk, and that was beautiful. I was exhausted and slept like a log."

BACK TO ADAK

"A DAY LATER a destroyer pulled alongside the *Middleton* and picked up Story, Upickson and me to return us to Adak.

"Later, the Alaska Scouts were back on Adak, training and preparing for the battle of Attu. Story, Upickson and I had been transferred back to our old outfit.

"We looked up Colonel Verbeck, second in command of the Scouts, and requested a transfer into the Alaska Scouts.

"Sure," Verbeck agreed. "Go on back to your units and put in requests. I'll see they go through."

"We put in for transfers to the Alaska Scouts, but nothing came of it.

"After a few days I asked a sergeant friend who worked at headquarters how our transfers were coming.

"The Colonel's not going to put in for it," he told me.

"Why?"

"He's not going to let them have his best men," was the answer.

"We went back to Colonel Verbeck. He wired General Buckner. Buckner then wired our regimental commander. "These three men are transferred to the Alaska Scouts as of receipt of this telegram."

"The Colonel still said he wasn't going to transfer us. He was going to make us wait two or three months for the usual paper transfer.

"My sergeant friend said, 'Colonel, I don't think I'd buck General Buckner."

"Our transfers went through," Leo smiled.

During the Battle of Attu, Land with a few other

Alaska Scouts were held in reserve aboard a troop ship anchored in Massacre Bay on the south side of Attu.

The battle of Attu was nearly over when Leo and several other Alaska Scouts were sent to nearby Shemya Island to set up tents and do other little chores—getting ready for fresh arriving troops.

Captain Thompson, of the Alaska Scouts, asked Leo if he would cook for a general and several other officers until their tents were set up and a routine established.

"Sure," Leo agreed. "Provided I can continue as an Alaska Scout."

"As Alaska Scouts we wore parts of uniforms with selected outdoor civilian clothing. We were allowed to arm ourselves with any issue weapon we wanted. We were just typical, independent Alaskans, and Captain Thompson knew it," Land told me.

"It didn't take long for one of the generals to tell Captain Thompson it was demoralizing for his troops to see the 'slovenly appearing' Alaska Scouts. He wanted us all clean shaven, in uniform, wearing ties—the works.

"Captain Thompson nodded his agreement with the general, then got our little group together and told us to head for nearby Alaid Island where there was an old trapper's cabin.

"We'll let the general run his army his way, we'll run the Alaska Scouts our way," Captain Thompson laughed.

"We were on standby on Alaid. We kept our rifles clean, and watched for possible enemy action—and spent a lot of time playing cards.

BEACHED LIBERTY SHIP

"One foggy night we heard a terrific crash. Next morning the fog cleared and we saw a new Liberty ship, high and dry, where it had run its bow up on the beach of Alaid Island.

"We walked over to the ship. The crew told us it had been evading a Jap submarine. Anyway, that was the excuse.

"Barges unloaded the stranded ship. It then backed off. A hole in the hull was above water, so it could travel. We went aboard and it headed for Adak. On the way, a destroyer astern of us kicked off a bunch of depth charges, and radioed our ship to speed up—they weren't sure they had sunk the Jap sub they had detected.

"From Adak we went to Amchitka to regroup for the Kiska invasion. Captain Thompson told those of us who weren't involved in the battle of Attu that we were to be the number one guys for Kiska—we could plan on being involved.

KISKA

Land traveled from Amchitka to Kiska aboard an LST [Landing Ship Tanks]. Alaska Scouts were assigned to the big rubber boats used in the landing—one Scout to a boat that held twelve or fourteen men. The Scout was captain until the boat hit the beach on Kiska.

Leo guided his boat to its assigned landing area in Gertrude Cove. "There was all kinds of stuff the Japs had abandoned scattered along the beach—machine gun tripods, rifles, parts of mortars," he remembered.

"We reached a command post with two trenches around it and waited there for troops to arrive from a troop ship. B-24 bombers were supposed to bomb Jap ships in Kiska Harbor. There weren't any, of course, but we heard them flying over. Regardless, the fog was too thick for them to see to safely drop bombs.

"However battleships and cruisers bombarded the empty harbor. When those big shells landed the whole island shook.

"When the troops landed, our job was over; we had gotten the early troops ashore, and had stood by until the main troops were ashore. We went back to the beach at Gertrude Cove.

"That night it sounded like a war, with rifles all over the island firing.

"Next morning we were organized into a platoon strength outfit of Alaska Scouts, mixed with American and Canadian soldiers. Our orders were to work toward Kiska Harbor until we ran into Japs.

"We didn't run into any Japs. We learned that during the previous night various units had fired at each other—each thinking the other was the enemy. It was a bad and confused situation in the dark and fog.

"We explored the Jap encampment at Kiska Harbor. There were many tunnels. Two midget submarines were on rails on the beach. The Japs had put demolition charges on the control panels.

"Some of the guys got hurt or killed by booby-traps.

"We Alaska Scouts went over to nearby Little Kiska Island to get out of the way. The Japs had artillery there. They had removed the firing bolts and tossed them into the harbor.

"A little leanto there had an oil stove, and some oil. We fixed it up and kept warm and dry while we waited for the next move.

"A few weeks later we were flown to Anchorage. I remember flying over the lights of Anchorage at night just before we landed. Next day General Buckner gave us all fifteen-day furloughs, and we got paid. Some of the guys had gone a year without pay.

"I hadn't heard from my wife for a year. During my time away from Anchorage I started with $4, and in card games managed to run it up to $2,800. That, plus my back-pay, gave us a nice cushion for a while.

"I was based at Fort Richardson with the Alaska Scouts for the next two years, field testing equipment, and doing search and rescue assignments," Leo concluded.

AUTHOR'S NOTES

THE TWO HOURS I spent with Leo Land provided me with some material I used in my historical novel *Castner's Cutthroats, Saga of the Alaska Scouts.*

Twenty-two years later in compiling this volume I regretted that I didn't question Leo more closely about his time with Castner's Cutthroats. Even so, his story is sufficiently compelling to include here.

I reached David Land, Leo's son, who lives in Haines, and learned a bit more about his father.

Leo earned a Bronze Star while in the Aleutians. He was too modest to tell me that.

Leo had planned to make a lifetime career of the Army. It wasn't to be. After six or seven years (David was unsure of the exact time) he received a medical discharge. He and his family then lived in Juneau for about eight years. Leo became a commercial fisherman, worked at construction, and was a mechanic.

He moved back to Haines where he remained for the rest of his life. He did some trapping in the Haines area, and raised his family of three sons and two daughters.

Leo Land died September 6, 2000, at Haines, and, with his wife Edna, who preceded him in death, is buried in the Jones Point cemetery at Haines. He was 82.

14
THE LEGENDARY SQUEAKY ANDERSON

By Stig W. Palm

I FIRST MET Carl "Squeaky" Anderson during the wartime winter of 1943 on the island of Adak, where he was captain of the port. It was easy to figure out how he got his nickname, for as I opened the door to his office he was railing at his yoeman in his high-pitched, squeaky voice. Whenever he was angry or excited, which was most of the time, his voice would assume a high crescendo.

In this instance the yoeman had apparently neglected to give Squeaky some information. Among the things Squeaky yelled, "I'd giff you a summerary (sic) court martial . . . iff I knew how!"

Squeaky's office was located on Sweeper Cove, where he had recently completed a magnificent wharf. Woe be unto him who so ever slightly damaged that wharf. From his office he was able to keep close watch, and no doubt he had watched me as I brought our little minesweeper YMS (Yard Minesweeper) alongside. Fortunately there was no wind, or I might have felt his wrath.

As is customary, I was there to pay my respect as a new arrival to his port. I recognized his accent immediately, for I am also of Swedish descent. In the confines of Squeaky's office I did a little apple-polishing and answered his questions in Swedish. He mellowed and inquired how come, so I explained that my mother had been born in Gothenburg and from her I had learned. It turned out Squeaky also had been born in that city, but he had left there at the age of 13 aboard a merchant vessel bound for the United States.

As I recall his story, which he told me over a period of time, he got to Honolulu where he jumped ship, thinking he could find a better job. His youth was against him, but being big for his age and strong, he was able to enlist in the U.S. Marines. He subsequently took part in the Nicaraguan campaign of 1912. He served out his enlistment, gravitated to Seattle, and later moved to Alaska. He ran the *Polar Star*, a small trading vessel in the Bering Sea, and was captain of the *Star* which hauled freight, passengers, and mail between Seward and the Aleutian Islands. For many years he roamed the Aleutians and became almost as well acquainted with those islands as were the Japanese in those times, which is saying a lot.

Squeaky was a successful salmon cannery operator at Seldovia, where he built up a fleet of boats. But he also got involved with other things, like highly illegal sea otter furs, which got him into trouble.

About the time that World War II rolled around he was under indictment for nineteen counts of such things as illegally running furs. But the Navy, recognizing his worth in knowledge of what had become a war zone, and his ability to get things done, was able to quash the indictments. Squeaky was commissioned as captain of the port at Dutch Harbor, where he was in charge of naval defenses when the Japanese attacked there in June 1942.

He did a marvelous job of that and, also, of building up the naval facilities in and around Dutch.

So he got the job as beachmaster when our forces landed on Adak. Later he was made captain of the Adak port, where he continued to get things done, and ahead of schedule at least partly because he disregarded spit and polish and regulations.

He was constantly under heavy pressure. We often discussed our navigational charts, which had some geographic features as much as eight miles out of place. The local magnetic disturbances were such that a magnetic compass was often worse than useless.

Outside of Sweeper Cove was huge Kuluk Bay, an anchorage for large ships, but it was usually rough. So in the various assignments made to our YMS, which included a lot more than minesweeping, he would tell us where to hole up when the weather got too bad for our topheavy shallow-draft wooden ship. One of these places was Scabbard Bay, off Kuluk. It was shaped like a scabbard with high cliffs on either side; while weather might be raging outside, it was usually like a millpond there.

We developed a soft spot for that little bay and used it many times. The first time there we found the old four-masted schooner, *Sophie Christensen*, at anchor. As usual we were short of water, so we came alongside and they were happy to give us 200 gallons—and then we played poker while the storm raged outside. Ostensibly *Sophie* was a fishing vessel, but I'm not sure what she was doing at the time. I understand she is still around, more than 100 years old. [Palm wrote this story in 1985. —JR].

As preparations for the May 1943 invasion of Attu built, Squeaky went almost without sleep. The battleships, cruisers and destroyers kept filling Kuluk Bay, and he had me sweeping for mines, although I assured him no mines could live in those waters very long.

It's not generally known, but when a minesweeper is sweeping and has the proper signals two-blocked (flying), it has the right of way over every other ship. Once we had the pleasure of making the huge battleship *USS Mississippi* veer out of our path. Squeaky got a big kick out of this.

On March 26, 1943, during the naval Battle of the Komandorski Islands, a U.S. task group of the heavy cruiser *Salt Lake City*, the light cruiser *Richmond*, and four destroyers, *Bailey, Coughlin, Dale*, and *Monaghan*, exchanged gunfire with a Japanese force twice its size. After three and a half hours the Japanese fled.

On our side, seven Americans were killed, with seven hospital cases, and thirteen minor injuries.

On March 28, the new 2,200-ton class destroyer *Bailey* arrived in Kuluk Bay, Adak, with its dead and wounded, and Squeaky sent us to pick up those unfortunates. It was very rough, but we managed a nice landing alongside their port side and tied up. But just as we were about to start loading, someone from the *Bailey* released our stern lines, causing our bow to move in on theirs so the destroyer's big steel scuppers gouged a huge hole in our starboard bow, which, of course, was wooden.

We stuffed mattresses and everything else we could find into the hole to keep from shipping water, but the rough seas made it a lost cause, so we backed off and headed for Sweeper Cove.

I hated to radio Squeaky, as he had enough troubles, but we needed repairs. He told me to get to the YR-38 for patching and then to report to him on the double. It was with heavy heart but still with my usual smile that I walked into his office. He greeted me at the door, "How in hell kin I git mad at you ven you are alvays smiling?"

He took me into his *sanctum sanctorum* and fed me some fresh strawberries and ice cream, my first in more than a year.

Squeaky, as Beachmaster for the North Force, was among the first Americans ashore at Attu. He faced a big challenge—getting materials across a narrow beach and up a cliff. He did so efficiently, and was promoted to Commander after Attu.

Squeaky had some personal scores to settle with the enemy, and he made make certain nothing got screwed up. Subsequently he became a beachmaster of legend throughout the Pacific.

A beachmaster is responsible for the intricate placing and allocation of materials piled on an invasion beach during and after a landing. After the Aleutian Campaign, Squeaky became a beachmaster in the Central Pacific. At Abemama, in the Gilbert Islands, according to historian

Commander Carl "Squeaky" Anderson, at Adak, June, 1943. A Swedish immigrant, during World War II, Anderson gained fame for his organizational ability as a port captain and as a beachmaster. He cut corners, ignored regulations, and knew how to get a job done. STIG PALM

Samuel Eliot Morison, Squeaky was . . . "troubled by beach and shore parties scattering through coconut groves sightseeing, instead of helping his crew. For, he [Squeaky] observed, 'De girls vos very pretty, und dey vear no vests around der chests!'".

Our Army was ill-equipped to fight on Attu. The men had improper clothing, especially footgear, and there were many frostbite and trenchfoot casualties. A battle that at first was estimated to take three days, took three weeks. Recapture of Attu became one of the bloodiest battles of the Pacific islands.

Next came the matter of recapturing Kiska, the other American island in the Aleutian group that had been occupied by the Japanese. Quite by accident, our little YMS had a hand in that.

Squeaky kept ordering us out on patrol to see what we could see, but mostly to see what we could *hear*, for the Aleutian fog is ceiling zero ninety-eight percent of the time. One night, despite my admonitions, the watch officer failed to advise me that he had doubts as to where we were. By the time I got topside we were hopelessly lost in the fog.

I took control and with our fathometer we found nothing resembling our location from our charts. The seas were relatively calm, so we kept cruising and looking for some kind of landmark or depth that we could identify, when suddenly there loomed a point of land.

The fog had lifted somewhat, so we could see quite well to a height of about thirty feet, but it was the usual tundra, with no distinguishing features. As we crept closer we searched our charts and watched the fathometer. We had been heading west, but now we turned north following the coastline. Suddenly we saw a peculiar outcropping of rock, and near it on the beach, was a small vessel that had all the earmarks of Japanese design.

Coupled with the rock, which was noted on our chart, we now knew we were off the Japanese-held island of Kiska. Our immediate inclination was to head east at flank speed, but I knew Squeaky needed all the information he could get. Since we saw no evidence of patrols by ship or plane, we cautiously inched northward hoping to catch a glimpse of the main harbor.

We eased into the harbor. All we could see were wrecked ships and buildings, with no sign of life. We high-tailed it back to Adak. En route I dictated a memo to Squeaky. When we docked I ran to his office to hand it to him.

I had never seen so much gold braid and scrambled eggs on military caps as were gathered in that little office, but I was able to deliver the memo to Squeaky, who by that time was a full commander.

The invasion of Kiska took place soon after, and, as we suspected, the Japanese had all left. We did find some mechanical mines in the harbor and some booby traps ashore. Also, there was considerable evidence that our bombing missions had been successful.

This was in August, 1943. The following month I was sent back to Dutch Harbor to take command of another minesweeper. In late November, while returning to Dutch for a mission, we saw a PBY-5 crash in the sea, and we were able to rescue ten of the eleven crew members. When we got them ashore I found my orders sending me back to the States, but suddenly, there had to be a board of investigation on the PBY crash, on which I was a prime witness. After that I was ordered to assist in locating the plane at the bottom of the bay for retrieval, for it contained the then highly secret Loran equipment. All told I was delayed two weeks, but when I finally left, instead of my having to take a ship to Seattle, the admiral got me a plane ride.

We stopped in Kodiak for fuel. While there I saw the infamous "Greenhouse," a house of ill repute, with its usual number of soldiers and sailors waiting outside in a long line. I mention this because it had a bearing on my last visit with Squeaky.

At Seattle I went to the 13th Naval District headquarters to wangle some leave to see my son for the first time. He was then almost a year old. Who did I meet but Squeaky Anderson, now resplendent with the four stripes of a captain. I asked about lunch, but he had to give a speech to a women's club at the Olympic Hotel. He invited me to accompany him for moral support. By now Squeaky was being lionized, and had little time for himself.

He was introduced as the hero of the Aleutian campaign, at which he shook his head, but he gave a fine speech, accent and all, depicting the hardships suffered by servicemen in Alaska. He spoke of "tundra fever" (tiredness of Alaska) and described some tragic episodes brought on by the monotony of duty in the North.

He received a standing ovation, after which was a question-and-answer period, which he fielded quite well until one dowager stood and asked, "Captain Anderson, what could we send those poor boys up there to do them the most good?"

Squeaky looked at her, blinked a few times, and replied, "Whores, lady, t'ousands of 'em!"

End of session.

Several ladies did stop to shake hands with him.

After that we went to his room where we shared a bottle. That was the last time I saw the great man.

Squeaky is gone now, but he's not forgotten.

I got my leave.

"The Legendary Squeeky Anderson," By Stig W. Palm was first printed in June 1985, in *Alaska Magazine* under the heading "People of the North." (Spelling was "Squeeky" in the magazine, probably based on the spelling at the Port of Adak—by Squeeky himself.)

AUTHOR'S NOTES

Before World War II and the Aleutian Campaign, Squeaky Anderson started a salmon cannery at Seldovia, Alaska, on the Kenai Peninsula. He emerged from the Navy after the war as a Rear Admiral, and returned to running his cannery.

He transplanted Squeakyville from Adak to Seldovia, and therein lies a tale.

In the 1950s he wanted a shortwave station at the cannery so he could talk to his tenders and fishermen. However, federal policy allowed only one shortwave station to an Alaskan community, and Adam Lipke, a pioneer Alaska radio operator, was already licensed for Seldovia.

Squeaky applied to the federal government for a radio license for Squeakyville, a place that existed only in his imagination—and he got it.

For years KWE 38 at Seldovia remained on from early morning until late at night. Anyone with a message to Seldovia could get through. In addition, during the commercial salmon fishing season, KWE 38 had four scheduled times on the air so tenders, boats that collected salmon from fishermen, could report.

One morning Squeaky called a tender on the fishing grounds.

"How many fish you got?" he demanded in strong Swedish accents.

"Seven hundred reds," the skipper answered.

"T'at's fine, Ted. Seven t'ousand reds," Squeaky warbled.

"No, Squeaky," the skipper corrected. "Seven hundred. Over."

"That's fine, Ted, that's fine. Seven t'ousand reds."

"No, Squeaky," the skipper repeated, "Seven zero zero."

"Okay, I heard you," Squeaky answered instantly. "Seven t'ousand reds. KWE 38 clear."

When the tender docked, Squeaky was there. The skipper climbed ashore and Squeaky confronted him, a finger on the man's chest.

"Ted, when I say you got seven t'ousand fish, you *got* seven t'ousand fish!"

The skipper nodded in confusion. Squeaky explained.

"Dese fishermen sit around town waiting for fish to hit. I want them to get out and fish instead of sitting here listening to me on the radio. Dey won't go out there for seven hunnert fish!"

There hasn't been a salmon cannery in Seldovia for many years, and KWE 38 is history. Squeaky is also history, but, as Stig Palm wrote, he is not forgotten.

15

STIG PALM: YMS SKIPPER

During the twenty years I was Outdoors Editor for ALASKA Magazine*, Stig Palm and I held a lengthy correspondence. Each of us wrote at least 40 letters. That correspondence led to friendship, and my wife Audrey and I once spent a pleasant week with Stig at his home at Sun Lakes, Arizona.*

As we corresponded and I learned of his nearly five years of naval service, most of it in the Aleutians in the early 1940s, I encouraged him to write about it for ALASKA Magazine*. His article on Squeaky Anderson (chapter fourteen) resulted.*

In his correspondence with me he often held forth on other of his Aleutian experiences. Those letters gave a human touch to that war, as revealed in the segments that follows, lifted directly from his letters.

Stig Palm died in April, 2003. He was 85.

Navy Reserve Ensign Minnesota-born Stig Palm, not long after being commissioned. He served in the Navy for nearly five years, most of it in the Aleutians during World War II.
STIG PALM

AT DUTCH HARBOR I was given command of the YMS-126 (Yard Mine Sweeper: these vessels were never named, only numbered), the crew of which had a terrible morale problem. I once found two of them waiting in bushes with .45 pistols planning to kill the then-skipper. He was the type to post a "Captain Queeg" notice to the effect, "No one shall have a coffee cup larger than that of the Captain."

When I replaced him I was an instant hero to the crew.

We were returning to Dutch Harbor from Akutan with YMS-126 after leading another Soviet coal burner to our coaling station there. I did this sort of thing a lot, as the Russians usually got lost in the Bering Sea fog. We had a sort of lend-lease arrangement to provide these ships with coal at Akutan. They couldn't make it all the way from the states to Russia without refueling.

Near Dutch, we saw a PBY-5 amphibian flying in a somewhat disoriented manner. It was understandable, for we were in the usual fog. They blinked at us, but the signal was not intelligible. We turned to follow. Shortly the airplane veered left, lowered wheels, and crashed into the water.

A nearby power barge, *Myrtle*, reached the plane first; we were there moments later. We launched our little wherry and picked up ten of the eleven-man crew. One crew member was jammed in a rear compartment. He couldn't get out. The plane was sinking and there was no time to pry him out. We heard his pitiful screams as the PBY disappeared beneath the water.

The surviving crew suffered from shock and exposure to the 42-degree water. The worst injury was to the copilot whose wrist was severed. My pharmacist did a fine job dressing the wrist until we could get the man ashore to a doctor. I recommended he be promoted to Chief Petty Officer.

The pilot of the PBY, Walt Means, was a fine guy, and he was on the hot seat. There was much testimony at a hearing on the crash. The copilot testified that the red wheels-down light was on. My helmsman, Knudsen, a former commercial fisherman, also testified that the wheels of the PBY were down (they were).

I testified immediately afterward. How could I refute the two of them? I tried to obfuscate by dwelling on the fog. Nevertheless, Walt was grounded.

You don't land a PBY amphibian on water with the wheels down.

NOTES FROM DUTCH HARBOR NEWS MONDAY, NOV. 29, 1943.

"The officers and crew of the USS YMS-126, Captain Stig Palm, and the crew of the Pontoon Power Barge *Myrtle* who assisted in a local airplane crash, are hereby commended for their prompt action and the expeditious manner which they exhibited during the process of rescuing survivors. In particular B.B. Baker, PhM1c [pharmacist mate first class], is to be commended for his prompt and efficient service in rendering assistance and supervision of the injured survivors from the time of their receipt aboard the YMS-126 until delivery to the station at Dutch Harbor.

"This conduct on the part of the above personnel is in keeping with the high standards and best traditions of the U.S. Navy."

One of the first Loran units, then still secret, was on the sunken PBY. It had to be retrieved. I was given the assignment with help from Lieutenant Wilfred Keene, an assistant to Rear Admiral John Reeves.

We found the airplane, and the Loran was retrieved.

ARMY COURT MARTIAL

Once we had to stop at Cold Bay for fresh water. An Army court martial was underway there, but there were difficulties. They had no recorder. I made the mistake of telling them that I had experience as a court martial recorder, assuming the Army system was similar to that of the Navy. So I became the recorder, which in a sense is the same as a prosecutor for civil law.

It seems that the first nurses to arrive at Cold Bay had been disembarking at the wharf, when a GI who had been there for three years with no leave, had the temerity to make an indecent proposal to one of the new nurses. He offered her $300. Cash, yet.

I was appalled when I learned the facts. The nurse, fresh from the states, was most indignant that an enlisted man could proposition her (was it ok for an officer?). I wasn't allowed to ask that, although I was on the side of the poor GI, so was a bit schizoid.

I tried to point out the three years of horrible conditions the man had endured. Cold Bay was one of the worst assignments in the Aleutian War Zone, and I saw most of them; there was nothing there.

I tried my best to prosecute and succeeded, to my dismay, and the poor guy got ten years at hard labor. I had hopes it wouldn't stick, but never knew. I avoided Cold Bay from then on.

YMS-134

In August 1943, I was skipper of the YMS-134 at Adak. Squeaky Anderson had us doing many things as sort of a jack-of- all-trades. One of these was to go on patrol, in this instance to see what we could see or hear about the Japs on Kiska, although we had strict orders to not go near the island, as he felt we would get blown out of the water with our tiny 136-foot wooden minesweeper. We drew about six feet of water and we had twin screws for the maneuverability required for sweeping. We had no radar. We did have a fathometer which we had scrounged from a beached patrol boat at King Cove. We also acquired anti-submarine underwater sound gear the same way.

My standard orders were for the officer of the deck to always notify me at any time there was doubt as to our position. It is important to understand that when the Japan Current, which is relatively warm, meets the cold water of the Bering Sea, a dense fog is created. Often the wind blows for days, sending the waters through the Aleutian Chain usually either north or south. When the wind lets up, the waters come rushing back, creating tremendous currents, and this condition is very treacherous, for usually you don't know you're being moved by those waters. With experience one does learn to cope with it.

On one trip from Adak eastward, I felt us being pushed southward by the rushing water and gradually changed our heading a total of 170 degrees to port and hit Amlia Island, my landmark, right on the button.

From Adak, Squeaky ordered us to patrol northward out of Kuluk Bay, then westward toward the Rat Islands. We were to keep radio silence, except in an emergency, for which we had codes.

A good skipper never really sleeps, especially in the Aleutians and especially with "Logheads" (Loghead was an ensign assigned to YMS-134. He was a nice kid, but he was green, and had no sea savvy, with little prospect for improvement). As we headed toward Kiska, the fog cleared intermittently and the sea was fairly calm, so it wasn't bad sailing.

After being on the bridge many hours I turned the watch over to Loghead at midnight, but I had qualms. Things seemed to go smoothly until about 0300 when I sensed some shuffling and signs of confusion on the bridge directly above my cabin. I went to the bridge. Loghead admitted he was lost.

Lieutenant Stig Palm, Captain of the YMS-134 (Yard Mine Sweeper) at Kiska, taking a bearing with a stadiometer from the bridge of his ship. STIG PALM

It was understandable, for with constant fog and unknown currents, and no sight of land, it is most difficult to be certain where you are. This is very stressful so, instead of the standard navy eight hours watches, we used four.

Loghead had stayed on course, but apparently currents had pushed us around, in what direction we knew not. The fathometer showed thirty two fathoms, which was no help except we knew we weren't close to land.

There wasn't much to do but follow our dead reckoning. I ordered a lookout to the forepeak in case we suddenly came upon an island. For fifty-six hours straight I stayed on the bridge, living on sandwiches and coffee. Finally, the forepeak watch reported land sighted about four miles away.

From the flying bridge with binoculars I tried to find a landmark that showed on charts.

It was not at all familiar to me, and I knew almost all of the major Aleutian Islands. We cruised closer and could see it was a headland. On a hunch I turned the ship northward and we sighted a peculiar rock outcropping and a beached vessel which had the typical Jap silhouette.

Could this be Kiska? The chart and the description in the *United States Coast Pilot* said so.

We slowed and kept to a northward course, which took us into Kiska Harbor. We saw wrecked ships in the harbor, and bombed out buildings on shore. There was no sign of life. We were amazed.

This was the kind of information I was supposed to get—in spades. We left at flank speed, thinking uneasily of the large caliber guns that had been reported on the ridges surrounding the harbor.

En route to Adak, I dictated a memo for Squeaky to my yeoman, Theodore Roosevelt Ross, making it clear that Kiska appeared to be deserted.

At Adak I ran to Squeaky's office, delivered the memo, and fled from the crowd of gold braid there.

The brass were unimpressed by my report. Squeaky later told me that gold braid from the trade school (Annapolis) didn't feel that a reserve officer could be depended upon, so plans to invade Kiska were unchanged.

THE ALEUTIAN STARE

MORALE WAS A major problem in the Aleutians. Men developed what they called, "The Aleutian Stare." Men simply stared, as if looking through things. Not a few were returned to the States in straitjackets.

There were many instances of GIs trying to get back to the states from the Aleutians. Some tried by sneaking aboard ships or airplanes headed stateside; most were caught immediately. One fellow leaped off the pier at Dutch and tried to swim for it.

A sergeant built a small boat from ammo crates and with an outboard motor took off, headed for

The 360-ton YMS-134, Stig Palm's ship, was 136 feet long and powered by twin 600 horsepower Cooper-Bessemer diesels that could push it to a flank speed of 17 knots. Because it was designed to sweep mines, some of which are magnetic and touched off by a steel hull, YMS hulls were wood. The cabin, however was steel, offering some protection in a gun battle.
U.S. NAVY/STIG PALM

Seattle. We were in the area and were ordered to keep a lookout for him. We sighted him as he was about to enter Unimak Pass, and we radioed for instructions. We were told a Navy Kingfisher (float plane) was on the way to pick him up. Which it did and just in time, for that pass was about to go into one of its furies.

A GROUNDED RUSSIAN

We once found a Russian freighter hung up on the rocks on the eastern end of Unimak pass, which is full of pinnacles. It was showing signs of breaking in two.

We signaled with our blinker, but apparently their electricity was out, for they didn't respond. Somehow they had managed to get a cable for a breeches buoy to shore, but the riding seat was out of order. The crew went hand over hand on steel cable, with the seas breaking over them all the way.

There couldn't have been much flesh left on their hands, but all twenty-two made it ashore. There was no way we could get to them. But in the hope that someone could read our blinker we signaled them to walk eastward and we would radio for help.

They understood and started to walk, so I radioed Mrs. Cohen at King Cove and she knew what to do. Later I heard the crew was picked up and arrangements made to get them back to Russia.

When the ship broke up, stuff poured out and we retrieved some large cheeses which floated toward us. Quite good.

USO TOUR

One morning at Dutch Harbor I went to see the new country club for the Navy, and went into the steam bath. And who did I meet there but movie star Errol Flynn. He was there on a USO tour with actress Martha O'Driscoll. Both had beautiful builds.

He asked all about mine sweeping, so I invited him aboard my YMS, hoping O'Driscoll would come too. Instead, he brought a half case of Scotch and some cases of beer. Booze isn't allowed aboard Navy vessels, but we somehow managed. He was a nice guy. I met him later at the Beverly Hills Hotel, and he remembered me and invited me to visit his movie set. Sadly, I had no time because I had to check in at San Pedro.

UP RELEASE BY RUSSELL ANNABEL. HEADQUARTERS, ALASKA DEPARTMENT, NOVEMBER 27, 1943.

Errol Flynn is here with a cast of four, billed as a Christmas-New Year's tour of army and navy camps in Alaska, including the Aleutians.

The first performance today was based on gags, humorous skits and Flynn's recent girl troubles. The troops liked him, his act and sample gags. "I like this cold climate. You know, it was getting plenty hot for me in Hollywood and I'm not kidding. You should've seen the crowd at the airport when I left. Hundreds of people. All my lawyers."

It was understood here that attorneys for blonde Shirley Evans Hassau who charged that Flynn is the father of her two-year-old daughter agreed to delay action for six months so Flynn could make the tour for the Hollywood Victory Committee.

The cast includes singer Martha O'Driscoll, magician Harry Mendoza, guitarist Jimmy Dodd and wife singer Ruth Carrell.

16 TWELVE RETURNED

UP RELEASE BY RUSSELL ANNABEL. HEADQUARTERS, ALASKA DEFENSE COMMAND, MARCH 24, 1943.

THIRTEEN SLIM, death-dealing Lockheed Lightning fighters were roaring through the smoke and fog above the bomb-torn Jap garrison at Kiska harbor.

Suddenly, Flight Leader Lieutenant Kyle A. Bean, Secor, Illinois, saw that one of the planes had been hit by anti-aircraft fire and that it was burning. The pilot of the burning fighter was Lieutenant John W. Livesay, Fort Worth, Texas, a veteran Aleutian combat airman—friend and long-time flying mate of every man in the squadron.

This was the morning of March 15, and the Lightnings, going in ahead of a flight of medium bombers, had strafed the camp area and the new fighter strip on which Jap workers were slowly and laboriously hauling earth in primitive pushcarts.

The fighters had poured their belts of explosive and incendiary bullets into buildings, into the revetted emplacements of Jap anti-aircraft guns, into the seaplane hangar perched on a cliff above the water, into the submarine base and into storage dumps.

It was when they had raged over the smoking garrison the last time, and swept out over North Head near the entrance to the harbor that the anti-aircraft burst smashed Livesay's right engine. Pilots behind him saw his plane zoom to clear the ridge, then saw it lurch under the terrific impact of the shell burst. They saw the first trailing scarf of black smoke, then the blossoming of flame as it whipped back in the propeller wash and enveloped the wing.

There was nothing they could do.

The bombers were coming in now, making their runs, and the Lightnings were scheduled as top cover for them. The pilots rendezvoused, hunting in their tiny glassed-in cockpits, weaving through the ack ack bursts at 300 miles an hour, as Lieutenant Livesay's plane lurched out to sea, headed toward the home base.

If they used their radios, no one has revealed what they said. But they knew they were probably saying goodbye, for it was a long over-water flight to the base and the smoke plume trailing Livesay's plane was growing.

Eleven of the pilots turned back into the hell of ack ack over Kiska. The twelfth, Lieutenant John K. Geddes, Altadena, California, followed Livesay. As the latter's plane approached a small, bleak, uninhabited islet it began going out of control. Probably the control cables were burning out. It wavered, lost altitude, tried to spin, but Livesay set it down in the surf 300 feet offshore.

Geddes, circling overhead, saw a life raft float clear, but did not see Livesay. The burning Lightning had sunk.

A search party later landed from a seaplane, found Livesay's body on the beach, and buried him in the side of a ridge overlooking the foggy Bering

Sea, with his identification tag on the rocks covering his grave.

Lieutenant Livesay's epitaph, in stilted official language, is in the operation files of the Alaska Fighter Command:

"Thirteen Lightning fighters of the Eleventh Air Force on this day staged one the most destructive strafing attacks ever carried out against the Japs of Kiska. Twelve of the fighters returned to base."

[From John H. Cloe's notes I found the following confirmation. Annabel had it mostly right: "15 March, 1943. Anti-aircraft fire hit the right engine of the P-38 flown by Lieut. John W. Livesay, 54th Fighter Squadron, while on a mission over North Head. He feathered the prop and managed to reach Rat Island where he bailed out. An OA-10 sent to rescue was unable to land due to rough water. The crew landed on the opposite side of the small island and hiked across. They found Lieut. Livesay face down in the surf, recovered his body, and buried it above the shoreline in a grave marked by a cairn and his dog tags. (Intel Summary, Field HQ 11AF, 15 Mar 1943). –jr]

AUTHOR'S NOTE

After the war, grave registration teams collected bodies of service men buried at various places in the Aleutians, and re-buried them in military cemeteries, or made arrangements with relatives for burial elsewhere.

When the U.S. entered World War II, the twin-engine P-38 Lockheed Lightning was the Army's fastest and most heavily armed fighter. The four fifty caliber machine guns and single 20mm cannon concentrated in the Lightning's nose could destroy an enemy plane with a one-second burst.

After the Japanese sneak attack on Pearl Har-

The twin engine Lockheed P-38 Lightning fighter was a large plane, as can be seen by this photo of one on the ground at Adak in 1943. The two engines provided added safety—the airplane flew well with one engine. The long range ability of the P-38 made it a better airplane for the Aleutians than the P-40s and P-39s that were also used there. NATIONAL ARCHIVES

The slim, streamlined, P-38, with its twin booms and tail, was unmistakable. Its firepower, all in the nose, was a concentrated four fifty-caliber machine guns, and one 20mm cannon. In summer, 1942, a federal stream guard at Kodiak cringed under a dock when a P-38 circled overhead. Because of its incongruous shape, he thought it a Japanese plane.
NATIONAL ARCHIVES

bor, and the discouraging string of Jap victories in the Pacific, U.S. Air Corp General George Kenney hustled to the Lockheed Aircraft plant in California, urging Lockheed administrators to rush what was code-named "Project Snowman," a special design of P-38 fighters for use in the Aleutians. He wanted the planes to be worked on twenty-four hours a day until the Lightnings were en route north. "Those ships will be fighting within thirty-six hours after they leave the factory," he said.

A squadron of P-38s was hastily formed and flew to Alaska. The P-40s and P-39s already in the Territory didn't have enough range to effectively fight in the Aleutians.

The first offensive mission by P-38s was on September 3, 1942, when two of these twin-engine fighters flown by Lieutenants George Laven and Victor Walton flew from Umnak Island to Kiska.

They dropped bombs on ships in Kiska Harbor, and shot up Japanese crews on shore and aboard ships. Both their planes were damaged by anti-aircraft fire, but they returned safely to Cape Field on Umnak Island.

At the time it was believed to have been the

longest distance fighter mission of the war. They had been in the air for eight hours.

After the war, retired Colonel Walton said that, "All but ten of the original thirty-one P-38 pilots in the Aleutians were killed there, most of them lost to the weather."

On one occasion, four P-38s were being escorted by a B-17 bomber on a flight to Adak. They flew a few feet off the water, and the fog was so thick that the number one man could not see numbers three and four of the formation.

"When we got to Adak, three and four were gone. They had hit a rock sticking out of the water," Walton said.

Another P-38 pilot, retired Lt. Colonel Richard Bracey, said, "The best thing I remember about the P-38 is that it brought me home single-engine three times."

REFERENCES

Christy, Joe, and Jeff Ethell, *P-38 Lightning at War*. Not dated. Charles Scribner's Sons, New York.

Caidin, Martin, *Fork-tailed Devil: The P38*. 1971, 1973, Ballantine Books, Inc.

Cloe, John, *A History of the 11th Air Force & Fleet Air Wing 4, Part I.* 1993. Anchorage Chapter—Air Force Association, and Pictorial Histories Publishing Company, Inc.

Jones, Lloyd, S., *U.S. Fighters. 1975*. Aero Publishers, Inc.

17

LANDING AT ATTU

UP RELEASE BY RUSSELL ANNABEL.
MASSACRE BAY, ATTU ISLAND,
MAY 12, 1943.

UNITED STATES TROOPS attached to a naval amphibious force struck swiftly and unexpectedly yesterday at Jap garrisons on Attu, making three landings: two on northern enemy concentrations at Holtz Bay and Chichagof Harbor, and one to the south.

The enemy was taken completely by surprise and there was no organized opposition until our troops took up positions at the foot of mountain passes leading to Jap strongholds. Here, machine gun nests and snipers had, for the time being, halted our advance.

The three landings were made at Massacre Bay on the south side of the island, at Blind Cove, and an unnamed beach near Holtz Bay on the north side of the island.

Rear Admiral F. W. Rockwell commands the amphibious force making the attack while Major General Albert E. Brown, Charleston, South Carolina, commands the Army troops attached to the task force.

Following up heavy, beautifully accurate barrages laid down by naval units and army artillery, troops advanced up Massacre Creek through blowing fog, waded icy streams and floundering through quaggy muskeg until machine gun fire, supplemented by occasional mortar fire, caused them to dig in at the junction of passes leading to Sarana and Holtz Bays.

The remainder of the first day was devoted to searching the foggy snow-striped crags for hidden snipers and machine gunners.

A platoon of Japs guarding Massacre Bay were surprised by the advancing troops. They were cleaning two 40mm guns near an outpost shack. The Japs set fire to the shack and fled hastily into the hills without firing the guns that were obviously placed to dominate approaches to the bay.

The force that landed at Blind Cove was also unopposed on the beach, but snipers and machine gun nests were encountered in the mountain pass leading to the Holtz Bay garrisons. Today, this force was reported to have reached a position within 1200 yards of the main Jap encampment.

Continuous heavy fog prevented air action save for two raids made by United States bombers which roared through the overcast today to unload their sticks of bombs on enemy emplacements on the south side of Massacre Pass. The effect of the bombardment was unobserved from our positions at the junction of the two passes.

Enemy strategy appears to be to hold the passes, making full use of the fog and bad terrain, with the idea of making the destruction of their forces as expensive as possible. Our intention is to continue to advance from the north and south until the jaws of the pincher are joined and the enemy is hemmed in on three sides on land, and with naval units and army aircraft guarding the fourth side.

Our patrols fanning out through fog-shrouded, cliff-hung valleys have been efficiently mopping

Japanese troops on high ground, Attu. Mountain heights of Attu are snow-covered year-round. Japanese were the only enemy troops to reach North American soil during World War II. The Japs encountered two enemies on Attu—American troops, and the Aleutian weather. JAPANESE PHOTO

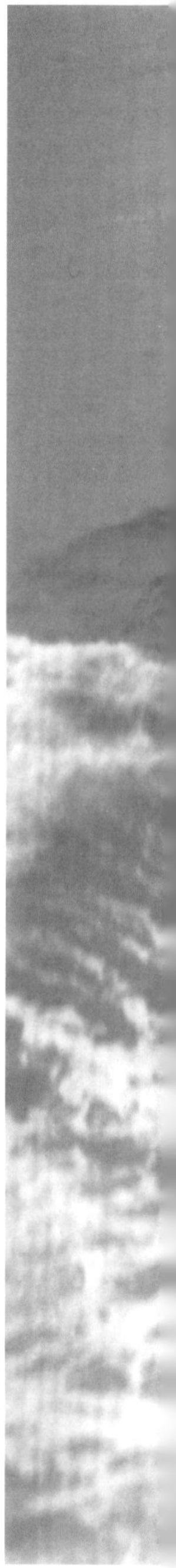

up isolated pockets of resistance left below the mountain passes.

One patrol, led by Captain Robin Goodfellow, of Salem, Oregon, threaded its way from Murder Point to the head of Temnac Bay, arriving there at midnight and finding a group of six Japs in an outpost guarded by three sentries. The latter were killed by rifle fire which went unheard by the Japs in the tent because of the continuous naval and army artillery fire.

Goodfellow and his men crept up to the tent where the Japs were sitting around a table in candlelight and threw in grenades, killing all but one Jap, who was surrounded shortly afterward and killed by rifle fire.

A large supply of sake was found in the tent, indicating the Japs had been drinking to buttress their courage. Papers on the Jap bodies revealed they had fought in the Burma campaign. The uniforms of the enlisted men were thin for the bitter Aleutian weather, but those of the officers were well made and of excellent material.

One officer, killed in a tent beside Massacre Creek when a machine gun squad infiladed the tent, wore a parka lined with silk and knee-length boots with fur-lined puttees. He carried a two-handed sword, and in the tent had a supply of sake, canned peaches and pears. His pistol was a Colt .32 automatic with clips of American-made ammunition.

American troops aboard the U.S.Transport *Bell* route to Attu, May 9, 1942. NATIONAL ARCHIVES

An additional unique item of equipment was a pair of short skis four feet long made of light yellow wood.

No booby traps or land mines were on the beaches or in the passes, further evidence that the Japs had not anticipated an attack on Attu. The lack of artillery in strategic spots supports this.

The only heavy gunfire encountered was on the east side of Massacre Creek, when a Jap mortar, firing from behind a ridge across the valley, temporarily disrupted our communication line.

The importance of taking Attu, according to military observers follows:

1. It will give us a striking base within 1100 miles of Japan and 700 miles of the Jap base at Paramushiro.

Howitzer and troops loading into a Higgins boat from the transport *Bell* for the first American amphibious landing of the war at Attu. NATIONAL ARCHIVES

The *USS Heywood*, lying off Attu Island on May 11, 1943. Diesel-powered Higgins boats push through fog toward the unseen beach, with alert soldiers, fearing a hostile greeting. There was no resistance by the Japs to the landing. NATIONAL ARCHIVES

2. It will isolate Kiska by placing it between two United States bases from which shuttle bombing probably can be carried out after development of the island.

3. It will advance the North Pacific front to a point where bombing of Alaska or the Continental United States by the Japs will be virtually impossible, save by seaborne carrier.

The morale of our troops here is splendid despite the difficult front line conditions in the world's worst weather. At an advanced sector where this is being written, the men have dug in in a shallow depression on a rocky mountain-top between spines of grey rock and deep winter snowdrifts. Fog blows over them constantly. Shells from our barrages scream overhead and machine guns rattle in the fog on both sides and on the slopes above, where scouts are combing the ledges for snipers and machine gunners.

There is no fuel here save for paper shell cases and the supply train hasn't yet brought up sleeping bags and pup tents. Nobody had any sleep or hot food, but the men are exhilarated by combat. They feel swell and eager for a chance to move ahead. All of these troops are highly trained for amphibious operations, but this is their first actual combat.

General Brown has the highest praise for them, and they for Brown, as he is constantly at the front, going everywhere the men go. In fact, the men are worried about him. This morning, a group of boys lying be-

Landing at Attu, May 11, 1942. This is not what the soldiers expected. A bulldozer crawls off a power barge, and soldiers casually stand around a pile of their rucksacks. Offshore is a troop transport and a bevy of landing craft bringing troops ashore. The sea is calm, and early morning fog has lifted. NATIONAL ARCHIVES

hind an outcropping of rock, waiting for a Jap gunner to open up so they could knock his nest out, said. "What in the hell do you suppose he wants to keep going up that damned Sarana Pass for? Isn't a General supposed to stay back a little and direct the battle?"

But the tall, lean 53-year-old General wants to see for himself what's going on, and you as likely will find him ahead with scouts trying to spot a foxholed Jap among the snowdrifts, as well as receiving reports at his command post.

Everyone has commendation for the remarkable barrages laid down by the warships and army batteries. This afternoon we lay on rock combing 1,000 feet above Massacre Creek, and watched the big guns blast the Jap position at the rim of a snowy hanging valley on the south side of steep Massacre Pass leading to Holtz Bay.

There were three earth huts silhouetted against the snow field and with glasses we could see the Japs moving between them. Our 105mm howitzers registered near them with the first few shots and we saw a lone Jap dash out on the snow to pick up a body which he carried into the hut, just as a 14-inch naval shell made a direct hit on it, blowing up earth, bodies and timbers.

For the following hour, navy guns and 105s played over the valley, seeking out hiding places with uncanny ease although naval units were far out at sea, hidden in fog banks, and army guns were three miles below us.

The Japs made extraordinarily little effort to fortify this side of the island, despite its vulnerability. Small outposts were found on Massacre, Temnac and Sarana Bays but they had few guns, and save for Massacre, where they had a shack, the Japs were living in tents haphazardly revetted.

There were no trenches on the beaches and no roads connecting these bays with the main Jap garrisons. Trails in the heavy Attu grass flats show there has been considerable travel over the passes, but our forces in the first few hours constructed more roads and bridges than the Japs had over the entire south side of the island.

At Massacre and Temnac, the Japs made an attempt to deceive aerial observers regarding their strength by making dummy gun emplacements and stripping turf off black soil for hundreds of yards so it would resemble trenches from the air.

Thus far there has been no indication of the fate of more than eighty Aleut men, women and children, plus a handful of army and navy personnel, and Mrs. and Mrs. Charles Foster Jones, of Marion,

A C-ration stockpile inland on Attu. Note that it is next to a gravel-bottomed stream. Tractors and Jeeps couldn't navigate the soggy tundra; they *could* travel on gravel stream bottoms. NATIONAL ARCHIVES

ABOVE: The first U.S. flag raised on Attu after the landing of our troops was reportedly on this abandoned Jap landing barge. NATIONAL ARCHIVES

LEFT: An Attu "highway." Gravel bottom streams were the only firm ground at lower elevations of Attu. Vehicles sank in the soft, nearly bottomless, tundra. NATIONAL ARCHIVES

A tractor pulling a trailer load of life preservers collected by the Navy along an Attu beach on May 16, 1943. They were worn by troops in assault boats. NATIONAL ARCHIVES

An Attu beach. Tons of supplies were scattered along the Attu Beaches. This is an ammunition dump. NATIONAL ARCHIVES

Ohio, Bureau of Indian Affairs school teachers who were on the island when the Japs seized it the first week of last June. [Fog of war: Forty Aleuts were taken to Japan. There were no Army personnel on Kiska when it was taken; only a ten-man Navy weather crew. —JR]

Jones is believed to have been heard once on a prisoner broadcast from Tokyo. [Jones died on Attu while in the hands of the Japs. —JR] The Attu chief, little Mike Hodikoff, for years had warned that the Japs intended to seize Attu.

He feared and hated the Japs as a result of his contacts with Jap seal and sea otter poachers, and personnel from Jap "cadet training ships" which prowled the island to collect rare flowers and plants.

The landing two miles northwest, on an arm of Holtz Bay, was preceded by a unit of the famed Alaska Scouts trained by Colonel L. V. Castner, and lead by Lieutenant Bob Thompson. Their mission was a perilous one, as they would have been under fire from the entire Holtz garrison if their landing was detected.

They scouted the beach, searched for opposing Japs, and signaled back vital information before the main body of troops was sent ashore.

18 ITCHYMOTO

UPS RELEASE BY RUSSELL ANNABEL.
MASSACRE BAY, ATTU ISLAND,
MAY 16, 1943.

ITCHYMOTO, THE ACE Japanese sniper of Sarana Pass, who for the past five days has been concentrating on stretcher bearers, died suddenly this noon in his cleverly camouflaged foxhole among the fog-wreathed drifts of a mountain peak.

Itchymoto's abrupt departure from this world was the result of a scientifically coordinated manhunt carried out by infantry scouts, the signal corp and a mortar crew.

The platoon scouts under Lieutenant George Murphy formed a long thin line at the base of the mountain this morning at daybreak, and began climbing toward the fog-hidden summit. By midmorning they were ant like dots visible only when crossing snow drifts, but with them was a radioman with a walkie talkie set, and also signal corp men laying thin telephone line as they climbed, which gave perfect two way communications.

At the base of the mountain, with the mortar crew, was Major Ernest H. Bearse, of Grants Pass, Oregon, watching the progress of the scouts with powerful binoculars.

Suddenly, from a rim of rolling fog close above the climbing men, a Japanese machine gun began firing, the orange tracers seeking out nooks and crannies among tumbled boulders where the scouts had taken cover. At the first burst, the mortar crew waited, kneeling beside their gun, until Lieutenant Murphy gave the location of the gun nest over the walkie talkie. They fired one shot for register and another for effect.

Major Bearse was asking questions over the telephone and walkie talkie simultaneously. He smiled suddenly and said, "That one got the damned machine gun."

The mortar crew relaxed. They were a hard looking lot, unshaven, plastered with mud and red-eyed from lack of sleep, but they smiled happily among themselves, enormously pleased with their marksmanship.

While they were waiting for another target, I took their names. They were Corporal Richard Hill, of McMechen, West Virginia, Private Lloyd Bullard, of Los Angeles, Corporal Lynn Meador, of Burnet, Texas, Private Norman White, of Cedar Grove, West Virginia, and Private Warren Withers, of Altoona, Pennsylvania.

Scouts moving up again are now converging toward a knife-sharp ridge on the rim of a savagely broken canyon in which a stream drops in a series of waterfalls. They broke trail across a snow pitch and disappeared into fog.

Major Bearse put down his binoculars and held the receivers of both the walkie talkie and the field

"Itchymoto," the name troops on Attu gave to a Jap sniper, was hated especially by medics. He fired on dressing stations so often that medics refused to mark them with their red cross insignia. The sniper also targeted the trail stretcher-bearers used. Here, stretcher bearers carry a wounded American out of the mountains—easy marks for a sniper. NATIONAL ARCHIVES

phone to his ears. Presently we heard a burst of rifle fire but no word came from Lieutenant Murphy.

A worried Major Bearse began requesting information over and over again. "Are you all right, Murphy, come in please."

The mortar crew knelt tensely by their gun, everyone was very quiet.

I thought that damned Itchymoto wasn't alone on the crest. Murphy must have walked into a trap. The machine gun fire tipped the Japs off and they

A thin line of American soldiers on an Attu mountain. Japs remained hidden in clouds and fog above our troops. When fog occasionally cleared, their snipers, machine gunners, and mortars fired on our forces. This is the situation under which the sniper nicknamed "Itchymoto" operated. NATIONAL ARCHIVES

were laying for him. Probably a whole company of them were coming up from the Sarana side and it was like shooting clay pigeons.

It wasn't the first time we had cursed Itchymoto. Of course that wasn't his name. I don't know who first started calling him Itchymoto. Probably it was one of the medics he had fired on so often.

We all hated him because he had his rifle targeted on the trail the stretcher bearers used, and he had worked on these people so often and so efficiently that the medics had refused to mark their dressing stations with their red cross insignia, knowing it would only draw fire.

We waited and finally one of the mortar crew went over to a fire he had built into the side of the bank and brought hot coffee. We gulped it without taking our eyes off the mountainside. Major Bearse was still calling for information. A half hour passed. A single rifle shot echoed down the can-

Japanese-killed American soldiers on Attu at Massacre Bay, June 1, 1943; "Comrades in arms, comrades in death." The terrible results of Jap snipers and machine gunners in the fog. NATIONAL ARCHIVES

yon walls, sounding faint and far away. Major Bearse reached swiftly for the volume control knob of the walkie talkie.

"I've got him," he said. "Here's your target."

The climax was swift and noisy and very efficient. The mortar went *pow-pow* as fast as the crew could load, its reports mingling with the sound of the shell bursts high on an unseen ridge crest.

The firing continued until Major Bearse announced that the target [Itchymoto] had been destroyed.

Lieutenant Murphy and his men haven't come down from the mountain yet, but when they do we are all going to congratulate him and his men. We are going to shake their hands and give them hot coffee and tell them what a swell job we think they did.

19

JAP PROPAGANDA

UP RELEASE BY RUSSELL ANNABEL.
HOLTZ BAY, ATTU ISLAND,
MAY 21, 1943.

PREFERRING DEATH to captivity in the hands of the Japs, two elderly Attu school teachers, Mr. and Mrs. Charles Foster Jones, of Marion, Ohio, made a suicide pact last June 7 when Japanese invaders landed at Chichagof Village [on the island of Attu].

This was revealed today when a copy of *The Aleutian Campaign Journal*, a book written by *Domei* correspondent Mikizo Fukazawa was found in the Holtz Bay garrison. Fukazawa was on Kiska, and wrote about Charlie House in July 1942.

The book stated that both of the Joneses slashed their wrists before the Japs could take them, Mr. Jones dying, but Mrs. Jones being saved. Fukazawa said Mr. Jones is in a burial plot near an ancient Russian Aleut church in the old village. Jones was 64. His wife was 63. No mention was made of where Mrs. Jones was taken.

Native Aleuts tried to stand off the Japs with hunting rifles, and, when they realized this was hopeless, fired the village, the book stated.

It went on to say that when the Aleuts realized the Japs were friendly, they greeted them with open arms. It said Attu chief, Mike Hodikoff, became reconciled to the Japanese and entered into a spirit of the friendliest cooperation.

The book was published for distribution in Japan and has had two printings. It is illustrated with photographs of Kiska and Attu but shows no military installations.

Fukuzawa states that Kiska and Attu were occupied purely as a defensive measure, as Japan knew the United States was going to fortify these islands with the intention of bombing Japan from Attu. Taking them was necessary to the defense of the Japanese empire, and Japan must at all costs hold Attu, the books says.

The correspondent, who spent two months on Attu and two on Kiska, says twenty Aleut women were captured and added that some of them "were very cute."

Fukazawa reported that between June 12 and October 31 [1942], Attu and Kiska were bombed eighty-one times. From the bombing Jap losses were one destroyer sunk, two transports heavily damaged, fifteen seaplanes lost, and damage done to shore installations.

Kiska was occupied June 6 and Attu June 7, both occupation forces being army troops. The book states that at Kiska, ten army weather men were captured, nine the first day, and the tenth man, William Charlshouse [Fukazawa spelling], of California, managed to escape and lived in the mountains for fifty-two days before hunger and exhaustion forced him to surrender to the Japanese.

The *Domei* correspondent says that it has been determined that Kiska is better suited to farming than Attu, but that Attu is valuable for raising blue foxes.

Stressing the hazards of weather and United States bombers and warships, Fukazawa narrates his experiences journeying to Kiska on a small Japanese cargo ship. He says the ship was torpedoed twice by an American submarine and left in sinking condition.

Crews took to lifeboats and tried to reach Kiska, but their radio had been damaged in the torpedoing and the lifeboats became lost in the fog and were carried to sea by strong ocean currents. After drifting several days, a Jap torpedo boat found them and gave them a course to Kiska harbor.

The book says early attacks on Attu and Kiska by navy Catalinas were very destructive, but were reduced materially when the Japs found the seaplane bombers were based at Nazan harbor on Atka Island, which they attacked with four-motored Kawanishi flying boats and submarines, sinking the United States cruiser *Northampton*. Previous to this, there had been an average of ten Catalina attacks a day, but afterward the Catalinas attacked only two or three times at wide intervals.

The narrative covers the period June 7 to November 19, 1942.

AUTHOR'S COMMENTS

Annabel followed this release with a post script to United Press editors, saying he had no way to check the accuracy of the claim of the sinking of the *Northhampton*, and would the editors check and add whatever was necessary.

Fukazawa was either naive, or he entered into the propaganda mode of the Japs when he wrote his book. If Annabel's report is accurate, the book was full of misinformation.

The Japs misidentified the seaplane tender *Casco*, torpedoed August 29, 1942 by the submarine RO-61 in Nazan Bay (Atka Island), calling it the *Northhampton*. The *Casco* was damaged, but didn't sink. It was repaired at Bremerton, Washington.

The military men captured on Kiska were not Army, but a weather crew of Navy personnel. Charlie House survived forty-nine days, not fifty-two, on his own. Other members of the weather crew surrendered over a period of about eleven days—they were not captured "the first day."

Village Aleuts buried Jones, who died while in Jap hands, near the Russian Orthodox church at Chichagof village. The reportedly "ancient church" at the village on Attu was built in 1932.

Mrs. Jones (Etta) was taken to Japan and held prisoner for the duration of the war. She survived to return to the States after the war.

Postwar accounts of Attu villagers made clear there was no attempt to "stand off the Japs with hunting rifles." The possibility was discussed, but wiser heads prevailed.

The Aleuts did not fire Chichagof Village on Attu. They lived in their houses in the village as prisoners for several months until they were transported to Japan in September, 1942.

The Aleuts greeted the Japs with open arms? That isn't the way the Chichagof Aleuts who managed to survive Japanese captivity reported it. Mike Hodikoff, their leader, detested the Japs. He had long warned the Coast Guard and others that the Japs would one day land in force on Attu. Cooperation came from him—and the others—because they had no choice. To say otherwise is pure propaganda.

20 DEATH OF A KID

UP RELEASE BY RUSSELL ANNABEL.
HOLTZ BAY, ATTU ISLAND.
MAY 21, 1943.

WHEN UNITED STATES troops stormed the bleak cliff sides and ridges between the east and west arms of Holtz Bay May 17, Seaman Claire McLeod, 17, of Los Angeles, went with them.

McLeod was supposed to aid in the unloading of equipment on the landing beach, but he wanted to go to the front and help fight the Japanese. He borrowed a navy helmet and an army Garand [rifle] and followed the troops through the hell of machine gun and 75mm fire up the side of the ridge. At the summit, where the Japanese made their final stand from networks of foxholes and pits dug under huge boulders, a major noticed McCleod's youth and becoming suspicious of his motley gear, ordered him to the rear.

McLeod started back but circled a buttress of the ridge and returned in time to help stand off a bayonet charge. He then took a sack of grenades from a fallen United States soldier and with them wiped out a Japanese machine gun nest.

The major ordered him back again. In fact, within the hour he ordered McLeod back seven times.

McLeod stayed until the ridge was taken and everyone who saw him during the action said he was a brave and efficient soldier, the equal of any present.

Shortly before the action ended and the Japanese garrison fell, a sniper centered his sight on McLeod. The bullet passed through the boy's head, killing him instantly.

Today McLeod's status was undetermined. Officially he deserted his post in time of war, one of the most serious offenses which can be committed by military personnel. Unofficially he is a hero. But the boys say McLeod probably wouldn't have cared what charge was laid against him. He had his wish. He wanted to help fight the Japanese and he did.

AUTHOR'S NOTE

WAR CORRESPONDENT Howard Handleman also told the story of Clair (Clair, without an e) McLeod in his book *Bridge to Victory* (Random House, 1943). He gave McLeod's home as Salt Lake City, and said he was a seaman second class in the U.S. Navy. He reported that McLeod was 19 years old.

According to Handleman, McLeod's boss, a Lieutenant Boyle of Seattle, said that he learned that McLeod, assigned to helping soldiers unload boats and stack supplies on the beach, was spending most of his time talking instead of working. His subject was the war fronts of Africa, China, Russia and England. McLeod told the other sailors, "We're all in this thing together. It doesn't make any difference whether you're Army or Navy or what, you got to get in and pitch."

The bodies of five American soldiers killed in action at Holtz Bay, Attu. Altogether 549 American soldiers died in the Battle of Attu—including the kid, Claire McLeod. NATIONAL ARCHIVES

Boyle ordered McLeod back to his ship.

Instead of complying, McLeod grabbed a carbine (not a Garand), some ammo, and K rations, and went to the front.

Handleman concluded that, "McLeod was a symbol of the spirit of Americans on Attu. They wanted to do whatever was necessary to accomplish their task, to engage and destroy the enemy."

21 THE HIGHEST HONOR

ONE CONGRESSIONAL Medal of Honor—the highest of all American military awards—was awarded to an American warrior for action in the Aleutian Campaign. Following is the official citation and, after that, a salute by writer Paul Gallico to Private Joe Martinez, the recipient of that medal.

MARTINEZ, JOE P.

RANK AND ORGANIZATION: Private, U.S. Army, Company K, 32nd Infantry, 7th Infantry Division.
PLACE AND DATE: On Attu, Aleutians, 26 May 1943.
ENTERED SERVICE AT: Ault, Colorado.
BIRTH: Taos, New Mexico
GOVERNMENT ORDER NO. 71, 27 October 1943.
CITATION: For conspicuous gallantry and intrepidity above and beyond the call of duty in action with the enemy.

Over a period of several days, repeated efforts to drive the enemy from a key defensive position high in the snow-covered precipitous mountains between East Arm Holtz Bay and Chichagof Harbor had failed.

On 26 May 1943, troop dispositions were readjusted and a trial coordinated attack on this position by a reinforced battalion was launched. Initially successful, the attack hesitated.

In the face of severe hostile machine gun, rifle, and mortar fire, Pvt. Martinez, an automatic rifleman, rose to his feet and resumed his advance. Occasionally he stopped to urge his comrades on. His example inspired others to follow.

After a most difficult climb, Pvt. Martinez eliminated resistance from part of the enemy position by BAR (Browning Automatic Rifle) fire and hand grenades, thus assisting the advance of other attacking elements.

This success only partially completed the action. The main Holtz-Chichagof Pass rose about 150 feet higher, flanked by steep rocky ridges and reached by a snow-filled defile. Passage was barred by enemy fire from either flank and from tiers of snow trenches in front. Despite these obstacles, and knowing of their existence, Pvt. Martinez again led the troops on and up, personally silencing several trenches with BAR fire and ultimately reaching the pass itself.

Here, just below the knifelike rim of the pass, Pvt. Martinez encountered a final enemy-occupied trench and as he was engaged in firing into it he was mortally wounded. The pass, however, was taken, and its capture was an important preliminary to the end of organized hostile resistance on the island.

THE STUBBORN MAN "ABSORBING ALL ENEMY FIRE," THE LATE PRIVATE JOE P.MARTINEZ LED THE ATTACK AT ATTU

BY PAUL GALLICO

Joe P. Martinez was born some twenty-three years ago in Taos, New Mexico, in a small, dusty, adobe house on the outskirts of the village. His round, dark eyes soon became used to the strange clear light, to staring off into the distances of the snow-capped peaks of the Rocky Mountains.

Joe's father was Manuel V. Martinez, and their forbears were the small dark men of Mexico. They were citizens of the United States. Time and history rolled over old Mexico, and a piece of it became New Mexico, and those born there were Americans.

At some time during Joe's life and growing up, the family moved northward into Colorado, into the little town of Ault, north of Denver, close to the border of Wyoming. Life was simple and uncomplicated. The Rockies still reared their distant, snowy heads. Joe Martinez became a farm laborer. They knew Joe locally as a good worker and a steady boy, albeit a little stubborn sometimes. But otherwise, neither he nor his being made so much as a ripple on the consciousness of the world or the nation. No one ever put the name of Joe Martinez into the papers.

Today the physical remains of Joe Martinez lie sealed in a grave on the flint-hard frozen slopes of Attu Island, the furthest outpost of the Aleutian chain off Alaska. But his name has been put into the papers. His name and his deed as an American soldier have gone into the archives of the nation as the wearer of the blue ribbon and gold medal of the Congressional Medal of Honor.

The war made Private Martinez out of plain Joe Martinez on August 7, 1942, when he was inducted into the Army at Denver, Colorado. Thereafter for many months his identity was submerged in the horde of G.I.'s at Camp Roberts, Camp Butner and Fort Ord.

We neither see nor hear from Private Joe Martinez again until May 25, 1943, when, still a private, he turned up on Attu Island with the American invasion forces in the guise of an automatic rifleman and grenadier, a member of a reinforced battalion whose task it was to drive the Japanese from the heights they held between the east arm of Holtz Bay and Chichagof Harbor.

Picture a snow-filled slope leading up over the crest of a pass between rugged ledges of rock on either side. The Japanese held the flanks and the center of the pass and covered the ground leading thereto with lead and steel from rifle, mortar and machine gun.

It was like walking into a meat grinder. But the position had to be taken. To fail might be to endanger the entire expedition. The footsloggers went up that slope as far as human flesh and nerve could carry them and then, as their dead and wounded fell all about them, bogged down and dug themselves in to escape the annihilation pouring down from the slopes and the flanking rocks above.

No one will ever know whether Private Joe Martinez knew and understood the tactical necessity for taking that ridge. No one, for that matter, will ever know just what did go on in the mind of that stubborn man Martinez when, alone, he arose and continued on up that hill in the face of the enemy fire.

Perhaps he was battle-happy. Perhaps he was seething with rage at the death of a friend. Perhaps he was a plain, brave, stubborn man who was turning a global war into an individual affair between himself and the Japanese.

Occasionally Private Martinez stopped, with the bullets whining and ricocheting off the rocks at his feet, to turn around and gesture to the rest of the men and shout, "Come on you bastards." Then the others would get out of the foxholes and follow him on up.

You might think it strange that the advance was not led by officers or ratings at the moment. But the men on Attu at the moment did not think it strange. The officers and non-coms who had been walking out in front of them were all dead or writhing on the ground with wounds.

Martinez attained a small plateau which harbored several foxholes and machine gun nests. These he cleaned out with his automatic rifle and a couple of hand grenades.

The Japs on the slopes and ridges increased their fire and the battalion could go no farther.

And so, after a moment, again that one lone figure, lugging his rifle and his bag of grenades, arose and began to move up through the snow, the orange spurts of flame, the mushroom smoke of bursting mortar shells and the singing streams of machine-gun bullets. It was that stubborn Martinez carrying the private war to the enemy. The men behind him could bear better the travail of following him than the agony of seeing him move up against the enemy alone. They followed him again.

Martinez reached the first of two trenches and cleaned it out with his rifle. Five dead Japs were found there. He went off again up the slope to the second trench and obliterated the enemy there. Then he continued up to the ridge overlooking the pass into Chichagof Harbor.

His citation reads that there he stood up alone and unafraid, emptying his rifle into the Japanese positions just below and beyond the pass and was mortally wounded with his rifle still at his shoulder, absorbing all enemy fire and permitting all units to move up behind him and successfully take and capture the pass.

In the simple words, "absorbing all enemy fire," lies the secret and the story of the capture of that deadly pass, an important preliminary on which eventually hinged the end of organized resistance on the island.

For the Japs answered the challenge of the one-man war of stubborn Joe Martinez and from the two sides of the pass they concentrated their fire on this lone man who was afraid neither of them nor of any of their work.

Their Oriental patience succumbed to irritation that one man could be so heedless of them and so stubborn in his determination to reach the top of the slope which they were turning into hell.

And so they warred against him alone and he "absorbed" their concentrated fire until he fell dead of the steel and lead that shredded his body.

They had their triumph over that lone man, for they won their war against his body. But it cost them Attu. For when they came to retrain their weapons, the pass was full of American riflemen and grenadiers who had accepted the example of the flaming spirit of Joe Martinez and followed him up during the time that Joe was busy with his absorption of enemy fire.

Then those Japs joined their riddled bodies to that of Martinez, and shortly after, Attu fell.

On Tuesday, November 16th last, great honor came to Manual V. Martinez, the old dark-eyed father of Joe on his little farm outside of Ault in Colorado. For there he was presented with the Congressional Medal of Honor which forever after would tell the world what that stubborn boy, Joe Martinez, had done for the country in which he had been born.

---

22 BATTLE'S END

**UP RELEASE BY RUSSELL ANNABEL.
LAKE CORIES, ATTU ISLAND,
MAY 30, 1943.**

"THEY'RE COMMITTING SUICIDE—blowing themselves up with grenades," shouted one of the American soldiers crouched on a bullet-scarred ledge above Lake Cories.

For some minutes now, the officers and men of the beleaguered United States outpost had heard muffled explosions from the tundra hollows and sinkholes in which several hundred Japs were apparently making ready for another maniacal attack. The explosions didn't make sense because no bullets, shells, or grenades were falling among the Americans now, or anywhere near them.

Everyone was tensed for another attack such as the Japs had been making for the past six hours. They were determined not to let the little yellow men get into the camp area as they had when they poured out of the foggy hills at daybreak, screaming like crazy men.

The American troops tell you the Japs behaved as though they had been doped, that they came straight into rifle and machine gun fire and dropped only when dead or blown off their feet by the impact of bullets.

The men who were sleeping in the open say the Japs were yelling, "We die, you die," and that their voices were so shrill with emotion they sounded like women.

They had crawled with the craftiness of wild animals to within a few hundred feet of the small post situated on the rim of a deep snow-patched canyon north of Lake Cories, and then had jumped to their feet with wild yells and charged into the camp.

They had bayoneted pup tents, stabbing the long slender Japanese bayonets through the canvas again and again. They had caught American soldiers in their sleeping bags and shot and stabbed them before they could extricate themselves and lay hands on a weapon.

They had surrounded the command tent, throwing grenades, while a Japanese machine gunner lifted the rear wall of the tent with the nose of his weapon and raked the interior with a hail of slugs.

Few American soldiers had time to finish dressing. The ones who had slept in their trousers and shirts were the lucky ones. They lacked only shoes. But there were some who had to fight in their underwear. But dressed or not, they fought and fought well. There was no way of telling the extent of the attack. They knew it wasn't confined to this outpost as they could hear shooting and yelling from an engineer outfit at the foot of the pass leading into Sarana Valley, from an advance camp on the hillside above Lake Cories, and from a medical clearing station across the valley near the summit of the Sarana Massacre Pass.

So they knew this was it; the Jap offensive everybody had talked about since the first landing on Attu May 11.

Watching for Japs in the heights on Attu. May, 1943. NATIONAL ARCHIVES

A group of Japs had manned a 37mm gun on a knoll above camp and were already sending shells crashing through the American outpost. It was our own gun, our own shells.

An unidentified sergeant ended that with a sack of grenades, pitching them at the gun until the Japs were killed.

Such of the men as hadn't been killed, or dispersed by the first surprise assault, had now found their weapons and were returning the Japanese fire with deadly effect.

The evidence of their accuracy is here today—Jap bodies lying everywhere in the encampment, a large percent of them shot through the head. The thirty caliber bullets from the American Garands shattered the Japanese helmets as if they were made of cast iron, breaking out large chunks and driving them into the skulls of the Japanese.

Somebody had manned a fifty caliber machine gun now and the sleet of slugs pouring into the Japs began forcing them back among the grey, wet, mossy hills from which they had charged.

For six hours, the Japs tried to wipe out the American camp. Then at 11:30 the Americans began hearing the muffled explosions in the Japanese positions, and a soldier occupying a vantage point on a rock outcropping above the camp shouted that the Japs were killing themselves.

At first the Americans couldn't believe it. That armed enemy troops would destroy themselves when they might have fought their way back down the Chichagof Valley to their base was incredible. But soon other lookouts verified the statement.

The explosions continued for half an hour. They could be heard all about the American camp in boggy creek beds and marshy potholes wherever a

Jap soldiers on Attu preferred suicide to surrender. This group held grenades next to their bodies and pulled the pins. NATIONAL ARCHIVES

depression in the bleak upland terrain had offered the Japs cover. Finally, the enemy rifle and machine gun fire died away completely, save for the occasional crack of a sniper's rifle on the mountainside above the camp.

A squad went out to investigate and returned with an almost unbelievable report. The Japs had committed mass suicide when their attack bogged down. Throughout the day patrols continued to find groups of Japs who had huddled together and killed themselves, apparently because they could no longer advance, and were unwilling to retreat or remain where they were and be overwhelmed by the Americans.

General Simon Bolivar Buckner (helmet without net) at Chichagof Harbor, June 2, 1943. He is talking with Colonel Frank Culin (with ski pole) and Major Womeldorf and Lt. Colonel J. M. Finn (back to camera) during inspection on the last days of the Battle of Attu. It was September before the last straggler Jap defender was found. U.S. ARMY, COURTESY JOHN CLOE.

By mid-afternoon, reports were coming in that Japanese attacks in Sarana Valley and in Massacre Pass had ended in the same manner—mass suicide on the part of the enemy troops. So far as could be determined by careful investigation, the Japanese in every case had killed themselves with their grenades. They were seen to pull the pins of the grenades, bang them against their helmets to arm them, and then hold them with both hands over their hearts.

The dead were found in groups of twenty to sixty, the bodies piled one on top of another, most of them blown nearly in half. Many of the Japs had been crouched to their waists in narrow ice-cold creeks for cover, and had been shooting at American camps through a screen of coarse dead grass on the stream banks. They had moved together in these places to kill themselves in groups and now their shattered bodies form bloody dams around which the dark, bitterly cold little mountain creeks flow.

It was first realized by the still incredulous Americans that the Jap attack had been one of sheer desperation when troops began recalling that many of the Japs hadn't been armed with rifles, but only

Corporal C. Hale stands vigil as the flag waves over Army headquarters at Chichagof Harbor on June 3, 1943. This headquarters was formerly occupied by Japs. Note the excellent camouflage. NATIONAL ARCHIVES

with spears made by tying bayonets to the ends of sticks and boards. One American private complained that a yelling Japanese had risen out of a ditch and hit him with a rock, breaking three ribs.

Then, as information from various posts began coming in, it was realized that the raiders had been a motley group composed of army troops, of navy personnel, and civilian employees. A considerable number of the attackers had old wounds. Several had recently suffered amputation of fingers, and even of hands. By this evening 300 Japs who had committed suicide were reported found in the hills.

Still, American officers could hardly believe what had happened. They refused to admit the enemy mass suicide actually had occurred until they had checked reports time and again, and interviewed eyewitnesses and personally examined dead bodies in bloody charnel pits.

The first corroborating information from the enemy was received when a young Japanese medical sergeant, who was captured and brought to headquarters for questioning, said that the attacking Japs had no orders to withdraw in the event their crazy drive through the American lines proved unsuccessful. No rendezvous point had been named for them by Colonel Yasuyo Yamasaki, who had sent them on their mission.

This prisoner, and another questioned during the afternoon, said that their orders were to crash through American lines to our artillery positions where they were to seize guns and ammunition and turn them against us. Presumably they were to obtain food by capturing it, as their kits contained only two or three small rice balls and occasionally a dried squid. They carried neither blankets nor mess kits.

Sixty of the Japs drove to within a few hundred yards of our guns where they were stopped by rifle and machine gun fire, and forced to take cover in foxholes and American tents. Others were halted on the east slope of Sarana Pass where their bodies today are strung along the tractor road which was being pushed ahead toward Chichagof Village as front line troops have advanced. Within the past twenty-four hours the last of the raiders either have been surrounded and killed, or had committed suicide.

Hopefully, but still skeptical that the backbone of Japanese resistance has been broken so swiftly and dramatically, American forces have moved down Chichagof Corridor. There was no organized opposition below recently won Buffalo Nose, the rocky ridge thrusting into Chichagof corridor from the east.

As troops continued along the bottom of the valley, and scouts combed the hillsides, only an occasional sniper was encountered. By twilight our troops were entering Chichagof Village unopposed.

The Jap base was deserted. In the long red shadows of the midnight sun men saw the terrain incredibly torn by naval and army artillery fire, and the bombs of the 11th Air Force.

No large stores of food such as had been taken at the Holtz Bay garrisons were found here. The village, which many of us had thought was a stronghold—probably with large underground barracks and warehouses—was primitive, small, and now in smoking ruins.

Smoke drifted through it from tundra fires started by bombs and shells. The men built beach fires of bullet-pocked boards and driftwood and lay down to rest and try to understand what had happened.

They had expected a big showdown battle for Chichagof, but this was an anticlimax. The few remaining Japs had been sighted fleeing into the snowy peaks above Khlebnikof Point. To the westward, the village did not even resemble a military base. Instead it looked like a wrecked Aleut fishing village.

In contrast with the high country where men had been fighting, this place was green and springlike with grass and flowers along the winding stream bank and little black-throated Attu song sparrows singing in long shadows, the late sun, and gulls crying over the reef-hemmed harbor.

Gradually, as they stoked their campfires with the wreckage of the shelled and bombed village, the men began to appreciate, so far as an organized resistance was concerned, that the battle for Attu was over. The wild, yelling, suicidal attacks made by the Japanese had been their last major effort.

Other guerrilla attacks probably will be made by the remaining bands of Japs hiding among the peaks, officers and men realize. But without food, artillery and a base from which to operate, they will be of minor importance, military authorities state.

There's nothing glamorous about war. During the battle, exhausted GIs on Attu try to get some sleep behind a makeshift sod wall. Their rifles are handy. NATIONAL ARCHIVES

UNEXPECTED END
UP RELEASE BY RUSSELL ANNABEL.
CHICHAGOF VILLAGE, ATTU ISLAND,
MAY 31, 1943.

THE BATTLE FOR Attu ended here today and it was a fine ending, but not what any of us had expected. We had supposed there would be a big battle with the Japanese making a last ditch stand behind their sod breastworks with their backs to the sea, and that it would probably be decided in hand-to-hand combat. With the Japanese suicide attacks on the high country outposts still vivid in their minds, the American troops knew now there would be no compromise, no mass surrender, that if they brought the Japs to bay it would be a matter of kill or be killed.

So it was surprising when so little resistance was encountered in the Chichagof corridor, the long open mountain valley which cuts deep into the backbone of the Attu Range, and which had been so desperately defended by the Japs. There were only a few snipers in the rounded hills above the valley and these were quickly cleaned out by the scouts. Some thought that the lack of resistance might be ominous, that the Japs might have laid a trap and were letting us walk into it. Others thought the Japs had concluded they couldn't defend both the corridor and the village, and so were concentrating their forces in the village itself.

But as the lines of troops and the flanking scouts pushed on down the valley into the lowlands and the snow drifts became scarcer and scarcer and flowers began to show on the creek banks and you could smell the ocean and hear gulls over the ridges shutting off the view of the village, the men began to wonder what it was all about. They saw the advance scouts cross the ridge ahead and go down the slope into the village. There were a few shots, then silence.

Not until the shell-torn bomb-cratered village had been occupied and outposts sent to hold the high ground above the village site did the men realize that the battle for Attu had been over for nearly twenty-four hours before their arrival here, and that occupying Chichagof Village was merely the final move on our part which made the victory official.

The battle-weary troops, keyed up for a hard fight, experienced mingled emotions. They were glad the battle was over, yet disappointed in the village and the anti-climactic way it had been taken. The village in no way resembled a military base. The Japanese had themselves erected only one building, a camouflaged hut which apparently had been Colonel Yamasaki's headquarters. They had used the dozen or more ancient Aleut barabaras, underground huts covered completely with sod on which wild grasses grow to the height of a man's waist, and the huddle of frame buildings which had been the Chichagof schoolhouse, the residence of the school teachers, the Russian Orthodox Church, and the dwelling of little Mike Hodikoff, the Russian Aleut chief of the island.

All the buildings, even the barabaras either have been completely destroyed by incendiary bombs and shell fire or are so badly wrecked as to be useless. Nearly a year of bombing by the 11th Air Force has torn up the ground in the narrow valley mouth so badly it is difficult to walk over it. The Japs hadn't even erected a hut for their weather station. They had elaborate weather equipment but it was set up in a tiny cave dug into a side bank, resembling an old-fashioned root cellar.

Scouts coming down off the mountain slopes reported they had seen a column of Japs of undetermined number withdrawing into the saw-toothed peaks above Khlebnikof Point which divides Chichagof and Sarana Valleys. American patrols were sent to locate the Japs, but the main body of our troops remained in the village, resting by campfires or prowling curiously through the charred smoking ruins of the old Aleut village.

On the beach they found a wrecked Jap landing barge, bomb-shattered and punctured by many machine gun bullets fired by strafing planes. In the creek mouth were two wrecked float Zeros. These were also bullet torn. About them were dozens of metal oil drums, all shot through and through.

Still trying to substantiate a rumor, which has been current among our troops since the first landing, that the Japs had women on the island, men searched through the wrecked huts for evidence that women had been here. They found children's and women's shoes, but they were old and obviously had belonged to the former Aleut inhabitants. The rumor that Aleut women may have been kept here was blasted when Japanese interpreters found documents stating that the Aleuts had been evacuated to Sakhalin Island north of Japan where their ability to speak Russian may serve the Japanese well as half of this island is owned by Russia.

The shortage of food stores in the village confirmed statements by prisoners who had said the Japs here faced starvation. In going through underground storage rooms I saw buckets of tea, a few sacks of rice, some canned salmon and a few sacks of carrots and potatoes, but no stores to compare with those taken at the Holtz Bay garrisons.

It is apparent that Holtz Bay was the main Jap stronghold and that when they lost it May 15 and 16, they had lost the battle of Attu.

23 LEARN OR DIE

**UP RELEASE BY RUSSELL ANNABEL.
HEADQUARTERS, ALASKA DEPARTMENT,
NOVEMBER 29, 1943.**

Pilots and crews of the big transport planes which for two years have carried men, supplies, arms and munitions to army posts in this theater, are convinced they are the forgotten men of the 11th Air Force.

Few stories have been written about them, they have not been mentioned in the majority of citations, yet they have pioneered aviation in the North, and have almost daily braved dangers as great as those faced by combat pilots. When the transport squadrons were first formed here to fly men and freight to the new Aleutian garrisons, few of the pilots had had any experience flying on instruments. They had to learn as they went along, and it was a desperate, nerve-wracking way of learning.

"Most of us couldn't even fly through a cloud without falling out of it," says flight officer J. J. Trevisani, San Francisco. "But we had to start out flying the Aleutian chain, the foggiest, stormiest air route in the world. Some of the boys crashed into mountains, some crashed in the sea."

One such mystery disappearance occurred last year when Lieutenant Francis Kearney, Tampa, Florida, and his copilot Lieutenant Bertram Diaz, Maplewood, New Jersey, took off from Cold Bay with a load of bombs for the new base on Adak, and was lost somewhere en route. No trace of the airplane was ever found.

Flight officer Trevisani had an experience while learning to fly on instruments which he thinks may account for some of the early day crashes in the Aleutians. Trevisani was flying between Atka and Umnak when he observed a vast thunderhead on his course. He attempted to fly under the cloud at a low altitude, but suddenly found his plane in a terrific updraft which sucked it straight up more than one thousand feet into the lower part of the thunderhead.

The incredible force of the wind turned the plane over and hurled it like a blown leaf out over the ocean. Before he was clear of the hurricane wind, Trevisani and his passengers observed a weird phenomena—inside the cloud rain was ascending, while on the outer circumference it was descending, like a giant fountain.

"We have since been informed," says Trevisani, who now holds the record for one thousand hours of flying the Aleutian chain, "that nobody has ever seen the heart of a thunderhead and lived to tell about it. Winds of more than 600 miles an hour velocity have been recorded in those clouds—that's strong enough to rip the wings off an airplane and tear the fuselage to shreds."

The transport pilots in the early months of the Aleutian war often flew seventeen or eighteen hours a day. They flew the garrison to Nome, with as many as ninety transports on the Nome field in a single day. Two weeks before the Japs hit Dutch Harbor, they were frantically transporting men, guns and ammunition to Cold Bay and Umnak.

The pilots assert they don't know how the army knew the Japs were going to attack, but they state that this obviously was the case, as every available aircraft, civilian and military, was pressed into service to supply, man, and arm the two outposts.

Weather is the chief adversary of the transport squadrons, and when it strikes, there usually is no one left to tell the tale. Recently Lieutenant Robert William Jones, Los Gatos, California, took off before daybreak from Elmendorf and crashed within a mile of the field. Nobody knows what caused the crash—perhaps it was ice, or maybe a williwaw downdraft hurled the big heavily loaded ship against the hillside. The plane plowed through the timber, a wing ripped off, and fuel tanks exploded.

"Just one of those things," the transport crews say, when you ask them about it. "It could happen to any of us."

The other day Lieutenant Herbert Twede, Willows, California, a veteran of the Aleutian run who was chosen for nearly a year to fly Lt. General Simon Bolivar Buckner, Jr., came within a hair of being a casualty. Coming in for a landing at Attu, he made a normal approach but found, too late, that the field was covered with glare ice. His big C-47 skated the length of the strip and piled up against a revetment. Lieutenant Twede shrugs when telling about it, and makes the usual comment of airmen who have survived such crashes.

"Well, it didn't burn," he says. "So I'm still here."

The pilots aren't flying such long hours now, partly through the recommendations of Captain James Bradford, Westwood, Provo, Utah, their flight surgeon, who felt the men were burning themselves out. But they still put an average of 125 hours a month in the air. Moreover, they are now experts at flying on instruments, probably the best in the world at this type of flying.

They are required to spend at least half their flying time "under the hood," and one result of this has been that they now have confidence in themselves.

"A good part of the time I find myself taking off on instruments even in good weather," says flight officer Trevisani. "It's just second nature. We really used to sweat out a landing when we were trapped out of a field by fog, but now getting down is often just routine. It's old stuff, plenty different from the old days. I guess you could say we had our choice of learning to do it or dying."

AUTHOR'S COMMENT

Annabel's claim that Air Corp pilots "pioneered aviation in the North," is stretching it; bush pilots pioneered Alaska flying decades before WWII. Also his report of C-47 transports hauling bombs is probably erroneous; most were barged to Nome, and into the Aleutians. Thunderheads are rare in the Aleutians; his reporting on that could be another is questionable. And williwaws are found in the Aleutians, not in southcentral Alaska near Elmendorf air force base, as he speculated. Military transport pilots, new to Alaska and Aleutian weather, did have to "learn or die," as Annabel put it. It was dangerous flying, and many pilots lost their lives.

24

KISKA AND THE BATTLE OF THE PIPS

On May 19, 1943, a week after the start of the Battle of Attu, the Japanese High Command decided to abandon the Aleutian Islands. The garrison on Kiska was to be evacuated by submarine as soon as possible.

It was obvious that when the U.S. regained Attu—and it was apparent we would do so—bypassed Kiska would be vulnerable, and probably next to fall.

In twelve attempts by submarine, 820 men were removed from Kiska, but by June 22, three Jap submarines on this assignment had been sunk by the U.S.

The next decision in Tokyo was to attempt to remove the Jap force on Kiska with cruisers and destroyers.

For several months Kiska had been under a U.S. Navy blockade of two task groups totalling sixteen warships—three battleships, five cruisers, seven destroyers, and a high speed minesweeper. Their specific task was to destroy enemy forces attempting to reinforce Kiska. Intelligence learned from intercepts of Jap radio traffic the likelihood of an attempt by Jap navy forces to reach Kiska on the night of July 25–26.

Code breakers had learned that the Japanese Fifth Fleet, believed to consist of four cruisers, several destroyers and auxiliaries, had left its base in the Kuriles and had been at sea for several days.

Navy PBYs constantly scouted the North Pacific, alert for any Japanese ship nearing Alaska.

Despite the U.S. blockade, the Japanese rescue fleet, sailing in close formation in dense fog, arrived at Kiska Harbor on July 29. Kiska Harbor was clear of fog, with a high ceiling. These were precisely the conditions that Orin Seybert, Charlie House, and I found when we arrived there in Orin's Widgeon airplane in early July 1985, forty-two years later.

Ten landing craft already at Kiska were each capable of carrying about 120 men; another thirteen landing craft were aboard the rescue fleet.

The troops on Kiska had gathered seven or eight times on the shores of the harbor, waiting for the rescue fleet, which had aborted those missions because of lack of concealing fog.

Many of the Jap soldiers were bearded. They were clad in odds and ends of uniforms. They were low on food, low on morale, and worn out from constant bombing and naval shelling by the U.S.

On July 29th, as the rescue fleet emerged from the fog into Kiska Harbor, some wept with joy; others leaped with excitement; others hugged each other gleefully. They knew their lives had been saved.

Personal belongings, including rifles, were abandoned, and in fifty-five minutes, 5,183 men were loaded on the two cruisers and eight destroyers. Landing craft were scuttled to destroy any trace of the evacuation.

Once at sea, the rescue ships rounded the north end of Kiska at up to twenty-six knots, heading home.

To their starboard, almost abeam, a submarine surfaced almost at the limit of visibility. Course was altered to prevent close contact with it. More on that sub later.

Why did the U.S. blockade fail to detect the Jap rescue fleet?

Answer: the battle of the pips.

An aerial view of the main camp of Fortress Kiska on September 28, 1942, about ten days after Charlie House left for Japan. Wind streaks on the harbor indicate a strong easterly wind. Float Zeros are anchored out; others are beached. A damaged Kawanishi (Mavis) four-engine seaplane, one wing under water, the other cut off, is on the upper right. NATIONAL ARCHIVES

On July 23, a PBY Catalina reported a radar contact through the fog of seven unidentified objects on the sea surface about 315 miles west-southwest of Kiska. Were they Jap ships bound for Kiska? No one knew, but based on the radio intercept, it seemed likely.

On July 26, the two task groups were about eighty miles south of Kiska, steaming easterly, zigzagging at sixteen knots. At 0045, the battleship *Mississippi* reported a radar contact at fifteen miles. The radar of the battleship *New Mexico* also reported six objects.

Radar of the time consisted of a cathode ray tube across which a straight line appeared. When a target was found—a ship, land, any solid object—a "pip" appeared. A pip was a peak rising from the straight line. The distance of the pip from the side of the tube indicated the distance to the target.

Plotting indicated the objects were moving north at about sixteen knots. Their destination appeared to be Kiska Harbor or nearby Vega Bay.

Everything jibed—these were no doubt Jap ships.

The two battleships and three of the cruisers opened fire at the objects, and, for half an hour, continued to fire with brief interludes of quiet. The gun flashes were seen by the Japs eighty miles away at Kiska during an unusual clear spell. They even heard the rumble of the big guns.

The five ships fired 518 fourteen-inch and 487 eight-inch shells.

Then the pips vanished.

At 0222 the two task groups reformed, and at twenty knots for four hours, painstakingly searched the area. A float plane was catapulted to assist.

There was no oil, debris, or survivors—nothing was found.

There had been no enemy force.

What produced the pips?

There were plenty of theories. Were the radar waves bouncing off of distant islands? Could the aurora borealis have somehow tweaked the radar signals? Peculiar cloud conditions?

At the "Alaska at War Symposium" at Anchorage November 11–13, 1993, Brian Garfield, author of *The Thousand Mile War; World War II in Alaska and the Aleutians*, was the featured banquet speaker. He gave a plausible explanation for the appearance of the pips.

That explanation, Garfield said, came from Captain George Fulton, a long-time commercial fisherman in the Aleutians. He wrote Garfield with what is probably the best and most simple explanation of the "pips."

Sooty shearwaters.

Millions of this seventeen-inch-long brown member of the albatross family commonly appear in the Aleutians during summer. A flock resting on the water may cover ten or more acres of closely-packed birds. All members of a flock may leap into flight at once as they seek fresh feeding areas. Called the mutton bird in New Zealand, they breed in the Southern Hemisphere, and commonly summer in Alaska waters.

There is no doubt that a large flock of these birds would cause a radar pip. Captain Fulton said that, in July, many large flocks of shearwaters commonly inhabit the exact area from which the radar echoes were received.

Following the "battle of the pips," as it has been called, on July 29, the sixteen U.S. ships rendezvoused to refuel 105 miles south-southeast of Kiska, leaving Kiska unguarded—at exactly the time the Japanese rescue ships, traveling in dense fog, slipped in and out of Kiska Harbor. It was pure good luck for the Japs; bad luck for the U.S.

Japs on Kiska await rescue on the shore of Kiska Harbor. All 5,000 gathered here seven or eight times to await arrival of naval ships to yank them off of Kiska. JAPANESE PHOTO, COURTESY JOHN CLOE

Part of the fleet assembled at Kuluk Bay, Adak Island, to assault the Jap-held island of Kiska in August1943. NATIONAL ARCHIVES

One day earlier, or a day later, the enemy ships would have been detected by the radar-equipped U.S. force.

For seventeen days after the Japanese slipped away, Americans bombed and shelled the island. There were many clues that the Japs had left, but no one could prove they were gone.

UP releases by Russell Annabel for the period after the Japs fled Kiska tell a story:

August 2: "United States warships steaming past Kiska sent hundreds of shells crashing into Japanese garrisons, softening up enemy defenses . . ."Great grey ships came out of the fog bank and made bombardment runs off the mouth of Kiska Harbor without drawing fire from enemy batteries, the seventh time in succession that the Japanese garrison was sullenly passive under the hammering of navy guns." [The *New Mexico* and the *Mississippi*, with five cruisers and nine destroyers, fired 200 tons into the deserted shore establishments]

August 3: "The Kiska Japanese are apparently either running short of ammunition or trying to conserve it as today's bombing mission of five Marauders and three Liberators received no ack ack. This is the second mission in a week to receive no fire . . .

August 4: "The heaviest aerial assault of the Aleutian war was made yesterday when 126 bombers

Troops landing on the beach on the northwest side of Kiska on August 23, 1943. Lines of soldiers can be seen on the beach and to the top of the distant ridge. NATIONAL ARCHIVES

and fighter bombers subjected Kiska to an all day blitz. As big wicked-looking planes howled down out of the blue Aleutian sky, Japanese ack ack gunners took cover. Only a few bursts dotted the sky while dive bombers peeled off again and again to blast buildings and installations."

August 7: "Softening up operations carried out against the Japanese on Kiska during the past two months by naval surface vessels and warplanes of the 11th Air Force are showing marked results, according to pilots who have been flying almost daily missions over the enemy garrisons.

". . . pilots observed the Japanese were apparently withdrawing into the hills.

"Japanese resistance has been negligible . . . surface vessels steamed within 2,000 yards of their target and delivered broadside after broadside without receiving return fire . . . anti-aircraft fire has been uniformly light."

WHEN I INTERVIEWED Admiral Russell at Adak in July 1985, he told me a story about the submarine sighted by the fleeing Jap fleet.

Russell, assigned to General Douglas MacArthur's staff in Japan after the war, interviewed Japanese military about the Aleutian Campaign. Two volumes resulted; the first included questions and answers; the second was "An analysis of what we figured was the total story," Russell told me.

He interviewed Captain Rokuji Arichika, assistant to Rear Admiral Masatomi Kumura, commander of the Kiska rescue ships.

"When you left Kiska harbor, did you see any American ships?" Russell asked.

According to Russell, Arichika thought for a minute and answered, "Yes."

"What was it?" Russell asked.

"A submarine."

"Where was it?"

He gave Russell a range and a bearing on Pillar Rock, a landmark to the west of Kiska.

"What did you do?"

"We made an emergency turn away."

When Russell arrived home he went through war diaries of the S-boats (submarines) assigned to the Aleutians that were in the Kiska blockade.

The S-33 was exactly where Arichika said it was.

In 1985 Russell was visiting with Clyde Stevens, a long-time naval friend, and told him the story.

"S-33 was my boat," Stevens told Russell (he was Captain).

"What were you doing on the west side of Kiska?" Russell asked.

"I was photographing through the periscope beaches that were possibilities for amphibious landings," he explained.

"Do you remember seeing anything?"

"I sure wasn't expecting to see a Japanese cruiser, but I did. It appeared out of the fog. The damned thing was making thirty knots, and I could make nine knots flat out on the surface. There wasn't anything I could do about it, except to report one Japanese cruiser," Stevens said.

"He reported it, but apparently the report was lost in the shuffle. When a cruiser is seen that close in you'd think the planners would realize it was something really different. But nobody apparently considered it could have been part of an evacuation force," Russell told me.

Then there was Stig Palm's report to Squeaky Anderson that with YMS-134 he had slipped into Kiska Harbor and found it and the Jap camp deserted (see chapter fourteen). Annapolis-trained officers apparently refused to accept his word because he was a reserve officer, according to Squeaky Anderson.

As bomber and fighter pilots repeatedly flew over Kiska, the evidence mounted that the Japs were gone. Captain George Ruddell, and three other P-40 fighter plane pilots landed on the under-construction Kiska runway by threading their way around bomb craters and debris. They got out of their fighters and walked around and saw no Japs. On return to Amchitka they reported their discovery, and got chewed out for it—they weren't authorized to land there.

In April 1987, I received a letter from retired Army Colonel Irving P. Payne, of West Long Branch, New Jersey, who, in August 1942, commanded an Alaska Intelligence Center on Adak, a radio intelligence outfit that received intercepted Japanese radio traffic.

He wrote, "We reached a point where we just about knew every Japanese operator by his first name. All intelligence [we] gathered was reported to G-2 [Army intelligence] and Naval Headquarters on Adak," Payne wrote.

"On the morning of 9 July, 1943, I reported that an evacuation order, dated 8 July, had been intercepted. On the 29th of July I reported that all radio traffic in and out of Kiska had ceased, and [their troops] had been evacuated by what appeared to be about seven submarines.

"When this information was presented to Rear Admiral Fletcher, U.S. Naval Force, Adak, his comment was, 'Impossible. I have a ring of steel around that island,'" Payne wrote me. [Payne probably meant Rear Admiral Kinkaid; Fletcher was in Seattle at the time.]

Lt. Colonel Verbeck, Castner's assistant, reasoned there were no Japs on Kiska because, "The Air Corp is reporting accuracy and results of bombing that is far too great even for them. They report locating a gun emplacement or radar site, then, with a single pass they bomb it, and it's no longer active.

"They can't be that good. The answer has to be—the enemy is gone."

Admiral Kinkaid thought the Japs had retreated into the hills to fight from the heights as had the defenders of Attu.

He refused to allow Alaska Scouts to be landed

Wrecked Zeros in a bombed-out hangar, Kiska. NATIONAL ARCHIVES

so they could investigate, fearing they would be overwhelmed and killed.

Anyway, he thought if the Japs were gone, a landing on Kiska would be a super dress rehearsal—good for training.

The invasion was on.

UP RELEASE BY RUSSELL ANNABEL. AUGUST 15, ABOARD AN ARMY TROOPSHIP EN ROUTE TO KISKA.

WITH FORTY-TWO correspondents, photographers and artists representing press associations news syndicates and individual newspapers and magazines accompanying this task force, the assault on Kiska will be one of the most closely and meticulously covered military operations of this war.

We are steaming westward through a fleece of Aleutian fog lying tight against a sea as smooth as silk and as clear as creme de menthe. There are warships ahead of us and behind us, and somewhere in the hidden sunlight above us warplanes of the navy and 11th Air Force are on patrol. We have been told that we will reach Kiska within twenty-four hours, and that it is probable our landing will be opposed by the Japanese. This can mean a red hell on the beaches and then a bitter day and night guerrilla battle across the cold tundra swamps and knife-sharp ridges to the enemy garrisons.

It can mean that for many aboard this is a one-way journey.

A camouflaged 76mm Japanese gun, Kiska, September 7, 1943. NATIONAL ARCHIVES

The Japanese power plant, Kiska, after the Allied landing. NATIONAL ARCHIVES

A grave marker left on Kiska by the Japanese. It reads, "Sleeping here, a brave air hero who lost youth and happiness for his motherland. July. Nippon Army." NATIONAL ARCHIVES

As usual, Castner's Cutthroats were among the first ashore. Ed ("Hiram") Walker recalled for me what it was like on the night of August 14, 1943. He was Technical Sergeant Walker then.

"About twenty-five of us—a handful of Alaska Scouts and the rest Special Service Force Troops—went ashore from a destroyer at night before the main landing," he said.

"We paddled in, towing boats filled with explosives. As we neared shore the moon came out, and I thought 'Oh Lordy, all it would take would be one little rifle bullet and we'd all blow up.' I spotted a rock that I was going to swim to and get behind if that happened.

"We guarded the beach while rubber-suited divers planted explosives on rocks near the beach so landing craft could come in. They blew them just before daylight."

No Japs appeared.

While the main landing force spread out in the fog and dug in, Alaska Scout Lieutenant Earl Acuff took an advance patrol across the mountains to Kiska Harbor. Other Scouts with him were Ed Walker, Charles O'Leary, Leonard (Quill) Peterson, Billy Buck, and Stanley Dayo. The first clue that the Japs were gone was the sight of hundreds of rifles and pistols in the shallows of Kiska Harbor.

"It was spooky," Acuff told me. "We saw all those unmanned anti-aircraft and machine guns and I don't know how many caves and other fortifications. But we couldn't find any Japanese."

Messages left on Kiska by the departing Japs. Photo taken September 7, 1943. NATIONAL ARCHIVES

Entrance to the cave-hospital of the Japanese on Kiska. More than fifty caves were dug at Kiska by the Japs for housing, storage, bomb shelters, and this hospital. NATIONAL ARCHIVES

O'Leary wrote me, "There were six Alaska Scouts in the group headed by Acuff. General Buckner had called on the Alaska Scouts to go out and make contact with the enemy. We traveled through the mountains until we came above the Japanese stronghold in Kiska harbor. After watching for about two hours and seeing no activity, we radioed our findings back and said we were heading down to the Jap camp, which we found to be deserted except for two dogs."

One of the dogs was Explosion—the one-time mascot of Charlie House's ten-man weather crew.

The "fog of war" was amplified by the very real fogs of Kiska. Nervous allied soldiers—35,000 of them—searching for Japs, meeting allies in the shifting fog, mistook each other for the enemy, and opened fire.

Seventeen American and four Canadian soldiers died from this "friendly fire." A mine crumpled the stern of the destroyer *Abner Read*, killing seventy-one and injuring another forty-seven navy personnel.

Booby traps killed four and injured other soldiers.

The Japs had scrawled messages on walls, "We shall come again and kill you separately yanki jokers," read one.

United Press correspondent Russell Annabel described the Jap camp as, "The most forlorn, dismal, utterly foreboding place I have ever visited."

Rainwater poured in icy streams through bullet holes in roofs. Window panes had been smashed by bomb concussions. Torrents of muddy water swirled down steep paths. Lying everywhere were heaps of blankets and winter clothing. Dishes with congealing food sat on low tables.

Kiska was an embarrassment to the military. Our invasion of Attu had almost immediately made the newspapers across the country. It took six days for news of the Kiska invasion to appear. Obviously the military didn't know what to say.

It took the military even longer to announce the loss of lives from the destroyer *Abner Read* at Kiska. On August 18, the ship struck a floating Jap mine off the northwestern landing beach. It blew the stern off and seventy one men in it died. Another forty-seven men were injured.

At the time, Americans were inclined to remember the Kiska fiasco if they remembered anything about the Aleutian Campaign, rather than the blood bath that was the Battle of Attu. Today, few

Float plane dollies on Kiska for hauling float-equipped Zeros (Rufes) out of the water for maintenance. Piles of supplies and tents in the background are American. NATIONAL ARCHIVES

A bomb-damaged midget Jap submarine on the marine railway at the head of Kiska Harbor, September 12, 1943. Tents on upper right are American. NATIONAL ARCHIVES

The same midget Jap submarine in July, 1985. The land heals rapidly in the Aleutians. AUTHOR

Explosion, the dog who saw history on Kiska Island, with a new buddy on August 30, 1943. He was originally a mascot for the Navy weather crew on Kiska. NATIONAL ARCHIVES

Americans are even aware there was an Aleutian Campaign, and that the Japanese seized two of Alaska's islands.

To the Japs, the stumbling about of the Americans on the abandoned island was a moral victory. Both sides, however, knew who the victor was.

REFERENCES

Acuff, Earl, Tape-recorded interview by author. October 16, 1989, 5 pp., plus correspondence.

Alaska at War, 1941–1945. The Forgotten War Remembered. Edited by Fern Chandonnet. Papers from the "Alaska at War Symposium," Anchorage, Alaska, November 11–13, 1993.

Armstrong, Robert H. *Guide to the Birds of Alaska.* 1983. Alaska Northwest Publishing Company.

Chihaya, Masataka, "Mysterious Withdrawal from Kiska," United States Naval Institute Proceedings, February, 1958.

Cloe, John, *The Aleutian Warriors; A History of the 11th Air Force and Fleet Wing 4. Part I.* 1991. Joint publication by Anchorage Chapter of the Air Force Association, and Pictorial Histories Publishing Company, Inc.

McCandless, Bruce (Rear Admiral), "The Battle of the Pips," United States Naval Institute Proceedings, February, 1958.

O'Leary, Charles (Alaska Scout). Letter of October 9, 1989 to the author.

Payne, Irving P., Letter of 22 April, 1987, to author.

Rearden, Jim. "Kiska: One Island's Moment in History," *Alaska Magazine,* September and October, 1986.

Russell, James S., Tape-recorded interview by the author, July 1985.

Walker, Ed. Interview by author. Written notes. October 1978.

25

LOST AT SEA

UP RELEASE BY RUSSELL ANNABEL. HEADQUARTERS FLEET AIRWING FOUR, APRIL 7, 1944 (DELAYED).

HOW EIGHT YOUNG airmen of this command, adrift at sea in two rubber life rafts after their Catalina patrol bomber had crashed in a storm, sacrificed their lives rather than imperil friends who were trying to rescue them, was revealed here today.

They were ninety miles off the coast of Attu, with a forty-five-knot wind ripping the tops off the bitter bottle-green swells, and their pilot, Lieutenant Newell Putnam Wyman, Canandaigua, New York—standing at dusk in his pitching, wave-washed raft, freezing, with death very close—waved away the Catalina which was being brought in for a rescue landing, because in his opinion as a pilot the plane could not have survived the landing.

When Lt. Wyman waved the plane off, he signed the death warrant of himself and his crew, but he knew, as a patrol plane commander, that he had saved the lives of the men, his friends, in the plane, airmen here state.

"It was a brave and gallant and heartbreaking thing," says Commodore Leslie E. Gehres, who commands Fleet Airwing, Four. "I can't tell you how strongly I feel about it."

The dead, three of them not recovered from the ocean, are Lt. Wyman; Ensign Anthony Manix Moriarty, copilot, Shakopee, Minnesota; Ensign Raymond Edwin Rozuk, navigator, Cleveland, Ohio; Arvo Arthur Ranta, flight engineer, Gilbert, Minnesota; Charles Leroy Olson, Jr., gunner, Beaumont, Texas; La Vere Marvin Ryther, flight engineer, Rapid City, South Dakota; George Leo Huschka, radioman, Hope, North Dakota; and Armestead Sigrest Hardee, radioman, Sandersville, Mississippi.

Their Catalina was returning from a patrol mission over Asiatic waters on March 31 when it was forced down either by weather or engine failure. Six of the eight men succeeded in getting into the two rubber rafts, while two presumably went down with the plane, which broke apart on impact with the water. Thirty minutes after the crash, the rafts were sighted by Lt. Commander Frank R. More, Sunbury, Pennsylvania, another Catalina pilot. More, aided by green dye released from the rafts, maintained contact with the men until a second Catalina, piloted by Squadron Commander Lt. Marshall C. Freerks, Cuyuna, Minnesota, nosed in through a wall of fog and found him.

For seven hours the two Catalinas circled the rafts. They lost them time and again but each time kept searching until they re-established contact. Freerks, who has the reputation among Aleutian pilots of being at least half seagull—an airmen's airman—dropped smoke bombs to mark the raft's position, and kept calling for surface craft to come and pick up the downed aviators. But dusk was coming on, and the weather was so thick it was difficult even to see the water. Moreover, the two Catalinas were running short of fuel, and the pilots had been informed by radio that Attu field was closed in, so that relief planes could not take off.

A PBY readying for patrol. A crewman stands by the engines with a fire extinguisher at startup. Another crew member is in the bow, ready to release the tie-up line when both engines are running. NATIONAL ARCHIVES

Finally, his fuel desperately low, Lt. Commander More decided to risk a landing and take Wyman and his crew aboard. He knew what would happen if he smashed into one of the big swells—his Catalina would split open and sink, as Wyman's had. But the men down there were his friends. They were his messmates, flying companions. So he went down for a landing. He did not think the men could survive a night at sea, and with the fog closing in thicker and thicker, he was afraid the surface vessels might not find them.

Lt. Wyman saw him coming in, the big lumbering Cat easing down through the slate-colored murk, wing floats down, engines backfiring, feeling for a place to safely land. Wyman was dying from exposure. He was a lonely figure on the tossing raft, hemmed in by the ghostly fog and the gathering darkness, and he had the responsibility of command. He was a naval patrol plane commander. He stood up, with the spray and the black streams from the smoke bombs blowing about him, and waved the Catalina away. He gave Lt. Commander

Little Falls Cemetery on Attu. During the Battle of Attu, and afterward, fallen soldiers and sailors were buried here. The bodies were later removed to other military, or private, cemeteries. NATIONAL ARCHIVES

More the signal to gun engines and climb out of his landing glide.

It was Wyman's decision as a pilot, and More accepted it. Overhead, his plane, phantom-like in the dusky fog, Squadron Commander Freerks saw this, and dipped his wings in salute, one airman to another, saying goodbye. Freerks and More roared over the rafts once more, then set course for land.

Three days later, when the storm had abated, surface vessels were guided to the raft by Venturas and Catalinas. Wyman and his crew were dead. Every resource of the Navy had been thrown into the search for them during the three days since they were first sighted, but the fog and wind and the vast distances of the North Pacific had won.

One of the bodies was lost taking it aboard a warship. The remaining five were buried here today, in Little Falls cemetery, beside the heroic dead brought down last spring from the bloody tundra hills of Massacre and Sarana Valleys.

Two Navy chaplains read the service, and the airmen of this station stood at attention while the gray fog wraiths blew in across the island and the bitter ocean wind cried among the rocks, and everybody was proud of the way the men had died because it was something out of the deep warp of American naval tradition.

Readers might wonder about the hesitancy of landing a rescue PBY. Robert R. Larson, who flew PBYs in the Aleutians during WWII (see chapter seven) reviewed Annabel's story for me. His comment: "With my recollection of how terribly rough the ocean can get in the Aleutians, I can agree with the decision that was made by the pilots involved to not risk a landing. The PBY was not very strong to withstand a full stall landing into rough seas. The fuselage depth was small, and it resulted in breakups and engines falling off in severe impacts."

AUTHOR'S NOTE

The above press release demonstrates Rusty Annabel's way with words. The story is basically true. Annabel got some names and other details wrong. Perhaps it is an example of the Fog of War?

John Cloe, Chief of History, Office of History, for the Eleventh Air Force at Elmendorf Air Force Base, Alaska, carefully researched this incident from multiple sources.

The following are Cloe's research notes, which he generously shared with me.

Accident 31 March, 1944. A PBY flown by Lt. Newell P. Wyman, VP-43, crashed into waters 90 miles west of Attu Island during an approaching storm that caught a number of Fleet Air Wing Four, aircraft in the air. Lieutenant Wyman was a veteran of Kurile missions and had requested permission to return to Casco Cove [at Attu Island]. The other PBY crews made it down.

A PV-1 crew spotted the down flyers in two rubber rafts, which had been lashed together, and reported it. Lieutenant (jg) Don Norton, pilot of another VP-43 PBY, and his crew took off from Attu, where they had just landed ahead of the approaching storm, and headed out to the reported site.

Lieutenant Norton and his crew spotted the downed flyers, and he made a low pass overhead, observing one of the men in a raft give the "do not attempt to land" wave off sign.

Lieutenant Marshall C. Freerks, VP-43's executive officer, arrived next. He and his crew were heading back to base when they received notification of the downed PBY. On their arrival Lieutenant Norton and his crew departed for Attu while Lieutenant Freerks and his crew orbited overhead and waited for a destroyer he was told had been dispatched from Attu.

The storm front arrived as Lieutenant Freerks maintained visual contact with the downed PBY crew. The command center for Fleet Air Wing Four on Adak, which was coordinating the rescue efforts, had issued orders for no one to attempt a landing.

With darkness approaching, no other relief PBY being dispatched, and observing a break in the weather, Lieutenant Freerks asked his crew if he should attempt a landing. The possibility of it succeeding was slim and the crew voted to return to Attu.

The PBY crew [Freerks] arrived at Attu to find Casco Cove closed and had to fly on to Shemya where they landed shortly before the field there closed.

For some reason, the destroyers *Badger* (DD 126) and *Luce* (DD 522), dispatched to search for the two rafts arrived too late and were not able to locate them due to reduced visibility and hard driving rain.

Two crash rescue recovery boat crews based at Casco Cove also attempted to reach the downed flyers but had to turn back when the storm threatened to swamp their boats.

When the storm cleared on the third day, 3 April, a destroyer crew spotted the two rafts. Lieutenant Freerks and his crew arrived over the scene as the destroyer crew were recovering the ice encrusted bodies.

Because of the difficulty of the operations, the recovery crew accidentally dropped one of the bodies into the sea where it sank.

In addition to Lieutenant Wyman, the other dead included Ensign Anthony M. Moriarty, copilot; Ens. Raymond O. Rozuk; AMM2c Arvo A. Ranta, flight engineer; AMM2c Lavere M. Ryther, flight engineer; ARM2c George L. Huschka, radio operator; ARM2c Armstead S. Hardee; and AOM2c Charles L. Olson.

The bodies of Wyman, Moriarty, Ranta, and Olson were buried in Attu's Little Falls Cemetery.

No record of burial is shown for Ryther, Hardee and Huschka. The surgeon who examined their bodies estimated the men had survived for eight to twelve hours before dying of exposure.

EPILOGUE

THE FIFTEEN-MONTH Aleutian Campaign was the only World War II struggle to take place on North American soil.

Each of the 144,000 American military personnel who fought in the Aleutians had a story. Few have been preserved. Those in this volume have hardly scratched the surface.

The immensity of the life or death struggle that was World War II is difficult to grasp. Those of us who lived during those nearly four years remember that virtually every American was somehow involved—either fighting, or working on the home front in some way to futher the war. It was also a time when Americans were united as never before—or since.

The Aleutian Campaign was a relatively minor conflict when compared with others then under way around the globe.

At peak numbers, 8,500 Japanese occupied Attu and Kiska. In the end, we realized this enemy posed no real threat to mainland North America, something we were unsure of at the beginning.

We made an air war out of it and learned that the Aleutian weather posed more danger to airplanes and pilots than did the Japanese. About 225 Allied (U.S. and Canadian) aircraft were lost in the Aleutians, of which only forty-one were lost to enemy action.

About 1,000 of our military men died by enemy action and accidents; 549 of these in the Battle of Attu.

About 3,850 Japanese were killed; 2,350 of these were on Attu; another 1,500 were on Kiska and at sea by our submarines, bombers, and surface ships.

General Simon Buckner's proposal for our military to reach Japan through the Aleutians was never seriously considered. Lessons learned by our troops from battling savage Aleutian weather weren't lost on our military strategists. Also, by the time the Aleutian Campaign ended, the island-hopping strategy in the eastern Pacific was beginning to succeed.

The campaign in the Aleutians was a waste of material and energy for both the U.S. and Japan. Tragically, the loss of life there also created a lifetime of heartbreak for many.

Bottom line? The Aleutian Campaign was a battle over two remote islands that were never strategically significant. That doesn't diminish in the least the luster of the heroism demonstrated by our warriors who fought in that tumultuous, lonely island province.

INDEX

(BOLD NUMBERS DESIGNATE PHOTOS)